STARTING A BUSINESS
QuickStart Guide®

Editor: Marilyn Burkley
Cover Illustration and Design: Katie Poorman, Copyright © 2019 by ClydeBank Media LLC
Interior Design and Graphics: Katie Poorman, Copyright © 2019 by ClydeBank Media LLC

First Edition – Last updated: March 23, 2023

ISBN-13: 9781945051821 (paperback) | 9781945051630 (hardcover) | 9781945051579 (eBook) | 99781945051746 (audiobook) | 9781636100180 (spiral bound)

Publisher's Cataloging-In-Publication Data
(Prepared by The Donohue Group, Inc.)

Names: Cowell, Ken, author.
Title: Starting a business : the simplified beginner's guide to launching a successful small business, turning your vision into reality, and achieving your entrepreneurial dream / Ken Colwell, PhD, MBA.
Description: Albany, NY : ClydeBank Business, [2019] | "QuickStart Guide." | Chapters 15-17 include step-by-step instructions and questions to consider when writing a business plan. | Includes bibliographical references and index.
Identifiers: ISBN 9781945051630 (hardcover) | ISBN 9781945051821 (paperback) | ISBN 9781945051579 (ebook)
Subjects: LCSH: New business enterprises. | Small business. | Business planning. | Success in business.
Classification: LCC HD62.5 .C69 2019 (print) | LCC HD62.5 (ebook) | DDC 658.11--dc23

Library of Congress Control Number: 2019930888
Author ISNI: 0000 0004 6515 9581

For bulk sales inquiries, please visit www.go.quickstartguides.com/wholesale, email us at orders@clydebankmedia.com, or call 800-340-3069. Special discounts are available on quantity purchases by corporations, associations, and others.

OVER
850,000

READERS **LOVE** *QuickStart Guides.*

Really well written with lots of practical information. These books have a very concise way of presenting each topic and everything inside is very actionable!

— ALAN F.

The book was a great resource, every page is packed with information, but [the book] never felt overly-wordy or repetitive. Every chapter was filled with very useful information.

— CURTIS W.

I appreciated how accessible and how insightful the material was and look forward to sharing the knowledge that I've learned [from this book].

— SCOTT B.

After reading this book, I must say that it has been one of the best decisions of my life!

— ROHIT R.

This book is one-thousand percent worth every single dollar!

— HUGO C.

The read itself was worth the cost of the book, but the additional tools and materials make this purchase a better value than most books.

— JAMES D.

I finally understand this topic ... this book has really opened doors for me!

— MISTY A.

Contents

PART III – YOUR VALUE PROPOSITION

PART IV – YOUR BUSINESS MODEL

PART V – WRITING YOUR BUSINESS PLAN

BEFORE YOU START READING, DOWNLOAD YOUR FREE DIGITAL ASSETS!

 Complete Sample Business Plans

 Business Plan Creation Checklist

 Pro Forma Financial Statement Template

Useful Cheat Sheets

TWO WAYS TO ACCESS YOUR FREE DIGITAL ASSETS

Use the camera app on your mobile phone to scan the QR code or visit the link below and instantly access your digital assets.

 SCAN ME

or go.quickstartguides.com/startingbusiness

VISIT URL

Introduction

This is a book for people who are interested in starting a business.

Maybe you have an unfulfilled passion that you want to transform into your livelihood. Maybe you hate your job and want to get off the corporate treadmill. Maybe you dream of financial independence and want to "be your own boss." Or perhaps you are a willing (or unwilling) participant in the "gig economy" and want to learn how to make a living at it. Perhaps you've even started a business before but aren't quite sure you've got everything figured out. Whatever your circumstance, you will find value in this book.

I've spent over twenty years in the new venture ecosystem as an entrepreneurship professor, consultant, business school dean, and founder of my own ventures. When I began working with entrepreneurs, starting a business was hard and expensive. The dot-com boom and bust of the late 1990s/early 2000s demystified the process for the general public and made successful entrepreneurs into rock stars. Since then, technology has made starting a business much easier and less expensive, and self-employment is now a highly desirable career path for many.

Yet there are still profound misunderstandings among the general public about how to start and run a successful business. These misunderstandings are amplified by fawning press accounts that make extreme outliers of entrepreneurial success seem like the norm, as well as lifestyle-oriented blogs, books, and podcasts that make starting and running a business seem as easy as falling off a log.

My intent is to interject a dose of reality into all the hype. Yes, starting a business can be tremendously rewarding both psychologically and (possibly) monetarily. But it is also very hard work and will completely dominate your life, especially at first. You will have to deal with constant risk and uncertainty. How you approach these things will largely determine how successful you can be.

How This Book Is Organized

This book starts at the most fundamental level—the mindset and cognitive factors critical to success as an entrepreneur. There's a reason for this. In my 20-plus years working in the entrepreneurial ecosystem, I've found time and again that the right mindset is far more important to the success of a new venture than economic factors, airtight intellectual property protection, or killer financial projections. Over and over again I've seen ventures fail that seemed to have everything going for them. I've also seen too many ventures to count that succeeded despite so-called "experts" (i.e., me) thinking they had no chance at all. The intangibles are usually far more important than the tangibles in all creative domains, and, as you will see, I view starting a new venture as the ultimate creative act.

The next section of the book outlines the strategic issues you're going to have to grapple with in order to determine the two most critical elements of a new venture—your value proposition and your business model. Your value proposition lays out who your customers are and how you distinguish yourself from your competition. Your business model addresses how you will run your business and how you will meet your profitability goals.

Finally, I include a basic outline of a traditional business plan with specific instructions for how to write it. Although many of you have no need for a formal business plan, there are good reasons to pull all of your thinking and planning into a series of concise, useful documents and other media, and I'll go over how to do so.

Although this book is intended for everyone in the entrepreneurial ecosystem, I am focusing on the 99 percent of entrepreneurs who are not looking to raise large amounts of capital to rapidly scale into an eight-figure company. I will certainly touch on the different ways to raise money and the venture capital process, but this is only relevant to the vast majority of nascent entrepreneurs as a point of interest.

If you are reading this book, chances are you're seriously considering delving into the complicated, exhilarating, frustrating, and rewarding world of entrepreneurship. Congratulations! It won't be easy, but it may just be the best thing you've ever done. I look forward to helping you begin your journey.

Chapter by Chapter

» "Chapter 1: Your Big Idea" discusses the nature of opportunities. Believe it or not, not all ideas are created equal, and being able to discern the difference between an *idea* and an *opportunity* is one of the first steps to getting started on your own entrepreneurial path. In this chapter you will learn where opportunities come from and what makes an opportunity great.

» It's no secret that starting your own business comes with significant risk and a mountain of hard work. For many new entrepreneurs their biggest obstacle is their own outlook and attitude. "Chapter 2: What Are You Afraid Of?" tackles some of the biggest misconceptions that hold back many would-be entrepreneurs. While it is true that the world of entrepreneurship is not for everyone, in many cases the fears of failure or the reluctance to start for various reasons are unfounded.

» Despite what a Google search might tell you, the "secret" to entrepreneurial success is much more than a list of generic traits such as hard work and vision. As you will learn in "Chapter 3: What You Really Need to Succeed as an Entrepreneur" it is often the intangible aspects of starting a business that are the best predictors of success—not the tangible ones.

» In "Chapter 4: Your Company – The First Steps" our discussion shifts to the practical aspects of starting your business including your company's legal form. Chapter 5: What Are You Selling?"covers your product or service, how to set prices, and the strategy behind different pricing methods.

» The next two chapters "Chapter 6: Markets and Customers" and "Chapter 7: Industries and Competitors" examine the people who will purchase what you are selling (your customers) and the firms that will compete with you. I'll tell you right now—no matter how new, groundbreaking, or disruptive your product is you have competitors!

» With the fundamentals regarding strategic positioning covered, "Chapter 8: Your Value Proposition" introduces the concept that makes or breaks many small businesses and startups—a robust and well-defined value proposition. In many cases, a startup's value proposition acts as a shorthand for the startup itself. The value of your value proposition cannot be overstated.

» "Chapter 9: Operations" dives into the nuts and bolts of how to structure your business with a focus on value, what to keep in house and what to outsource, and how to find and exploit efficiencies within your value chain—no matter what kind of business you are starting.

» "Chapter 10: Marketing" explores the methods your business will use to reach more customers in your target demographic. In this chapter we discuss the promotional mix, distribution channels, and the sales cycle. Marketing plays a role in every business—new or well-established—and in this chapter you will learn how to use the promotional mix to grow your business.

» Becoming an entrepreneur means embracing change. In "Chapter 11: Planning for Growth and Change" we discuss the myriad factors that impact growth and the trajectory of a startup. This chapter serves as a primer to growing your business and planning for the inevitability of change.

» Business is done by people, for people. Your startup is no exception. "Chapter 12: Management, Staffing, and the Founding Team" covers everything you need to know regarding the people who will help you get your new business up and running.

» "Chapter 13: Where Does the Money Come From?" addresses the topic that seems to be at the forefront of every new entrepreneur's mind—funding. There is much more to a successful venture than money, but a venture won't go too far without significant funding. This chapter delves into the various forms of funding including the truth about venture capital and angel investment.

» Despite some of the anecdotal evidence you may have heard, if you are starting a business you need to produce a business plan. This is true *even if* you aren't seeking funding. "Chapter 14: Do You *Really* Need a Business Plan?" discusses the advantageous uses of a business plan and debunks some of the common misconceptions surrounding their necessity and implementation.

» The remainder of this book "Chapter 15: Introducing Your Venture, Chapter 16: Your Value Proposition," and "Chapter 17: Your Business Model" explore the exact steps to take when constructing your own business plan. Each step-by-step section delves into what to include, what to omit, and how to compile the information you will need to write your own winning business plan.

Let's get started.

PART I

THINKING LIKE AN ENTREPRENEUR

| 1 |
Your Big Idea

Chapter Overview
  » The difference between an idea and an opportunity
  » What makes a great opportunity?
  » The nature of competitive advantage and distinctive competencies

You're a brand-new entrepreneur who has a big idea and a boatload of passion. You wanted to start your first million-dollar business yesterday, because you know your idea is so big that it will thrill your customers and fulfill your dreams in the process. The first question you have: how much is this idea worth?

Nothing.

Ideas are numerous, and they exist without inherent value. An idea—no matter how big or small—is a series of electrochemical reactions inside your brain. No one purchases ideas, and ideas cannot be assigned a dollar value. This does not mean that ideas are without potential—ideas are critical first steps toward developing opportunities. Unlike ideas, opportunities are the stock and trade of successful entrepreneurs. Opportunities are actionable, and they have the potential to provide value both to customers and to you. The distinction might seem subtle, but the difference between an idea and an opportunity is a critical one. Attempting to follow through with ideas that have not become opportunities will spell disaster for your venture. It will be doomed before it even begins.

fig. 1

IDEA	OPPORTUNITY
Concept	Actionable
Notion	Provides value
Impression	Can be commercially validated
Seed	Can be executed

Ideas and opportunities do not exist independently of one another, and they do not exist independently of people. Everything that has been created by people started out as an idea, but not everything that has been an idea has been created. This is the root of the value assigned to opportunities: execution. Opportunities are valuable in their execution. Just as an idea that is trapped in your head has no value on its own, an opportunity that cannot be executed has no value either.

There is no such thing as a new idea. It is impossible. We simply take a lot of old ideas and put them into a sort of mental kaleidoscope. We give them a turn and they make new and curious combinations. We keep on turning and making new combinations indefinitely; but they are the same old pieces of colored glass that have been in use through all the ages.

- MARK TWAIN

Mr. Twain was correct. There are no new ideas. Every business idea is a permutation of existing ideas and conditions. Whether or not an idea can be evolved into an opportunity determines whether it will become reality, or whether it will just be another series of electrochemical reactions.

How Are Opportunities Cultivated?

A common misconception is that opportunities simply "occur" to entrepreneurs in a flash of insight. That may be how ideas come to us, but the process of uncovering opportunities is a little more complex. Opportunities aren't just waiting around for an enterprising entrepreneur to come and find them. They are an *extension* of the entrepreneur.

Each person is a unique blend of his or her background, talent, insight, and perspective. Together these facets form a kind of "thumbprint" that is just as unique to each of us as our actual fingerprint. The concept of an *entrepreneurial thumbprint* is essential to understanding how opportunities interact with the entrepreneurs who cultivate them.

First, where do opportunities come from? Opportunities are cultivated through a variety of methods, and each of these methods is dependent entirely on the entrepreneur and his or her entrepreneurial thumbprint.

Opportunities Come from Active Search

An engaged, structured, and disciplined process of searching for ways to evolve ideas into opportunities will yield better results than a passive process. Instead of searching for new ideas or new knowledge, focus on solutions to existing problems. The simpler the better. A compliment that an entrepreneur should love to hear after pitching an idea is *"That's obvious!"* Simple solutions to common problems have a higher potential for success.

Quick Case: Jazzercise, a legacy name in active fitness programs, was founded in 1969 by Judi Sheppard Missett. Judi was a teacher at a dance studio in Chicago when she noticed abysmal dropout rates among her students. Young women would attend dance classes to get a workout, but as the lessons progressed, students who had little interest in becoming professional dancers would abandon the class. To keep fees flowing in, Judi began holding warm-up classes with a focus on fun and fitness rather than honing dancing skills. These classes were later rebranded "Jazzercize" and developed into a fitness phenomenon.

Opportunities Come from Information

Entrepreneurial opportunities exist because different people have access to different information. What is an idea for one entrepreneur may be an opportunity for another who has the resources and the means to execute it. An opportunity that exists without the means to execute it does not have value. It is simply an idea.

Quick Case: Qualcomm is a name that for many doesn't immediately ring a bell, despite the fact that the company is responsible for the functionality of devices that we rely on every day. Qualcomm is the telecommunications and semiconductor company responsible for— among other things—3G cellular technology. Qualcomm also holds patents for the technology that powers 4G connectivity and is a leader in the 5G space. When the company was founded in July of 1985 by former University of California, San Diego professor Irwin Jacobs, he didn't have a business plan or a particular product in mind.

What the founding team *did* have, however, was an abundance of engineering talent in their small team and the vision that wireless connectivity would change the world in even more dramatic ways. Former Qualcomm CEO Paul Jacobs (son of founder Irwin Jacobs) said of the company's foundation, *"Having visions which are out there allows people to have creativity. The main force of a company is shaped by a vision."*[1]

The takeaway from Qualcomm's story is that Jacobs and the rest of the founding team started a company knowing what they wanted to do and how they wanted to change the world. They did this knowing that they had a well of technical knowledge and a firm belief in their vision.

Opportunities Come from Change

External changes can create opportunities in two ways:

» Change that makes it possible to do things that haven't been done before
» Change that makes it possible to do something in a more valuable way

An external change that makes it possible to do something in a more valuable way could be the catalyst that makes an idea that otherwise would not have been actionable into an opportunity that has the potential to provide value.

Opportunities Come from the Process of Effectuation

Effectuation is essentially the opposite of causation. It is a process used to identify entrepreneurial opportunity when the future is unknown or unpredictable. We often think of new ventures as starting with a goal, then gathering the resources needed to achieve that goal. Effectuation, on the other hand, starts with the resources at hand and then assembles them to build the goal.

The difference between causation and effectuation may seem subtle, but it is important. A great example of the difference is your approach to making dinner. If you were to take a *causal* approach, you would carefully plan out a menu in advance, then check your kitchen to see what you have, then go to the store to buy any missing items. In an *effectual* approach, you would look in your refrigerator and pantry, see what you have, and plan your menu accordingly.

MY TAKE

Causation versus effectuation—which is the "right" method to use when developing an idea into an opportunity? The answer is both. When it comes to making dinner on an average weekday night, you probably use the latter. If you're planning a dinner party, the former is probably best. The moral of the story is that sometimes the best opportunities are found by just looking around and seeing what skills and resources are available to you.

Active Search	Information
• Engaged, structured, and disciplined search will yeild better results than a passive process	• Different people have access to different information. This creates opportunities

Change	Effectuation
• Changes that make it possible to do things that have not been done before, or possible to do them in a more valuable way create opportunities	• The opposite of starting with a goal in mind, effectuation is the process of fitting the resources at hand to develop or uncover an opportunity

fig. 2

What's in a Thumbprint?

An entrepreneurial thumbprint—like an actual fingerprint—is unique to each person. Fingerprints all look similar at a glance, but upon closer inspection we see that no two are alike. Unlike our fingerprints, however, we are not born with entrepreneurial thumbprints. Furthermore, unlike fingerprints, an entrepreneurial thumbprint evolves over time. It is a blend of our skills, talents, connections, and experience.

In exactly the same way that an opportunity cannot exist independently of an entrepreneur, your entrepreneurial thumbprint cannot exist independently of you. In fact, it *is* you! To uncover the ridges and whorls of your own entrepreneurial thumbprint, ask yourself the following questions:

» **What are you passionate about?**
The topic of passion comes up frequently in this book and in any conversation involving entrepreneurship and the act of starting a business. If you're not passionate about an idea, it will stay an idea. It may be a good idea, it may be an interesting idea, but if you aren't inspired to make it a reality or passionate about its execution, then it will never manifest into an opportunity. Conversely, where you may lack passion for an idea or a business concept, another would-be entrepreneur may be excited about bringing it to fruition. Your personality, interests, inspirations, and passions contribute to forming your entrepreneurial thumbprint.

» **What do you know well?**
It's okay not to have an advanced understanding of business concepts at first. In fact, many successful entrepreneurs are not MBA holders.

Starting a business isn't as simple as monetizing your passion, but that underlying passion and knowledge forms the solid core of your entrepreneurial thumbprint. Someone who travels avidly and has a lot of experience navigating the world of rental cars, air travel, and hotel bookings is better suited to starting a travel agency than someone who has never left the country.

» **Who do you know?**
Having a huge social network isn't a prerequisite to success, but a long contact list can certainly help. A portion of your unique entrepreneurial thumbprint is composed of your network—both personal and professional. These people may be the first ones you reach out to when it's time to start funding your venture, but when it comes to distinguishing the difference between an idea and an opportunity, you'll find that your network is worth more than a round of financing. Who do you know that has skills or knowledge that complement your own? Better yet, who do you know that has skills or knowledge that fills in gaps in your own experience? Do you know anyone who could act as a mentor or provide other forms of guidance on your entrepreneurial journey? Are there members of your network who can get the word out about your new venture, or lend a hand getting you off the ground?

Ultimately, your personal/professional network plays a large role in defining your entrepreneurial thumbprint.

» **Is there a particular problem you want to solve?**
If you are familiar with a particular field or industry, it is more than likely that aspects of it that frustrate you also frustrate others. Inconveniences, limitations, and frustrations—collectively referred to as pain points—are tremendous drivers of entrepreneurial opportunity. This is true even if you don't know exactly how to fix the problem right now. As you explore the idea, discuss the issue with others, and gain a greater understanding of the how and why of the problem, it will become clear whether the other aspects of your entrepreneurial thumbprint can help you transform this into a real opportunity.

NOTE

If the elements of an entrepreneurial thumbprint seem circumstantial and subject to change, that's because they are. Nothing is set in stone. Entrepreneurs aren't born to start new ventures. Entrepreneurs are people, and as we learn and grow, our entrepreneurial thumbprints become better defined along the way.

A final note on the topic of entrepreneurial thumbprints: keep in mind that at the end of the day, starting a business is a creative act. As with any act that stimulates us creatively, inspiration can come from anywhere, even places that surprise us. As you will see in the next chapter, the idea that entrepreneurs are born, not made, is not only erroneous, but self-limiting. The sheer number of ideas matched with the sheer diversity of entrepreneurial thumbprints completely turns this idea on its head.

What Makes a Great Opportunity?

We know that opportunities start as ideas and that they can be cultivated though several different processes, but the critical question is "What makes a great opportunity?" After all the thinking, searching, and analysis, how do you separate opportunities that have real, actionable value from those that simply don't make the cut?

A *great* opportunity:

» Solves a problem for a customer
» Exists in a strategic space that isn't too crowded
» Can be executed in a strategic space where you can maintain a competitive advantage
» Has a reasonable potential to help you achieve your goals
» Fills a critical customer need that may or may not be obvious to them
» Is not obvious to others who don't have your background, experience, or insight
» Does not exist independently of you, the entrepreneur

Let's take a closer look at what makes an opportunity great.

It Solves Problems for Customers

This may seem obvious, but in practice it's not. The word "problem" indicates a negative emotion, but that's not necessarily the case. Customer problems fall into two broad categories—resolving pain and creating delight. Really great products do both at the same time. Products that do neither have little potential for success.

Customers buy *benefits*, not *features*. All the flashy features in the world will not help if they don't provide concrete benefits for the customer. This is why it's so critical for entrepreneurs to think in terms of solving customers' problems. Pain and delight are extreme emotions, and these are the sorts of emotions that cause customers to adopt new products. Incremental improvements and flashy features without benefits are unlikely to sway potential customers.

Quick Case: The smartphone market is littered with new entrants that ultimately failed due to the overzealous adding of features without tangible benefits. In 2005, ESPN, the Entertainment and Sports Programming Network, decided that what the smartphone users of the day were missing was an ESPN-branded phone. In the days before apps were the established standard, the ESPN phone could receive up-to-the-minute sports alerts and was truly a cut above other phones for the sports enthusiast when it came to sports news and scores. The phone flopped and was discontinued nine months later after reaching 30,000 customers—well below the 500,000 ESPN needed to break even on their investment.[2]

While the sports alerts *feature* certainly did provide enthusiasts with the *benefit* of very current news and scores, the phone fell short of consumer expectations in nearly every other way. The high price tag, cut-rate hardware, and restrictive contract failed to impress. Furthermore, ESPN committed to the release of this phone while simultaneously offering sports news and scores through services available from Verizon, Sprint, and other wireless carriers.

In the end, the phone did not do enough to solve the problems faced by its prospective customers, and it also failed to thrill. ESPN relied on brand recognition and a high-powered marketing campaign to pick up the slack in their value proposition—never a good idea.

It Exists in a Strategic Space That Isn't Too Crowded

It's no secret that new ventures are entering a business landscape that is already crowded with established competitors. This means that the best way for new ventures to survive is to carve out a niche that they can dominate rather than compete as a small fish in a big pond. The space that your venture occupies can't be written on a scrap of paper and pulled out of a hat. You must position yourself strategically.

What this means is that while passion about your venture is a necessary prerequisite for success, it isn't enough. Just because you're passionate about fitness does not mean that your gym will be successful. There are a lot of gyms out there—what sets yours apart?

It Maintains a Competitive Advantage

Competitive advantage is what makes your venture better at doing whatever it is you do than your rivals in the same space. Competitive advantage is detailed in the next section, but for now, know that if your opportunity can't be executed strategically in a manner that allows you to maintain competitive advantage, then it isn't a great opportunity.

It Has a Reasonable Potential to Help You Achieve Your Goals

Successful entrepreneurs don't start new ventures because they believe it's good for their health, and they don't start new ventures to get rich. When it comes to moneymaking potential, starting your own business is one of the *worst* ways to become independently wealthy. In fact, once your venture clears the startup stage and begins courting investors, remember that professional investors tend to shy away from entrepreneurs who are looking to get rich from their business.

Obviously you want to benefit financially from your successful venture. However, the road to startup wealth is long and extremely uncertain. If your primary goal is to get rich fast, this isn't the path for you. The stories you've read about tech "unicorns" that exploded into high growth and profitability are the extreme exception to the rule.

Investors look for talent, passion, and proof that your business can win. When assessing an opportunity, consider the ways in which it has the potential to achieve your goals. Of course, there are no guarantees, but if an opportunity isn't likely to help you achieve your personal goals, then why would you follow through with it at all?

It Is Not Obvious to Others

The unique blend of experience, insight, and passion that each entrepreneur brings to the table—his or her entrepreneurial thumbprint—is a key decider in what makes an opportunity great for that person and not for another. If a problem exists that a customer is aware of, then the idea of solving that problem is an obvious one, along with some ideas about *how* to solve it.

Remember that ideas are not opportunities. An entrepreneur with the right background, experience, and talent may see an executable solution to a problem. Because of his or her unique thumbprint, this executable solution might be a good opportunity. Others who are looking at the same problem may not see an opportunity so easily, if at all.

Q: What about problems that customers may not be aware of? How do you solve a problem for a customer that they themselves don't have in focus?

Answer: A great example is the story of the iPod. iPods solved a number of problems for consumers that they hadn't even realized were problems. The ability to keep a library of songs right on your device, to make custom playlists, and to deliver via download instead of making a trip to the store made products the iPod a clear winner over traditional CD players. The consumers who purchased iPod didn't have a burning need to replace their CD players. They were responding to the ways in which new technology provided a superior solution to how they wanted to experience music.

It Doesn't Exist Independently of the Entrepreneur

In the same way that great opportunities are not obvious to others, great opportunities do not exist independently of the entrepreneur. The ability to develop the idea into an opportunity and to see the ways in which it provides value and can be executed (and ultimately is executed) are completely reliant on the entrepreneur and his or her entrepreneurial thumbprint. A popular misconception is that opportunities are like cars—plop anyone with a license in the driver's seat and the vehicle will get to its destination. Nothing could be further from the truth.

Some Considerations About Opportunities

With the number of buzzwords and conflicting information that gets thrown around regarding the sources of opportunities and how to cultivate them, it is worth looking at the answers to common questions concerning the nature of opportunities.

» **Should I be looking for opportunities in growth industries?**
If your passion and skill set take you there, then yes. What makes the opportunity valuable is its ability to be executed, to provide value to customers, and to be accomplished in a strategic manner, all within the context of your entrepreneurial thumbprint. In that respect, the type of industry isn't as crucial to the value of the opportunity. Seeking opportunity in a "hot" industry just to be in a hot industry will do more harm than good, especially if that industry is at odds with your entrepreneurial thumbprint.

» **What about established markets that are dominated by entrenched competitors?**

Keep in mind that new ventures can almost never compete on price. A new market entrant simply can't tackle an entrenched competitor head on. If there is a strategic position that your venture can occupy that allows you to compete indirectly with existing market players, then the opportunity might not be a bad one.

» **Should I be looking for "disruptive" opportunities?**

"Disruption" is a buzzword that is popular in tech startups from Silicon Valley. The term originated from Harvard Business School professor Clayton Christensen in the late '90s.[3] He defined the concept of "disruptive innovation" as a principle whereby entrenched market players could be unseated by smaller rivals who offered simpler or less costly solutions. The popularity of the term's use to sell Silicon Valley tech startups to investors has eroded the meaning of the term to the point that it is irrelevant to entrepreneurs at large. Don't get me wrong—disruptive technologies are a real thing and have a profound effect on shaping industries over the long term. However, disruption is not a strategy, and it shouldn't be a major consideration when assessing an opportunity.

The Nature of Competitive Advantage

Competitive advantage is the sum of conditions that put one business in a superior or favorable position over another. Competitive advantage is something of a law of the jungle for the business world. If an opportunity cannot be strategically executed in a space where you can maintain competitive advantage over rivals, then the opportunity is not a good one. In his often-cited 1991 paper in the *Journal of Management*, economist and professor Jay Barney laid out a comprehensive look at competitive advantage by examining how it is formed, how it is sustained, and how it is exploited by firms. Competitive advantage stems from resources, competencies, or capabilities possessed by your company that have the following attributes:

» **Valuable to the customer**

Value is the name of the game. It is critical that what you do better than your rivals also provide value to your customers (otherwise it doesn't produce much of an advantage).

» **Rare, or hard to come by**
The rarer your sources of competitive advantage, the more difficult they are to duplicate and the more differentiated your business will be from competitors.

» **Not easily imitated**
A source of competitive advantage that is easily imitated isn't very robust. The rarer and more unique your sources of competitive advantage, the better.

» **Not easily substituted**
If a competitor can overcome your competitive advantage by doing something else that they are good at, your advantage is not sustainable.

Q: Where does competitive advantage come from?

Answer: The biggest source of competitive advantage is generated by what are known as *distinctive competencies*, which are a combination of best practices and technical skills that come together in a valuable and creative way that is difficult to beat by your competitors. For some organizations, distinctive competencies can be less tangible aspects of their business, such as their culture. An organization's culture is the culmination of its vision, way of doing things, and perspective, or worldview. For others, superior execution that allows them to provide overwhelming value to the customer is their source of distinctive advantage. Ideally, as many organizational aspects as possible come together as distinctive competencies.

For new ventures, competitive advantage rarely stems from a narrow skill set or intellectual property such as a patent. New ventures do have a few tricks up their sleeves, however, when it comes to distinctive competencies:

» **Agility**
Startups can—and often must—change direction completely at the drop of a hat. This is an inherent advantage over larger, more established businesses that must respond to changes in a much slower way. Is there a new customer segment that can be targeted? A startup can jump on top of openings like that very quickly. The same goes for emerging trends or new technology. Startups are speedboats compared to the ocean liners that are their established competition.

» **Specialized Knowledge**
As we have discussed, every entrepreneur has their own unique thumbprint of skills, knowledge, experience, and perspective. These are often an initial source of competitive advantage.

» **Team Cohesion**
Startups are made up of smaller teams than their larger competitors, out of necessity. Often, team members are cross-trained or take an active role in multiple areas of the business, meaning that each is very familiar with many aspects of the business. Additionally, working in smaller groups means that the team is often very close-knit and can respond faster to challenges.

» **Less Bureaucracy**
Red tape and "formal business practices" are a necessity of running larger, established businesses, but the size and agility of startups means that critical decisions can be made faster, and with less back-and-forth.

Distinctive competencies come together to form the competitive advantages that allow new ventures to compete. For example, if a firm competes on price, that's a competitive advantage. That advantage is made possible through distinctive competencies such as superior execution or improved processing techniques. But remember, *new ventures can almost never compete on price!*

Quick Case: To find a clear example of fierce competition and the need to maintain a sustainable competitive edge, one need not look further than their own internet browser. In August of 1995, computer services company Netscape launched what was, at the time, one of the largest IPOs on Wall Street. Netscape's decision to go public was buoyed by the popularity of their flagship internet browser, Navigator. Netscape's entrance into the public market caught the attention of competitor Microsoft. Microsoft didn't have a strong internet browser at the time, but they did have a robust operating system in the form of the Windows suite. They also had massive reserves of cash.

Microsoft released a competing product called Internet Explorer. Both Navigator and Internet Explorer were free products, but the key difference (and overwhelming advantage for Microsoft) was that Internet Explorer came bundled with the popular Windows operating system suite. To compete, Netscape infused their browser with newer and better features. A veritable features arms race ensued, and when the dust cleared Microsoft emerged the victor.

Given a second chance, could things have gone differently for Netscape? We will never know, but a clue can be found in today's iteration of the browser wars of the early 2000s. Internet Explorer's successor Edge is duking it out with Chrome, Firefox, and others who have managed to survive (and thrive) using Netscape's own tactic of relying on features to produce competencies in the areas of browsing speed, privacy, compatibility, and functionality.

Chapter Recap

» Ideas do not have inherent value until they are developed into opportunities. Opportunities are actionable, and they have the potential to provide value both to customers and to you.

» Opportunities are cultivated from a number of sources including active search, different or new information, change, and the process of effectuation.

» Opportunities that are executable, that are not obvious to others, and that solve problems for customers—regardless of whether or not the customer was aware of the problem—have the potential to be great opportunities.

» If an opportunity can be executed in a strategic space that isn't too crowded and where your entrepreneurial thumbprint and competitive advantage converge, you may have the foundation of a business that is successful and sustainable.

» Competitive advantage is the sum of conditions that put one business in a superior or favorable position over another. The elements that make up a winning competitive advantage are valuable to customers, rare, difficult to imitate, and not easily substituted.

» A startup's distinctive competencies are a key driver of that venture's competitive advantage. Small firms are agile, and they often benefit from specialized knowledge, a high degree of team cohesion, and fewer internal bureaucratic barriers.

| 2 |
What Are You Afraid Of?

Chapter Overview
  » Self-limiting beliefs that hold back would-be entrepreneurs
  » The fear of failure and the role of luck
  » Do you need a business plan?

Starting a business is a big step, and would-be entrepreneurs must ask themselves difficult questions. Many people have fundamental self-limiting beliefs and misunderstandings that prevent them from taking even the first steps. Before you begin, think carefully about the following items. Which of them apply to you? Are they holding you back from achieving your dreams? What can you do about it?

Self-Limiting Beliefs

One of the main barriers that holds us back is strongly held internal beliefs about ourselves and our ability to succeed as entrepreneurs. These beliefs are almost always based on generalizations or stereotypes about what "real" entrepreneurs are like or what the process of starting a business entails.

Here are some of the most common misconceptions that lead to self-limiting beliefs:

Entrepreneurs Are Born, Not Made

Everyone has an idea in their mind about what a "typical" entrepreneur is like. What is yours? Are they brilliant? Driven? Self-made? Charismatic? The answer may surprise you. In his 2003 book *The Change Makers*, Maury Klein profiled twenty-six of the greatest US entrepreneurs of all time. His conclusion? Outside of some very superficial characteristics such as "hard worker," they really don't have much in common. Some succeed in school. Some are dropouts. Some come from great families and others from broken homes. Some are very popular and sociable while others are loners and misfits. There simply isn't an overarching "entrepreneurial personality." Klein summarized what each of these men have in common as a series of intersections.

QUOTE

> *Every man had his own vision, his own style, and his own obsessions. Their common ground seems little more than a series of intersections where their ways of doing business crossed. No single explanation could embrace their roads to success or the routes by which they reached their destination. No formula or set of rules can transform one into a great entrepreneur any more than it could produce a great artist or scientist.[4]*

- MAURY KLEIN

Does this mean that successful entrepreneurs don't share any common mindsets? Absolutely not. The remainder of this chapter explores not only the misconceptions that form the foundation of the self-limiting beliefs that hold would-be entrepreneurs back, but also the mindset changes that can help them approach their endeavors in a realistic and successful way.

MY TAKE

The talent necessary to successfully launch a venture is the same that's needed for any other creative endeavor. Think about learning to play the piano. A few people are born tone-deaf, and no amount of work will result in their being competent musicians. A few are blessed with natural talent and can become world-class pianists without the need for extensive formal training. The vast, vast majority of us fall somewhere in the middle. Maybe we'll never play Carnegie Hall, but with enough practice and the right coaching, we can reach some level of competence. We can't all be Mark Zuckerberg, but that's okay. We should be following our dream, not his.

EXAMPLE

Quick Case: To illustrate the range of personalities that are no obstacle to success, consider the stories of three titans with entrepreneurial roots: Warren Buffett, Mark Zuckerberg, and Thomas Edison. Buffett was born in 1930 as the son of a congressman in Omaha, Nebraska. He expressed an interest in entrepreneurial activities as a child and worked in his grandfather's grocery at a young age. He also dabbled in various other entrepreneurial undertakings, to the point of amassing a considerable amount of money as a child. His intention was to skip the world of higher education and instead head straight into the world of business; however, he was overruled by his father, who insisted Buffett receive a college education. Decades later, Buffett—in addition to being considered one of the most successful investors in the world—is worth over $80B. Despite his outsized wealth, Buffett famously lives frugally and is a noted philanthropist. His success has been built on building a plan, sticking to it, and repeating that process.

Contrast this approach with that of Facebook founder and CEO Mark Zuckerberg. Zuckerberg was born in 1984 in White Plains, New York. At a young age he became interested in computer programming, and by the time he graduated high school he had developed a reputation for being a programming prodigy. He attended Harvard to study psychology and computer science, and it was from his dorm room there that he famously created the first iteration of Facebook. Zuckerberg dropped out of Harvard to lead Facebook and has championed an approach to success that largely consists of the ethos "Move fast and break things." Unlike Buffett, who sticks to the course he has laid out for himself, Zuckerberg channels what has become the Silicon Valley mentality of constant change, growth prioritized above all else, and what has been called "the hacker mindset."

In 1847—eighty-three years before Warren Buffett was born—inventor and entrepreneur Thomas Edison entered the world as the last of seven children. He received only a small amount of formal schooling; he was homeschooled by his mother after attending public school for only a few months. After working for the railroad as a young man, Edison struck out on his own and obtained the exclusive right to sell newspapers on his local railroad. This endeavor morphed into a series of jobs that provided him income while he continued to dabble in his true twin passions of reading and experimenting. Edison's legacy is that of a prolific inventor with over 1,000 patents to his name, but he was also a shrewd and successful businessman who founded fourteen companies. The most notable of these is General Electric, which to this day continues to be an internationally successful company. In his personal life, Edison followed a strict doctrine of nonviolence and lived as a vegetarian.

All three of these men have made an indelible mark on the world despite the differences in their background, education, and personal style that got them to their lifetime of accomplishment. All three worked hard, but, more importantly, a common thread that ties them together is a deep passion for the path that they chose.

I Don't Have Any Business Skills

News flash—most entrepreneurs don't have a business degree, and often their first experience in the business world is when they start their own venture. Business skills do help make the process an easier one, however, and will be required once you become established. This means you will have to acquire them yourself, create a team of people with the right skill sets, or hire experts. The contributions of your founding team are critical, and I cover founding teams at length in chapter 12.

Business skills aren't a must-have, but there are two major skills that you will need. The good news is that, though some people are born with a natural aptitude for these skills, anyone can learn them. Even more good news: learning these skills won't just help you become a successful entrepreneur. They are the foundation of a healthy and happy life regardless of your career path.

Self-Awareness

In what is sometimes called "the paradox of leadership," effective leaders must balance humility and confidence. These two character attributes are often seen as opposites that are incompatible with one another, but that assessment leaves out a critical component of the equation—self-awareness. The Stoic philosopher Epictetus sums up the need for humility thusly: *It is impossible for a man to learn what he thinks he already knows.*

A healthy level of humility and self-awareness helps you to understand your strengths and weaknesses. Life in general is a long learning process, and the undertaking of starting your own business even more so. Humility is an expression of self-awareness that allows us to say, "I do not yet know enough." Humility is what allows us to be willing to ask for and accept help when needed. No one does anything significant in life alone. We all need help and support along the way.

Successful entrepreneurs know that they don't have all the answers, and they actively seek out advice and good ideas. The worst characteristic for an entrepreneur to have is suspicion and paranoia that everyone is out to get them and steal their great ideas. Not only is this behavior unbecoming, it also reflects another major misconception regarding ideas and opportunities. As discussed in the previous chapter, ideas do not have inherent worth. Only when they evolve into actionable opportunities do they develop a value, and this evolution is due in no small part to the composition of your entrepreneurial thumbprint.

Confidence is also an expression of self-awareness. Not to be confused with arrogance, recklessness, or egotism, confidence is the side of self-awareness that allows us to say, "Knowing the challenge in front of me, and knowing my experience, learning, and skills, I think I have a good chance of overcoming this challenge." If self-awareness is something that you haven't thought about before picking up this book, that's okay. Self-awareness—and by extension humility and confidence—are not hardwired character traits. They are aspects of the dialogue you have with yourself and elements of the frame through which you see the world. As with any other skill, self-aware living can be cultivated through intent and practice.

Interpersonal Skills

Interpersonal skills such as communication, listening, empathy, and conflict resolution often get lumped into the category of "soft skills." Soft skills are often seen as less valuable than "hard skills," or the explicit skill sets required to execute a professional role. This book is not a debate about the relationship between hard and soft skills, but in the realm of entrepreneurship, traditionally "soft" interpersonal skills become essential hard skills for success.

Dealing with people and making connections is an unavoidable part of being a successful entrepreneur. Successful entrepreneurs are assiduous networkers and connection-makers. This doesn't mean that you have to be an extreme extrovert or super salesperson. What it does mean is that business is done by people, with people, and for people. Avoiding contact with humans is not a recipe for entrepreneurial success. At times it may *feel* as though interpersonal skills are impossible to teach someone who doesn't have a knack for communication. Either you're born being comfortable talking to strangers or you simply aren't, right? Not really. Unlike hard skills such as computer programming or accounting, interpersonal skills are tough to measure and evaluate, but that doesn't mean that someone who isn't a strong communicator is doomed to never improve.

I Don't Have Enough Money to Start a Business.

Twenty years ago, this wasn't just a self-limiting belief—it was a reality for the vast majority of entrepreneurs. There were tremendous fixed costs in starting a business, such as leasing and equipping office space, purchasing plant and equipment assets, covering material and inventory costs, and hiring employees, not to mention numerous legal and regulatory hurdles.

In the last two decades or so, these costs have been either eliminated or largely mitigated. The typical twenty-first century startup doesn't require any of the above items. There are many businesses you can literally start right from your laptop while sitting in your local Starbucks.

This doesn't mean that you won't require *any* funds. There are certainly costs associated with the startup process. Depending on the type of business you want to operate, your startup costs can run into a few thousand dollars, spread over time. Your baseline needs will include the following:

1. Connectivity
A laptop, cell phone, and good internet connection are a must. (You probably already have these anyway, right?)

2. Registration
Incorporation, along with state registration, incurs some basic legal fees. A lawyer is usually not necessary for a startup in the earliest stages, but if you are unsure about your needs or the specifics of your industry, contact a lawyer who specializes in incorporation and business law.

3. A Web Presence
A web presence has never been easier to establish or more necessary for modern businesses. Collectively, your web presence refers to your domain name, web hosting, and website. Vendors who offer these services make it easy to establish a web presence for your business even if you have no technical experience.

4. A Graphic Identity
The *graphic identity* of a business is the sum of that business's visual design elements such as logos, business cards, visual messaging, color palette, and visual themes.

5. A Social Presence
Your web presence can be a two-way communication tool, but nothing beats social media for creating a dialogue with your customers. Now more than ever, consumers expect that the brands they do business with will have a social presence. This is true even if your business doesn't sell a "sexy" product. Social media accounts for businesses are usually free, but they can incur cost in the form of content production, management, and

management software that reduces the time requirements that an active social media presence can produce.

Here are some things you think you will need, but probably won't:

1. A phone service or answering service
2. A lawyer, accountant, marketing agency, or other high-priced professional service provider
3. A retail storefront, inventory, or storage space
4. Employees

Of course, there are many businesses, such as restaurants, retail stores, gyms, etc., that will require significant up-front funding. In the case of those types of businesses, you need to think carefully about where this money will come from and whether this is the right kind of business for you. This will be discussed at much greater length in chapter 4.

Now Is Not the Right Time

An internet search will provide you with the "scientific" answer to the question "what is the best age at which to start a business?" The answer is 39. I have no idea how that age was arrived at, but the internet believes it, so it must be true!

The fact is, there is no right time. Younger people have less experience in business and in life, but also fewer family and professional obligations holding them back. Older folks have wisdom, networks, and experience, but also may have a lot of other demands on their time. The fact is, there is no "best" time. Any time you choose to jump in is going to lead to a lot of hard work and demands on your time. If you know that you're passionate about your venture, and your strategic analysis leads you to believe the opportunity is there, go for it!

This *doesn't* mean you should throw caution to the wind, quit your job, and hope for the best. Careful planning is in order, and you're going to have to cover all of your other obligations as well. The topic of work-life balance will be explored in greater detail, but suffice it to say it will be a strain for the foreseeable future. You probably won't be able to quit your day job right away, which means you'll have to deal with two jobs. You'll have to do a lot of juggling to keep all the balls in the air.

A WORD ABOUT MULTITASKING: It is received wisdom these days that we live in a constant state of distraction and that people's attention spans are getting shorter. I don't know whether or not this is actually true, but I do know that modern technology is both a blessing and a curse when it comes to productivity. I'm writing this section on my laptop in MS Word. Besides Word, I currently have nine other apps open, including my productivity app. On my two browsers, I have eighteen tabs open to different websites. How does my desk compare to yours? I bet you're looking at something similar.

The good news is that this unprecedented power frees you to organize your work however you'd like. The bad news is that it gives you ample opportunity to screw around. The choice of how you work best is entirely up to you. Some people prefer to plan out every waking hour extensively. Some like to make lists of tasks to accomplish. Some like to focus on one task at a time. Others like to switch rapidly between tasks. Some of you are morning people, and some like burning the midnight oil. Any regimen that works for you can be effective. The trick is to know when you're being effective and when you're wasting time and energy on nonproductive tasks. If you're not accomplishing what you're setting out to do during the day, you're either setting unrealistic expectations or you need a new system.

What If I Fail?

A fear of failure is natural for many first-time entrepreneurs, but successful entrepreneurs think about failure in an entirely different way. To them, failure is not only a part of the process of starting and growing a new business, but it is also an important marker signifying growth and movement. Part of this perspective shift comes from the inherent optimism that all entrepreneurs share, but a mindset that embraces failure is a realistic and holistic look at what it means to find success starting your own business.

It doesn't matter how many times you fail. It doesn't matter how many times you almost get it right. No one is going to know or care about your failures, and neither should you. All you have to do is learn from them and those around you because all that matters in business is that you get it right once.

- MARK CUBAN

The best way to understand failure in the context of your own business is to operate under the assumption that you will fail. Failure in some capacity is guaranteed when entering uncharted territory. If failure is guaranteed, then that means the way you handle failure becomes the most important element of your entrepreneurial success. Pick any successful business today that started out as a startup. The founding team of that business met numerous failures, but today the business is alive and well. Where would that business be today if those founders had seen failure as a dead end?

Failure is an inevitability of the testing and experimentation process. For entrepreneurs who are starting out, a large portion of what they do is experimentation. If an entrepreneur doesn't experiment with a new way of doing things, how can the business grow? In this way, failure is not a dead end, but an indicator that growth and learning are taking place.

The way in which a person views failure is a mindset, not a personality trait. Personality traits can be difficult to change, but you are in complete control over your own mindset. Don't be paralyzed by a fear of what people will think. Failures are the learning tools through which we reach successes.

Within the entrepreneurial world, failure is the means by which businesses find their way. Harnessing this concept as a driver of innovation and growth can seem difficult at first, but it can be developed through key activities.

» **Change your mindset**
Welcome failure as a learning opportunity, and try to fail fast so as to not waste time chasing a poor business model. The faster you can put inevitable failures behind you, the faster you will be along the path toward success.

» **Be ready to pivot rapidly**
Failing just for the sake of failing won't get you anywhere. When you reach the realization that the current course isn't working, be ready to pivot. Understanding failure as a learning tool means that flexibility is important. Don't cling to an original idea, especially in the face of evidence that it isn't the best course of action. It's better to "fail fast" than continue on a course that's not working.

» **Experiment constantly**
Constantly experiment with new ideas and initiatives but realize that many aren't going to work out. Try to inject a healthy dose of natural

curiosity about new ideas into the way you think about your business, and the good ones will morph into opportunities.

In practice, this set of activities changes the path to success from the straight line that many people envision to the branching and divergent path that is a more accurate representation of the journey to success that you will encounter. The twisting path pictured is a visual representation of the entrepreneurial mindset and its relationship to failure. In short, each point of failure along the way is an opportunity to pivot toward a new path to success.

fig. 3

Risk and the Entrepreneurial Mindset

Starting your own venture obviously carries a considerable amount of risk. Embracing failure and aiming to fail fast does not mean being reckless with risk. Instead, it means understanding and accepting risk as an inherent quality related to starting your own business and managing that risk by improving your odds.

Think of risk in these ways:

»   **Entrepreneurs interpret the risk vs. reward calculation differently.**
    No one who is starting their own business believes that their actions aren't risky compared to choosing another path. What they do believe, however, is that the reward justifies the increased levels of assumed risk.

» **The entrepreneurial mindset changes a person's perception of risk.**
When failure is seen as a steppingstone and the path to success is understood to be nonlinear, an individual's perception of risk changes dramatically. Compare that mindset with someone who sees failure as a dead end, or any path to success that is not a straight line as invalid.

Calculating risk based on a massive reward, perceiving risk through the lens of failure as an opportunity, and being comfortable with risk all differentiate an entrepreneur from a speculator or a gambler. In this way, risk can be seen less as static odds and more as a condition that can be influenced.

The Role of Luck

Many entrepreneurs scoff at the notion of luck, preferring rugged slogans like "I make my own luck," "the harder I work, the luckier I get," or "luck is where preparation meets opportunity." Despite this self-made motif, self-reflective entrepreneurs will often readily acknowledge that luck has had a profound role in their success. I will say this about luck—you're much more likely to find it if you're out there trying to make things happen rather than passively waiting for fortune to smile down upon you.

That being said, if you scratch a little below the surface of any entrepreneurial success story, chances are you will find some sort of chance meeting, lucky break, great timing, etc., that just can't be explained as anything else but luck. Sometimes it's hard to sift out the "luck" because successful entrepreneurs and the adoring financial press that follow them have no incentive to admit to any sort of good fortune, and every reason to imply that every good thing that happened to them was the result of their intelligence, hard work, and careful planning.

Like many nascent entrepreneurs, you probably like to read stories about successful entrepreneurs as a form of motivation, but the stories you read are often hopelessly skewed and self-serving. They are, in the words of Rudyard Kipling, "just-so stories." The phrase stems from Kipling's famous book of children's tales by the same name. I am not the first person to trust Wikipedia; however, the entry for just-so stories sums them up quite nicely. They are "an unverifiable narrative explanation for a cultural practice, a biological trait, or behavior of humans or other animals." Such tales are common in folklore and mythology. Just-so stories are the effectuation version of narratives—they start with the end result and work their way backwards rather than truly examining the root cause of the phenomenon.

Entrepreneurs are this generation's folk heroes and myths, and we like to believe they have superhuman skills and abilities. We view them as the ultimate self-made men and women. However, that's often just not the case. Going back to our Quick Case on page 24, Mark Zuckerberg was the product of an affluent household and an Ivy League pedigree. Bill Gates' story follows much the same narrative. Warren Buffett's father was a member of Congress, and he has a degree from Columbia. Jeff Bezos went to Princeton. These are not exactly Horatio Alger stories. This isn't to say they aren't admirable people—it's just that their success stories are more nuanced than is generally acknowledged.

The best way to deal with the prevalence of luck is to not worry about it, because you can't control it anyway. Worrying about things outside your control is a surefire path to stress and anxiety, neither of which are conducive to success. It's also not very mindful. Mindfulness, the importance of living a self-actualized life, is discussed at length in the next chapter.

Do I Need a Business Plan?

Every business should have a business plan—even if your business isn't seeking funding. As with many aspects of the entrepreneurial universe, there are many misconceptions surrounding business plans, their utility, and the scope of their function. Because of this, business plans are often seen as a waste of time. However, nothing could be further from the truth.

The last part of this book is dedicated to helping you build your business plan in a comprehensive and strategic manner, but for now, suffice it to say that your business plan is much more than just a summary of your business. It is also each of the following:

» **Communication tool:** The business plan communicates your opportunity to potential founding team members, stakeholders, family members, and prospective employees.

» **Planning tool:** In addition to helping you develop strategy, the business plan construction process forces you to become fluent in your opportunity, your market, and your industry.

» **Discovery tool:** Oftentimes we simply don't know what we don't know. The business plan construction process uncovers knowledge gaps relating to your opportunity, market, and industry in an organized and systematic way.

Also understand that despite its utility, a business plan is not a magic bullet. Even the most well-written and well-constructed business plan is not a guarantee of success or even a guarantee that your opportunity will receive funding.

Q: Is it okay to outsource the writing/construction of my business plan?

Answer: No. The whole point of the business plan writing process is to ensure that you know the ins and outs of your business like the back of your hand. A critical component of your value proposition—the backbone of your business—is identifying *who* will be buying your product or service and *why* (chapter 8). A consultant will be able to point you in the right direction, check your work, and recommend ways to collect information, but he or she should not be doing the work. There is simply no substitute for rolling up your sleeves—even if you are the only person who will ever read the plan.

Chapter Recap

» Many self-limiting beliefs that hold would-be entrepreneurs back are based on misconceptions.

» The common idea of a "typical" entrepreneur is also usually based on a misconception. There is no single path that will guarantee success. Successful entrepreneurs come from a variety of backgrounds and take diverse paths to reach their success.

» A lack of "business skills" does not disqualify someone from being an entrepreneur—many famously successful entrepreneurs started their businesses with a lack of formal training (but having a business background certainly helps!) Two key skills to develop are self-awareness and interpersonal skills.

» Startup costs are much lower than they once were. Some businesses can be started with low financial commitments or commitments that are spread over time, and with little more than a laptop and an internet connection.

» There is no "right" time to start a business. Younger entrepreneurs have freedom of time but lack experience and a developed network. Conversely, entrepreneurs who are older tend to have more experience and developed networks but more time constraints.

» Failure is by no means the end of an entrepreneur's journey. It is important to reframe your conception of failure as a learning tool and an indicator of progress and experimentation rather than a brick wall.

» Every new venture should take the time to construct and maintain a business plan. Business plans are important strategic documents as well as discovery, measuring, and communication tools.

| 3 |

Reaching Success
What You Really Need to Succeed as an Entrepreneur

Chapter Overview
- » Intangible versus tangible aspects of starting a business
- » The intangible aspects that have the greatest impact on success
- » The importance of mindfulness, achieving a state of flow, work-life balance, and living a self-actualized life

This is the part of the book where I'm supposed to give you a list of traits you need to be successful as an entrepreneur. Or I would if I was writing clickbait rather than a serious book. I recently googled "Do I have the entrepreneurial spirit?" and got nearly 65 million results. Most of the relevant results were lists of traits. Some common themes:

- » Passion
- » Resiliency
- » Vision
- » Calculated risk-taking
- » Hard work

I don't dispute the importance of any of these characteristics for entrepreneurial success, but these traits are widely held by many people and they certainly don't guarantee success. I've been observing successful entrepreneurs for a long time, and I believe there is one characteristic that's most critical for success: mindfulness.

Mindfulness

Mindfulness is a term that seems to be everywhere these days. It is used to the point where it can seem meaningless. At its most basic, mindfulness means being focused on what's actually happening in the present, without spinning a narrative about what it means, or comparing it to what other people are doing or thinking. It also means not continually regretting or reliving the past or worrying about things that might possibly happen in the future.

Truly mindful individuals always know exactly what they are doing and why they are doing it. This may seem simple, but if you really think about it, a lot of the things we do on a day-to-day basis are essentially mindless. We do them out of habit, because someone told us to, or just because they are part of a routine. If you are looking at your day mindfully, you are carefully considering the purpose and desired outcome of all your actions and making sure you're doing them for the right reasons rather than chasing false hopes and expectations.

Approaching your life this way will profoundly change your perspective in very fundamental ways. Let's take a simple example—driving. People have a tendency to get angry and aggressive when they drive, for no good reason. And it only hurts them. Let's say the light you're waiting at turns green and the car in front of you is slow to start moving. You get furious and curse at the other driver, maybe even blow your horn. Where does the anger come from, and what purpose does it serve? Mindful individuals realize that their anger does not help them in any way. They're not going to get where they're going any faster, and the aggravation just raises their blood pressure and makes their day worse.

As you can see, mindfulness encourages you to examine your thoughts and emotions to truly understand where they're coming from. Doing so allows you to see much more clearly why you're doing what you're doing, and whether it fits into your goals or even whether it makes sense at all.

With this in mind, let's examine how mindfulness informs the internet's list of "essential entrepreneurial traits."

Passion

Are you doing what you're excited about? Is it meaningful to you? Do you feel strongly that it's what gives your life purpose? If not, you're probably pursuing entrepreneurship for the wrong reasons. Many people are attracted to entrepreneurship because they want to make a lot of money, but starting a business purely to make money is a mistake. The road to entrepreneurial success is long, hard, and extremely uncertain. Chances are good that you will fail, at least at first. Not to mention that the process of starting a new business will take up most of your time and energy. If you're not passionate about what you're doing, chances are you'll lose interest, and at the very least you'll waste a lot of time being unhappy.

You may have heard that many people are attracted to entrepreneurship because they are independent and want to work for themselves. This is largely a myth. There is no such thing as a "lone wolf" in business. You are always accountable to someone, even if you don't have a boss. Entrepreneurs are accountable to stakeholders such as customers, suppliers, investors, and employees. You can't just do whatever you want, and the more your business grows, the less freedom you will have. There are occupations that are essentially solitary, but the domain of business is largely a social network.

Being mindful means understanding what you're passionate about and why. If you love what you're doing, you'll excel at it. If you don't, you'll be miserable. It's important to make major life decisions for the right reasons.

Resiliency

Starting a business is hard, and there will be many failures and frustrations for each success. This is simply a reality of starting a new business. Mindful individuals accept these bumps in the road for what they are—setbacks on the path to achieving larger goals. They don't worry about things they can't control, stress out about possible future outcomes, or engage in negative self-talk when things don't go their way. No one is perfect, and we all make many mistakes throughout our lives.

Mindful people recognize this and are quick to forgive themselves when they screw up. The past has already happened. The future is unknown. The only thing we can control is what we do in the present moment.

Vision

Mindful individuals keep an eye on long-term goals, without being distracted by day-to-day hindrances or the doubts and negative feedback of well-meaning individuals. This doesn't mean that mindful entrepreneurs don't take advice. The trick is to know the difference between advice and negativity. Amazon founder and CEO Jeff Bezos once referred to this mindset as "stubborn but flexible."

Everyone has advice for those starting their own businesses. That advice can be particularly insistent from people who have never started a business themselves. It also tends to be overwhelmingly negative. Everyone is in a rush to tell you why you aren't doing the right thing. That doesn't mean they are wrong. Successful entrepreneurs have the capacity to mentally sift through the feedback they're getting, ignoring the unhelpful advice but being ready, willing, and able to act quickly when they hear something that makes sense to them.

This mental sifting is an important part of the decision-making process, but it also invites falling prey to *shiny object syndrome*. Like a magpie that lines its nest with every shiny object it can find, entrepreneurs who fall victim to shiny object syndrome chase after every new opportunity that looks promising to them without thinking through their choices or asking critical questions about utility and need. Instead, mindful entrepreneurs maintain their long-term vision about where they are headed and what they want their venture to ultimately look like, but they recognize that they don't have all the answers, and that changing conditions may warrant changing tactics or strategies along the way.

Calculated Risk-Taking

I addressed the concept of risk at length in the previous chapter, so I won't belabor those points here. Adopting a mindfulness perspective leads people to favor action over endless analysis. The perpetual analysis hamster wheel that exhaustively explores every option and postpones action indefinitely has aptly been referred to as "paralysis by analysis." It should go without saying that talking about taking action is a lot less helpful than taking action.

Mindful individuals are not afraid to fail; in fact, they prefer to adopt a scientific approach of constant experimentation in which failures teach you as much as successes do. If something isn't going to work, it's much better to "fail fast" and find it out quickly rather than waste time on a path that will not lead you to achieving your goals.

Hard Work

It takes a lot of hard work to start a business successfully. Then again, it takes a lot of hard work to do almost anything worthwhile in life. This is what makes a mindful approach to entrepreneurship so essential—the key is to know what you're doing and why you're doing it. This is what mindful people do.

The notion of hard work really has to do with work-life balance, and there is no right or wrong answer to the topic. Some people feel the need to "#hustle" 24/7 in order to be successful. This obviously depends on a multitude of factors such as the type of business you are starting or your personal skills (to name a few) but there is no way around it—you are undoubtedly going to have to sacrifice much of your leisure time. Not to mention potentially much of your disposable income and/or savings.

Mindful people adopt the mentality of sacrificing in the short term for the long-term gains. If everything you do is in furtherance of where you want to be, and you're working in an area that you're passionate about, you won't perceive your activities as "work." Rather, they're simply what you do. This quote, while perhaps cliché, sums up the mindful entrepreneur's approach to hard work:

"Find a job you enjoy doing,
and you will never have to work a day in your life."

- MARK TWAIN

Flow

It turns out that mindfulness has an analog in psychology: the concept of *flow*.[5] If you have ever felt like you were "in the zone," congratulations—you have achieved a state of flow. Flow is the focused, productive, and uplifting feeling that comes with being totally immersed in a task. When you are in a state of flow, you lose track of time. Your concentration and focus are completely dedicated to the task at hand. What kinds of tasks produce a flow state? Those that present a challenge and that are intrinsically rewarding. Flow is mindfulness in real time.

Another way to think about flow is to define it based on what it's not: anxiety, apathy, arousal, boredom, control, relaxation, and worry are states of mind that contrast with flow. When a task is much too difficult for our skill level it can cause feelings of worry and anxiety, as well as a feeling that we are not in control. Conversely, tasks that are no challenge at all or those that do not have outcomes that we view as valuable can cause boredom and apathy. Flow, then, is the sweet spot between a task that is too challenging and one that is too easy—and has an outcome that we are invested in.

Obviously, flow is the optimal state for learning and productivity. More than simply being a tool for getting the most out of your time, being in a state of flow feels *good*. It is a goal not only in the sense that it allows us to work at peak performance, but in the sense that it leaves us feeling tremendously fulfilled by the work that we do. Psychologists have conducted large amounts of research on how to achieve the flow state, but the short answer is mindfulness. When you exhibit the mindful approaches to vision, passion, and resiliency outlined above, you're inviting the flow state.

There are eight characteristics of flow:

fig. 4

Complete Concentration on the Task at Hand

- Focus to the point that the rest of the world fades away

Transformation of Time

- Time seems to speed up or slow down

Clarity of Goals, Reward in Mind, and Immediate Feedback

- An understanding of what needs to be done
- An understanding and desire for a successful outcome
- Immediate feedback to guide further actions

The Experience Is Intrinsically Rewarding and an End in Itself

- The task and its outcome have value for the person performing it

Balance Between Challenge & Skill

- Often a pairing of high skill with high, manageable challenge

A Feeling of Control over the Task

- The difficulty of the task is matched to the skill level of the person performing it

A Feeling of Effortlessness & Ease

- Despite varying challenges or difficulties, the overall rate of fatigue is low

Actions & Awareness Are Merged

- Performance of tasks feels like second nature
- One has a feeling of truly living in the moment

Work-Life Balance and Working for Yourself

Life is all about tradeoffs and compromise. Everyone has to find their own balance. I like to visualize life as a triangle consisting of work life, home life, and personal life. Your work life is all of the things you do to pursue your vocation and make a living. Your home life consists of your family, your living space, and all of the things you do to maintain them. Your personal life is everything else; all of the social, spiritual, physical, and intellectual activities that make your life complete.

fig. 5

Figure 5 shows an equilateral triangle, with all sides completely in balance, but that's rarely the case. Usually, one or two dominate your activities at a given time, and the other one or two take a back seat. This balance shifts constantly. Maybe you have young children and your home life is your main priority. Maybe you just started your business and work takes up most of your time. Maybe you're at a point where your social life preoccupies you. If you spend more time on one, you have less to spend on the others. Time is a zero-sum concept. We each only have twenty-four hours in the day, and we each choose how to spend them.

The thing about being self-employed is that these areas tend to blend together. Despite the fact that it may not feel like it at times, there is much more to life than your business. Yes, your business is an expression of your passion and creativity. Yes, your business is an important part of your life. And yes, your work life is a big part of the triangle that makes up your life. But your business *isn't* your life. To wax philosophical for a moment, if you and your business are one and the same, what does it mean for your health and well-being if your business hits a speed bump? Being able to separate yourself from your business will allow you to make smarter decisions and will have a positive effect on your mental health.

At times, the advice to take a step back seems counterintuitive. A few pages back, I myself told you something that isn't a secret: starting a business takes a lot of work. But completing a "lot of work" doesn't have to equate to working frantically and burning yourself out while alienating friends and family in the process. Many contemporary articles and social media posts don't do much in the way of helping dispel the notion of entrepreneurs as mythical figures. Advocating for the "hustle" mindset, casting entrepreneurs as never-fail heroes, and fetishizing high stress levels and a lack of sleep as success metrics do not help those launching their own ventures to make better choices when it comes to work-life balance.

Quick Case: Digital media mogul and founder of The Huffington Post (now HuffPost), Arianna Huffington poured her heart and soul into her fledgling media company to get it off the ground. For Huffington, eighteen-hour workdays were the norm and sleep deprivation simply came with the territory. After two years of running herself into the ground—though building a very successful company—Huffington had an epiphany, which she shares publicly. Returning home from the office one night, she collapsed in her apartment and hit her head on the way down. She woke up to find herself lying on the floor with blood on her face. Medically, the only thing that was discernibly wrong with her was that she suffered from sheer exhaustion. Now, Huffington has a complete one-eighty position on work-life balance.

By professional definitions of success, I was successful. By any sane definition of success, if you are lying in a pool full of blood on the floor of your office, you are not successful.[6]

- ARIANNA HUFFINGTON

Arianna Huffington is far from being the only successful entrepreneur to encourage those who are starting new ventures to carefully consider their work-life balance. Ultimately, there is no single answer for everyone. Some people simply perform better when they can lose themselves in their work, and that's okay. Working hard and working too hard can seem like a nonsensical distinction until working too hard leads to burnout and dissatisfaction with something that was once your passion.

It all goes back to the triangle. Ideally, all three facets of your life—work life, home life, and personal life—exist in harmony without too much pushing and pulling. This harmonious state allows you to shift focus between each aspect without too much friction. But if you are consumed by an obsessive focus solely on your work life, that part of the triangle pulls heavily on the other two and stretches into an unrecognizable shape. With your life triangle out of balance, shifting focus away from your business causes feelings of guilt—guilt that stems from focusing on anything other than your business. The best way to combat this? Mindful living supplemented by healthy doses of self-awareness.

Living a Self-Actualized Life

Together, mindfulness and self-awareness culminate in what could be called a self-actualized life. This may sound like something out of a *Kung Fu* movie, but the reality is that time and time again the *intangible* aspects of entrepreneurship have the greatest impact on success. Just like self-awareness, mindfulness, and interpersonal skills, the recipe for living a self-actualized life is made up of ingredients that can be learned by anyone.

A person (entrepreneur or otherwise) who lives a self-actualized life is someone who has an appreciation for life and is guided by a set of inner goals and values. More than any other aspect, what is generally referred to as "the entrepreneurial mindset" is really a description of self-actualized living.

Creativity

The act of entrepreneurship is the ultimate creative act. Forming something that is successful, durable, and makes an impact on people's lives out of the randomness, ambiguity, and uncertainty that is the entrepreneurial ecosystem can't be called anything *but* creative. To some, that may sound intimidating, but even people who don't consider themselves "the creative type" find ways to let their imaginations soar. Creativity is an enduring human trait and can be both very powerful and very personal.

Quick Case: *Eddie Huang, Baohaus* – The son of Taiwanese immigrants, Huang has had a diverse entrepreneurial career. He lost his job as an attorney during the Financial Crisis of 2007-2008. Instead of hopping to another employer, Huang changed gears completely and turned to stand-up comedy to pay the bills. Over the next decade he started a clothing design company and became a chef and restaurateur, author, and TV personality. He is best known for his Manhattan restaurant Baohaus and his TV show *Huang's World*. Regarding his education, he said, "I wasn't meant to be an attorney, but I was meant to go to law school." His ventures have seen varying levels of success, but the sheer range of industries and markets Eddie Huang has participated in is a testament to his creativity and perseverance.

Authenticity

Whether they are well-meaning or not, those around you will have something to say about your choice to pursue an entrepreneurial path. Don't be surprised if this solicited and unsolicited input is overwhelmingly negative. Authenticity, at its core, means choosing your path and knowing *why* you're on that path regardless of the opinions of others. Authenticity isn't contrarianism, and it isn't an excuse to ignore good advice. Rather, it is a way of staying true to yourself, your goals, and your own happiness and success.

Quick Case: *Whitney Wolfe Herd, Bumble* – Featured on both the *Forbes* 30 Under 30 list and the *Fortune* 40 Under 40, Whitney Wolfe Herd was on the founding team for the uber-successful dating app Tinder. After she left the team in 2014, she began her own dating app called Bumble. Bumble's tagline is "Make the first move" and features a twist on the traditional dating app: matches between users are only truly matches if the woman messages first. This shift in functionality has paid off in a big way. Bumble reported 30 million users in June of 2018, which trails the 50 million reported by Tinder, but despite lagging, Bumble has demonstrated impressive growth. On the topic of success: *"Being able to put your blinders on, ignore negative opinions, and follow your strong intuition is what's validating to me. It's a great feeling to know you can trust your gut."*

Continuous Improvement

In our world, the only true constant is change. A philosophy of continuous improvement not only embraces change as a constant but reframes it as driver of improvement. This philosophy is referred to as **kaizen**, a Japanese word that translates as "continuous improvement." More than a doctrine of ongoing development, kaizen prioritizes incremental improvement over broad, sweeping changes. Incremental changes are easier to implement—they require fewer resources and can begin making an impact right away (albeit a small impact). Over time, incremental improvements add up and result in the same gains that broad sweeping changes might, but without causing the disruption that a total change of course can lead to.

In a professional capacity, this means incessantly and obsessively looking for more ways to provide value to your target customers and enhance your core capabilities. In a personal capacity it means applying the same logic of incremental improvement to find better ways to meet your goals. That may mean learning something new every day, honing your skills, working toward living a self-actualized life, or all of the above. More than just a tool to spur personal, professional, and organizational growth, the philosophy of kaizen has the additional benefit of encouraging comfort with ongoing change—an attitude that is not only healthy at the personal level, but absolutely critical for a new venture.

Sudden vs. Incremental Change

fig. 6

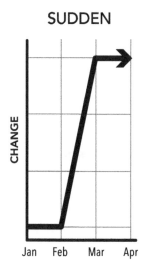

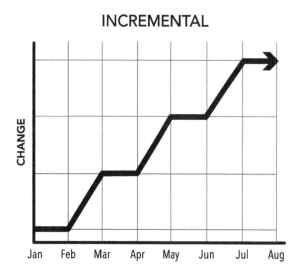

MY TAKE

Entrepreneurs often make lousy employees. They will never fully commit to an organizational culture or go all in to achieve organizational goals, because they don't see the payoff for them. They also tend to butt heads with their supervisors because they have strong opinions about the right way to do things that are often at odds with the status quo. Because they are intelligent and driven, they don't usually fail outright (although some entrepreneurs are so "out there" that they are conventionally unemployable), but they often drift from job to job, getting easily bored and restless and looking for the next thing. Does this sound like you? You should give serious thought to starting your own business.

Chapter Recap

» Entrepreneurial success is less about a list of traits and more about focusing on the present. Mindfulness, specifically knowing what you are doing and why you are doing it, brings out the best in what are often thought of as "entrepreneurial traits."

» Understanding the benefits of achieving a state of flow and working toward this condition on a regular basis will improve your feeling of fulfillment along with increasing your productivity and learning capacity.

» There is no question that starting a new venture requires hard work but allowing work life to overtake home and personal life can have very detrimental effects, not only on your feelings of personal fulfillment, but on the success of your venture as well.

» Mindful, self-aware living culminates in leading a self-actualized life. A self-actualized life is defined by an appreciation for life and guided by a set of inner goals and values. This, more than anything else, is the best definition of the "entrepreneurial mindset." It is marked by creativity, authenticity, and a desire for continuous improvement.

PART II

GETTING STARTED

| 4 |
Your Company
The First Steps

Chapter Overview

» Where exactly to get started
» Your first steps and important considerations
» Your name, legal form, and brand collateral discussed in detail

A Note on Strategic Planning

Regardless of whether or not you write a formal business plan, the beginning stages of starting a business are a strategic planning process. At its most basic, a strategy is a plan to achieve a specific desired outcome, and that's a good place to start. You need to have a specific end goal or set of goals for your venture. Otherwise, you won't know if you're successful, and you'll have no way of determining whether you're making progress. Now is the time to consider this carefully—*what are you actually trying to achieve?*

As I discussed in the previous section, just trying to make a lot of money is not a sufficient reason to devote your life to a venture. You need specific goals and desired outcomes. Take some time at this stage to think this through.

Visualization Exercise

Imagine your business at several discrete milestones: one year, two years, and five years. Imagine that you've been wildly successful. What exactly does "success" look like? Be as specific as you possibly can and use as many metrics as you need. These will become your goals. You need to develop a specific plan to achieve them. That's what this section of the book is all about.

YOUR GOALS NEED TO BE SMART – There is a well-known acronym in strategic planning regarding the nature of effective goal setting. Effective goals are *SMART*—specific, measurable, achievable, relevant, and time-bound. The meaning of each of these items is self-evident, so I won't spend a lot of time defining them. The important thing is to understand that your end goals have to be tangible things that you can actually achieve within a reasonable amount of time.

Some examples of SMART goals:
- *Achieve 90 percent customer satisfaction as measured by post-sale surveys.*
- *Grow sales to existing customers by 10 percent in the next year.*
- *Hire three new salespeople this quarter.*

Some examples of goals that aren't so SMART:
- *Be the next Google.*
- *Be the Uber of XX (pick an industry).*
- *Make a million dollars.*

Before you can really get started delivering value to your customers, you need to make some key decisions about your company. In this chapter we'll examine the first steps that are critical for every business, along with some of the more creative stuff like websites, logos, and business cards.

What Do I Do First?

If you are not familiar with what it takes to legally start a company, the process can seem complicated, but it really isn't. In fact, you may be surprised at how easy it can be. *But* this doesn't mean that it's a decision that should be made lightly. When it comes to the process of actually starting your business, it is always a good idea to do so under the advisement of a business or corporate lawyer. Let's take a look at some of the preliminary steps required to get your new venture off the ground.

What's Your Name?

What's in a name? After all, a rose by any other name would smell as sweet, right? While it is true that the problem you solve for your customers is more important than what you call your venture, that doesn't mean you should pick your startup's name out of a hat. There is no book out there that can tell *you* what to call *your* company. That being said, don't fall into some common traps that afflict new ventures. The longer you go on with a name you don't like, the harder it becomes to make a change.

» **Pick a Sticky Name**
A business name that is unique, memorable, stands out from the crowd, and stays fresh over time is as close as you can come to the perfect business name. In the brand-building industry, this is called a "sticky" name. Of course, coming up with a name that is perfectly sticky, totally encapsulates the problem you solve for your customers, and has a timeless quality is a sticky endeavor in its own way. No question—coming up with the perfectly sticky brand name is tough.

A truly sticky name can be a differentiator in its own right. A name that zigs while all of your competitors zag might help your venture stand out from the crowd, but there is a point where what you call yourself is so different from what your customers expect that your other messaging has to backtrack and spend time explaining what it is you do. Brainstorm, get inspiration, and (most importantly) get as much feedback as possible while attempting to come up with a name for your venture. Put yourself in the shoes of your customer. What first impressions do the name you are working on conjure up?

» **But Don't Get Too Sticky**
A name that is very long or has a very unusual spelling is memorable and unique, right? Not really. You're better off shooting for something shorter that is spelled in a way that your customers will expect. Acronyms might seem like a healthy compromise, but for new ventures they likely won't mean anything to your customers. Also keep in mind that your venture's name will be transformed into a logo or wordmark, meaning it will be on packaging, sales materials, business cards, and your website (which will be seen on a variety of screen sizes and resolutions).

Your brand's identity will ultimately be more than just your name, but the name will ultimately be a big part of what your customers associate with your brand—and rightly so.

» **Make Sure the Name Is Available**
Before going too far down the rabbit hole, check to make sure that you aren't duplicating a name that already exists in your industry. In some cases, your name may be legally distinct, but that doesn't mean it won't be embarrassing or difficult to do business in that industry. A name that is a clear—though distinct—duplicate of an existing industry player can lead to a venture that is perceived as always playing second fiddle. Not only

that, but how much can you *really* differentiate your offering from that of your competitors if customers are confused about who is who?

Now is also the time to ensure that the domain name for your desired company name is available (we'll discuss websites later in this chapter). If it's not, you probably need to rethink your choice. If customers can't find you via internet search, chances are you won't be successful.

» **Don't Name Yourself into a Corner**
Picking a name that's ultra-specific and doesn't leave you with any room to grow can cause friction and growing pains down the road. There is no need to be a clairvoyant but be on the lookout for business names that don't allow you room to grow. A good example of this principle is the tendency of small business owners to name their company after the geographic region where it was started. This is perhaps less common in the digital age, but when Springfield Star Cleaners expands into nearby Shelbyville, it might wish it had chosen a different name. Additionally, naming your business after a specific product offering or service can make branching out difficult; Smith's Radiators is much more restrictive than Smith's Auto Repair. Focus on the solution you provide and not the product—products may come and go, but the solution you provide is (hopefully) going to stick around for a while.

A word of caution regarding getting too cute with your name. Your business name is a critical part of your brand, and you should consider it carefully. Although you can always change it later, once you've invested in a website, logos, etc., and started acquiring customers, it gets harder and harder to do. You want a name that is memorable and fun (i.e., "sticky"), but you also want to come across as a serious business. A nonsense name worked well for Google, but it probably won't work as well for you. It's tough to establish a brand with a name that doesn't evoke anything to a potential customer. Similarly, "funny" names may work okay for certain businesses, such as ones that cater to younger people, but you run the risk of the joke wearing thin over time. And the less said about trendy names (I see you, ".ly companies"!), the better.

Picking a name for your venture is no easy task, but it is a crucial first step in forming the organization, getting the ball rolling, and getting off the ground. It is also not a decision to take lightly. As you will see, your logo, marketing materials, website, domain name, and social media presence will all be tied to your company name. Changing it midstream can become very complex very quickly.

Quick Case: Have you ever heard a brand name that just rubbed you the wrong way? Newspaper publisher and online media company Tribune Publishing was facing a declining brand image in a tough industry. In 2016 the Chicago-based company rebranded itself when the digital media component was spun off as Tribune Media. Their new name? Tronc. Oddly spelled, oddly pronounced, and widely ridiculed, Tronc eventually caved two years later and announced plans to revert to their original Tribune branding. The company formerly known as Tronc is a prime example of a clumsy attempt to refresh a brand without a deeper connection to its products or its market.

Decide on a Legal Form

The *entity classification*, or legal form of your business, matters for a couple of reasons. The entity structure that your venture selects can have important ramifications on the ways in which your business grows and expands, not to mention the amount of personal liability that your founding team could face. Let's take a closer look at the entity structure options available to entrepreneurs.

The following summary of legal entity structures should be considered simplified information and not legal advice.

» **Sole Proprietorship**
A sole proprietorship is a business where the owner *is* the business. It is an unincorporated business with a single owner. There may be some state or local filing requirements for business licenses and, if applicable, the ability to collect sales tax, but there is no other burden of filing for a sole proprietorship. Because sole proprietorships are unincorporated, the profits and losses from the business are reported directly on the owner's personal tax returns.

This may make a sole proprietorship seem like an attractive entity classification; however, there is one big reason why it is very ill-advised for entrepreneurs to start their businesses as sole proprietors: liability protection.

Legally speaking, a sole proprietor is one and the same with his or her business. There is no legal shield protecting the assets of someone who elects to use this legal form. This means that in the event the business is found liable for damages, the sole proprietor's personal assets can be targeted. If the business assets do not cover the extent of the claim, the sole proprietor's bank accounts, home, vehicle, and other assets are all fair game.

Many business owners who find themselves subject to a lawsuit thought it would never happen to them. A single suit can completely devastate the accounts and assets of a fledgling business, not to mention the personal accounts and assets of a sole proprietor. Additionally, when it comes time to seek funding, investors are wary of the risk that sole proprietors carry and will pass on these opportunities.

» **Partnership**

A sole proprietorship consists of a single business owner; partnerships consist of more than one owner. Partnerships, like sole proprietorships, are pass-through entities (profits and losses are recorded on the personal taxes of the partners), and partnerships offer no legal shield for each partner's personal assets.

Partnerships are governed by written agreements. By default, each partner has the right to participate in the management and profits of the business equally, but this can be overridden via contracts. These partnerships are known as general partnerships, or agreements where partners are on equal liability footing.

Groups of two or more individuals can also file to become limited partnerships, those with two classes of partner. In a limited partnership, general partners see no change in treatment. However, some partners may be designated "limited partners," partners who contribute financially but do not participate in the management of the business. Limited partners are liable only up to the amount of money they have contributed to the limited partnership.

» **LLC**

LLC stands for limited liability company, and LLCs are a common entity classification for small businesses. LLCs *do* require filing at the state level, and this application comes with a nominal fee and often a yearly corporate tax. LLCs are governed by their operating agreements—written rules that serve as bylaws for the business and dictate aspects such as ownership, profit sharing, and the roles and responsibilities of the owner(s). In a single-member LLC (one owner), a standard operating agreement will often suffice; however, when multiple members are involved, operating agreements must become more complex to reflect the needs, interests, and circumstances of each co-owner.

LLCs are uniquely structured in the sense that while they do provide a large degree of liability protection to business owners, for tax purposes they are considered pass-through entities. This means that the business itself does not pay taxes, and that profits and losses *pass through* the business on to the tax filings of the owner(s).

» **S Corporation**
IRS Subchapter S corporations, or S corps as they are commonly called, bridge the gap between an LLC and a fully-fledged corporation (C corp). They have a higher burden of eligibility than an LLC; while nearly anyone can form an LLC, S corps can only be formed and owned by US citizens or permanent residents. Additionally, S corps can raise funds through the sale of stock, although they are only permitted one class of stock, distributed to a maximum of 100 shareholders who are US citizens and only natural persons (that is, not other business entities).

Like LLCs, S corps are taxed as pass-through entities. Unlike LLCs, formation is a little more involved and requires the filing of articles of incorporation, which can incur ongoing expenses at the state level. Additionally, S corps are required to elect a board of directors. An LLC *may* have a board of directors but is not legally compelled to as S corps are. LLCs generally have more flexibility than corporations regarding how the entity is structured.

» **C Corporation**
IRS Subchapter C corps are full corporations, and this status comes with a range of benefits and considerations. C corps are not limited in the number of shareholders they can have, there are few restrictions on who can purchase shares, and stock can be divided into classes. C corps as a whole benefit from a number of favorable tax circumstances.

C corporations are *not* pass-through entities, and this means that revenue is subject to a "double tax." It is taxed once at the company level, and then dividends are taxed again as personal income. If the owner takes a salary, it's subject to income tax as well. In addition to being compelled to maintain a board of directors, C corps are subject to more oversight and a slew of other regulations and expenses.

S corps and LLCs are readily converted to C corps, so startups usually begin as one of these simpler structures and switch to the more complex C corp as they grow and their needs change.

fig. 7

LLCs
• Limited liability
• Pass-through entity
• Can have multiple member classes and a flexible corporate structure

S CORPORATIONS
• Limited liability
• Pass-through entity
• Can issue stock to a maximum of 100 shareholders

C CORPORATIONS
• Taxed separately from personal income (double taxation)
• No limit to number of shareholders
• Complex stucture for larger entities

SOLE PROPRIETORSHIPS
• No liability protection
• Owner is the business
• Income is reported on personal taxes

Where Will You Incorporate?

Currently, new businesses are under no obligation to incorporate in the state where the owner lives or where the business's physical headquarters are located. There is no question that it is *easier* to incorporate in your home state, but this doesn't take into account the business-friendly policies of some states.

For example, in 2015 as many as 86 percent of US-based initial public offerings (IPOs) chose Delaware as their state of incorporation regardless of the state in which their headquarters was located.[7] Delaware is the second-smallest state in the US, but because of its long history of being friendly to incorporated businesses, it is commonly used as a state of incorporation. Delaware's permissive tax law combined with its unique Court of Chancery—a state-level court that only hears cases pertaining to corporate law—mean that many corporations can substantially reduce their tax burden. Not only that, but cases pertaining to corporate law in the state of Delaware have a long history of case law attached to them. This robust legal history means that the outcome of similar cases can often be anticipated in advance.

Incorporation in Delaware is faster than in most other states, and if that's not enough to tilt the scales, Delaware state law does not require the disclosure of the names of a new corporation's directors or shareholders.

There are drawbacks to incorporating outside of the state where your headquarters are located. The practice of registering your business in a state where it is not based is known as *foreign qualification*. Many states charge fees for incorporation in other states, and there are additional reporting burdens; your venture is obligated to report to each of the states it does business in. This means that, at a minimum, you will have to report to your home state and to the state of incorporation. Not only that, but Delaware requires your business to name a "registering agent," which is a business that has an address in the state of Delaware and (for a fee) will receive and forward legal documents and state correspondence on your behalf.

Lastly, to pick up some of the lost revenue that its permissive tax structure bleeds, the state of Delaware charges a franchise fee (currently $300 per year) to businesses that are incorporated in the state. Taking everything into consideration, does this mean that your venture should be incorporated in Delaware? It could. An attorney who specializes in the formation of corporations can answer that question definitively. He or she may also recommend another business-friendly state, such as Nevada, or recommend that you simply incorporate in the state where your headquarters are located.

Register with the State and Get Appropriate Licenses

No matter where you choose to incorporate, you will likely be required to register with the state where you are incorporated and potentially any other states where you operate. And, depending on the nature of your business, you may be required to apply for state- or industry-specific licenses. These are not the kinds of things that can be ignored. Penalties for failure to acquire the necessary license can result in fines and other unpleasant consequences.

Other Business Essentials

Despite being quite dry, the topics of entity classification, compliance, and licensing are essential aspects of starting your own venture. Fortunately, there are many other important aspects to starting your own venture that are a lot more fun.

A good way to think about the following tasks is to consider them rewards or pacing breaks. Taking time to design a unique business card or to explore what your logo could look like can be downright fun. All of these tasks—including the dry ones—have to be completed at some point, and what I have found is that a "fun" task almost serves as a reward for completing one of the not-quite-so-fun tasks. After reading about your state's licensing requirements or wrapping up a call with a lawyer regarding your most favorable incorporation options, getting lost in the task of building the perfect business card can feel like stress release rather than a task to be crossed off your list.

Digital and Physical Brand Collateral

In the world of marketing, sales sheets, brochures, articles, and case studies that are used to promote a product are collectively known as *marketing collateral*. This concept, expanded to your startup's logo, website, business phone number, and networking and business cards, can be considered *brand collateral*.

All of your brand collateral should come together to tell the story of how your venture solves the problem that your customers face. When it comes to the intricacies of brand building, there is simply no substitute for having an experienced marketer on your founding team. If marketing isn't your strong suit, consider the ways in which you can attract marketing talent to your managerial team, or, at the very least, familiarize yourself with the key concepts.

When it comes to actually getting your collateral produced, using your home or office printer and copy paper doesn't exactly convey the professional touch. On-demand printing services like Vistaprint offer a range of products and leverage economies of scale to keep prices low. Upload a design, confirm a proof, and your finished brand collateral products are shipped straight to you. Vistaprint isn't the only game in town, but they are well-known and don't force buyers to adhere to overly restrictive order minimums.

» **Logo**
Your startup's logo comes together with color palette, typography, and style choices to form your graphic identity. This is the visual representation of your startup, and as your venture matures, the logo will become a sort of shorthand for the products you offer. If your founding team is short on design talent, there is a veritable army of professional freelancers standing by to work with you to develop a logo that expresses your identity and helps differentiate your offering from those of your competitors.

The modern gig economy has produced a glut of freelancers who specialize in niche contract work. The freelance marketplace Fiverr is a cost-effective source of design work, and an entire cottage industry has sprung up that is focused on producing logos for startups, between Fiverr and others.

Your Brand's Graphic Identity

fig. 8

LOGO	COLORS	FONTS	VISUALS
Memorable but not trendy	No more than four main colors	Stay away from trends	Photos, images, graphics, etc.
Makes an impression but isn't too complicated	Use complimentary palettes	Prioritize readability and cohesion	Used on your site, in marketing materials, on packaging, etc.
Consider your target demographic	Keep color scheme consistent	Don't use too many fonts; limit yourself to three	Emulate your brand and persona when possible

» **Business Cards**
Business is generally done between people, and people need to communicate. Business cards are a simple solution to this problem, and despite the overwhelming presence that digital technology has in our lives, business cards are still highly effective tools. Business cards are foundational pieces of brand collateral—cheap and easy to have made but glaring in their absence if you forget to order them.

Interesting and memorable business cards can be ordered quickly and cheaply through online service providers, or if you are at a loss for design options, the same freelancers who are available to produce your logo can often recommend business card designs. In their attempt to become a one-stop shop for on-demand printing, Vistaprint maintains a sophisticated business card production solution, but numerous printers can be found with a basic web search. When ordering a business card design, above all else be sure that the card is legible. If your pitch made an impression, your audience will keep the card whether it makes them say "wow" or just "meh." The value is in what the card conveys, not in the paper stock it is printed on. On the other hand, who doesn't like to make a great first impression?

» **Web Hosting**

It may have been forgivable for a business not to have a website back in the 1990s, but that is no longer the case. How many times have you heard about a company and then immediately punched their name into your favorite search engine? What happens if nothing comes up? Having a web presence is a necessity of living in the digital age, it's as simple as that.

Companies like Bluehost, SiteGround, and HostGator offer inexpensive hosting solutions that scale with your business as needed. When shopping for hosting services, look for round-the-clock support and technical features that lend themselves to speed and reliability.

The focus on a company's digital presence adds another dimension to the process of coming up with a name for your startup. Not only do you need a short, easy-to-spell, easy-to-remember company name, but there is another element to consider—your domain name, the part of a web address that comes after the "www." In addition to checking whether your business name is available, a quick web search can verify whether or not an associated domain is available. The shorter, easier to remember, and easier to spell your domain name is, the better.

The process of purchasing a domain and hosting, and of designing a site, is easier (and more critical) than it has ever been. Popular domain services include Domainr, GoDaddy, and WordPress—but try to stay away from purchasing your domain name from your hosting service. This helps increase security and can be a time saver if you need to change hosts (easy) without transferring domains (a bit of a hassle). Just like the process of logo creation, talented freelancers are standing by to help walk you through every step of the process, if creating and maintaining a digital presence isn't your strong suit.

Q: What's the difference between .com and .org and .info, etc.?

Answer: The ".com" is known as a *top-level domain* and it indicates the purpose of the site—a commercial site in the case of a .com top-level domain—though there are no restrictions on other top-level domains such as .info, .org, or .biz. If you're not sure which is best for your venture, consult with an SEO professional. (SEO stands for search engine optimization, and it encompasses a set of practices that businesses can use to encourage search engines like Google to rank their sites higher in the results for relevant searches.) The days of having to pick between .com, .org, and .info are over. Now, nearly any word can be used in place of the top-level domain (even ".sucks"). The intricacies of why one top-level domain is a better choice than another represent insight from a number of different disciplines, including marketing, branding, SEO, and web design.

In addition to the business necessity of maintaining even a basic website, owning your own domain allows you to use it as the domain in your email address instead of using one of the popular personal email providers; this goes miles when it comes to professionalism.

Phone Number

Being able to separate your personal phone number from your business line isn't just a measure of professionalism—it is also a move that will preserve your sanity as an entrepreneur. Digitally integrated business phone lines are powerful solutions that allow team members to take calls to a business line on their personal phones without the caller being any wiser. Google Voice is a freemium internet-based phone system that provides users with a phone number that allows calls to be forwarded to a number of different phones. Services such as Grasshopper that cater to small businesses include a virtual phone number as well as other phone services.

Social Media

On one hand, the world of social media is fickle and difficult to predict. On the other hand, social media is so ubiquitous that your customers almost definitely use it. Despite the fact that social media has slowly encroached on every aspect of our lives, many businesses still don't understand the best ways to leverage the sheer power of maintaining a social presence. What it means for a brand to "own" their social channels is an eternally shifting goalpost, but there are a few basic truisms for new ventures that are considering a social presence.

» **Don't Spread Yourself Too Thin.**
Different social platforms have different purposes. Some are all about sharing photos, some are all about sharing videos. Some are for connecting with friends and family, and some are for connecting with professional contacts. Unless your startup has a sophisticated social media team, it is better to pick the platform(s) that are most relevant to your customers and invest your time and money there. Nothing says your venture is out of touch like a clumsily executed social campaign that is a poor fit for the platform it appears on.

» **Don't Pick a Losing Battle.**
Social media is not something that should receive a half-measure of effort. Being noncommittal about a social channel can have a net negative effect on brand perception. If you are unprepared to fully commit to a social channel, it is often better to wait until your brand has the resources to project itself on a platform where your customers congregate than to under-commit and invite negative sentiment.

» **Don't Lose Sight of the Goal.**
When you log on to your personal social media accounts, it's okay to click on this or that. But for a business—at a time when your reputation can go up in smoke in minutes flat—everything that your public-facing account does must reflect a higher goal and a set of rules. The conversation between companies and their customers has never been more reciprocal— or more public—and brands need to be more conscientious than ever when navigating the social space.

You probably already know this, but not all social media platforms are the same. For example, LinkedIn is dedicated to professional audiences, so lifestyle brands and shopping-forward content don't resonate there. The Pinterest audience skews female (though this demographic is shifting).[8] Instagram is used by younger audiences, and Facebook users cross a number of demographics but tend to be older than many Instagram users and most Snapchat users.

Here's something you may not know: maintaining a social presence for your brand is time-consuming. Social management software, extensions, and plugins can save considerable time and effort in managing social channels. Options such as Buffer and Hootsuite simplify the monitoring and administration of numerous platforms, and other tools such as Hashtagify cut through the noise and allow you to track important trends.

Chapter Recap

» When deciding on a name for your company, it is important that be "sticky." Here, sticky means that it is a unique, memorable name that stands out from the crowd and stays fresh over time. There is such a thing as a name that is too sticky, however—keep it simple and to the point. Also take the time to check that the name you want to select is available in your region or industry before committing to a legal form.

» After a name has been chosen, select an appropriate legal form for your venture. A sole proprietorship is a business where the owner is the business. This legal form offers no liability protection, and business revenue is reported on the owner's personal taxes. An LLC offers a legal shield for personal liability and a more robust structure. It is a pass-through entity, meaning that business revenue is reported on the personal taxes of the owner(s). S corps are also pass-through entities, and they also provide liability protection. S corps do allow the issuance of shares of stock to a limited number of shareholders. C corps are full corporations. They are governed by a number of corporation-specific laws and have no limit on the number of shareholders who may hold stock in the company. C corps are not pass-through entities, meaning that personal income is taxed twice.

» Deciding where to incorporate is an important consideration along with legal form. Many businesses elect to incorporate in Delaware regardless of where their physical headquarters are located, due to Delaware's cost-effective and business-friendly legislation.

» The days of expensive business startup are in the past. Unless your startup is in an industry that is equipment-intensive or requires large amounts of physical space, you can likely get started with little more than a laptop and a reliable high-speed internet connection. Once your business exists legally, the next steps include digital and physical brand collateral. That means a logo, business cards, web hosting, a business phone number, and a social media presence. All of these brand collateral elements are cheaper and easier than ever to acquire, thanks to modern technology.

| 5 |
What Are You Selling?

Chapter Overview
- » The solution-oriented nature of products and services
- » Pricing methods, including markup pricing, going-rate pricing, break-even pricing, and perceived-value pricing
- » Pricing strategies to accomplish business and market positioning goals

The nature of commerce and trade is as old as human civilization itself. Stretching back to ancient Mesopotamia and beyond, the forces of supply and demand have shaped our lives, our shared history, and our shared future. The essence of commerce is the exchange of goods or services for some form of compensation. In this chapter, we examine what your product or service specifically is and how to determine the appropriate compensation for it.

A note regarding terminology. In this book, for the sake of simplicity, the *thing* that a business has for sale will often be referred to as that business's product, even if that product happens to be a service. Going forward, read "products" as "products and services."

Thinking of Your Product as a Solution

In the same way that opportunities can't exist independently of the entrepreneur, successful businesses (and the products they sell) can't exist independently of the problems they solve for their customers—the two are intertwined. Remember, too, that customer problems don't always have to be "pain points." Products that exist to solve problems *but don't accentuate customer passion to the fullest* aren't solving problems in the way that we normally think of. If a new product comes along and thrills these customers by speaking to their passion or reframing their previous experiences as less-than-ideal, that product essentially solves a problem for that customer. In this context, a pain point may not represent a negative aspect, but instead simply a barrier to a much more fulfilling experience.

Quick Case: Earlier in this book we discussed iPods as solving a problem that consumers didn't know they had. In the same way, adjustable golf clubs are a perfect example of a product that enhanced the ways consumers experienced their passion while solving a problem that they didn't know they had.

Golf enthusiasts are known for their willingness to spend lots of money to achieve even modest improvements in their game, and because the sport of golf is equipment-intensive, players keep a close eye on new product developments. When using traditional clubs, players are locked into using the equipment they brought with them on the course, based on a guess at the conditions that may arise during play. Adjustable clubs changed the equation by allowing players to adjust the characteristics of their equipment to match the conditions they encountered on the course.

In the same way that an MP3 player enhanced music listeners' experience by providing them with benefits they didn't realize they wanted, adjustable golf clubs provided golf enthusiasts with benefits that changed the way they enjoy the sport they are passionate about by reframing regular playing conditions as a problem with adjustable clubs as the solution.

Don't Become a Solution in Search of a Problem

In the case of the chicken and the egg, there is no definitive answer to which came first. When it comes to the development of your products or services, however, you don't want to become a solution in search of a problem. Designing products with a specific solution to a specific customer problem will always produce stronger products, but that's not the only reason you should start with the problem and work backward from there.

The products or services that your venture offers are a central part of your *value proposition*. The importance of your startup's value proposition cannot be overstated. If your processes, your operations, and your financial model are the *how* of your business, then your value proposition is the *why*. Your value proposition, what it entails, and its importance are covered in chapter 8, but for now keep it in the back of your head as consisting of the answers to two key questions:

» Who is your target customer?
» How are you different from your competition?

In later chapters, this book explores a number of ways to define, segment, and delight your customers, but a fundamental first step in understanding exactly who your target customers are is identifying the problem you will solve for them. As you will see, your value proposition is the core of your business; a venture that doesn't solve a problem for its target customers (or doesn't *have* target customers) will waste significant resources struggling to find its way and will ultimately never get off the ground.

"Build it and they will come" is not a business strategy. A common pitfall of new entrepreneurs is to think that their product or service is so attractive that it will "sell itself." Not only is this not a viable business strategy, *it never works!* It doesn't matter how many bells and whistles, how tech-enabled, or how sexy your offering is—no one will purchase it unless it solves a problem for them and they fully understand its features and benefits.

Think critically about the problem that you want to solve for people. Does the offering you have in mind follow through on solving their problem? If not, you have a solution in search of a problem, which is a lot like putting the cart before the horse. Or the chicken before the egg.

How Do I Price My Product?

Like many of the decisions you will face as an entrepreneur, the process of setting prices for your products/services should be executed in a strategic way. A pricing strategy starts with defined objectives. It is too simplistic to say that a company's strategy is to make as much money as possible. There are all kinds of reasons to adopt a pricing strategy besides profit maximization. The nature of the objectives that you select for your pricing strategy depend on the nature of your business model, your product or service, and the characteristics of the industry you operate in. The following are some common pricing strategy goals:

» Increasing sales
» Maximizing profit
» Discouraging market entrants
» Gaining market share

» Establishing market position
» Paying back investors
» Increasing cash flow

Once you have determined your pricing objectives, you can identify your range of potential prices. Your range of pricing flexibility is the space between your price floor and your price ceiling—the lowest and highest prices you can charge for your product or service. Your *price floor* is set by your minimum margin. It is the bare minimum you must receive for each unit in order to cover costs and make a reasonable profit. Your *price ceiling* is impacted by a number of factors, but the most influential are your market position, the prices of competitive products, and the *price sensitivity* of customers in your target market.

A market that is price sensitive is one where buyers have a lot of power—they can choose from many different options. This condition forces companies within the space to compete with one another on price, which is an area where new ventures are at a disadvantage.

Keep in mind that market position has a huge impact on your price ceiling. If you are positioned within your market as a luxury or premium brand, you can charge more for your product based on its perceived value. Economy or discount brands often have a much lower pricing flexibility as they compete more intensely on price.

The convergence of strategy, market perception, and competitive factors make determining an optimal price something of an art. The most important thing to keep in mind is that your pricing strategy needs to be grounded in solid rationales and constructed with a strategic approach in mind. Under no circumstances should the price that you charge for your products be a *WAG* (wild-ass guess)!

Strategically Establishing Your Prices

There are four basic ways to establish pricing:

» **Markup Pricing**

Markup pricing (also known as "cost-plus pricing") is a simple pricing calculation that totals the costs to produce and distribute a product (or to execute a service) and adds a markup to those costs to generate a margin. This markup should place the selling price somewhere within your selling price flexibility range (the difference between your price floor and price ceiling) and generate enough profit to sustain the business.

» **Break-Even Pricing**

Break-even pricing is centered on the business's *break-even point*. The break-even point is the equilibrium point where costs equal revenue. If the money going out equals the money coming in, that means profit is zero. Break-even pricing is not a sustainable strategy in the long term, but it can be an effective tool to gain a large amount of market share in a short time (known as penetration pricing) or to edge out and discourage new market entrants.

» **Going-Rate Pricing**
Going-rate pricing is a method that sets a product or service's price based on the prevailing market price for similar offerings. This method of establishing prices is common with products that have few differences, such as commodities or other homogenous markets. Because new ventures can rarely compete on price, being able to differentiate your product from others in the same space is a lifeline for many startups.

It can be dangerous to your bottom line to base your prices solely on the pricing of your competitors. This is especially the case if your competitors have been in business longer than you have, which is likely the case for many new ventures.

» **Perceived-Value Pricing**
Perceived-value pricing is a method that assigns a price to a product or service based on its perceived value rather than on costs, historical prices, or the prices of competitor offerings. Perceived-value pricing is a tactic commonly associated with luxury or premium brands that are highly differentiated from one another.

Positioning and the Price/Quality Matrix

A helpful tool for determining a pricing strategy is the price/quality matrix. It is a basic four-quadrant matrix that compares the price versus quality (or perceived quality) of others in the same space.

Low quality in a price/quality matrix isn't necessarily describing poorly made products or marked-up junk. Instead, it is a description of the price versus the perceived quality. If the price and quality are commensurate with each other and both are lower than other similar products in the market, then the product belongs on the bottom left quadrant. Likewise, if the price and perceived quality are proportionate and both are higher than others in the market, then they belong in the top right quadrant. When the price is higher than that of other products of a similar quality, then the price and quality are incommensurate; these are the products that belong in the top left quadrant.

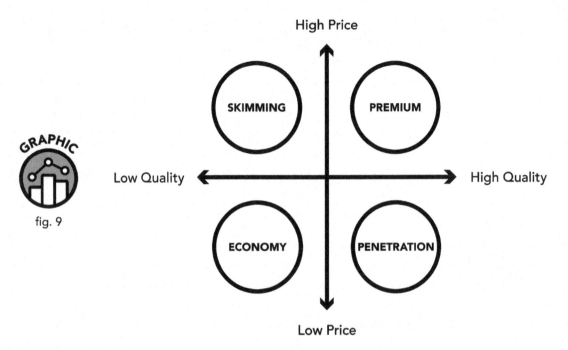

High Price

SKIMMING

PREMIUM

Low Quality ⟵⟶ High Quality

ECONOMY

PENETRATION

Low Price

fig. 9

Each of the four quadrants represents a defined positioning strategy through pricing.

Let's examine each in greater detail, moving clockwise from the top left.

Skimming – High Price, Low Quality

Price skimming is a strategy of charging a price that is not commensurate with the product's quality compared to similar offerings. The goal of this strategy is to collect as much revenue as possible from the small market segment that is willing to pay the inflated price. This tactic has a predictably short life span, and as the number of people willing to pay the price of the product falls, the seller brings the price down as well. In this way, the seller can "skim" revenues from a wider range of market segments. After a price reduction, a new market segment will be willing to purchase the product, and the process resets. After that segment is exhausted, the price will be reduced again until it matches the quality of the product.

This strategy is an effective way to recoup high development costs and is most effective in markets where new product launches are frequent. But it is not without downsides. A skimming price strategy effectively penalizes customers who buy the product when it is first introduced; they can (understandably) become frustrated to find out that the same product they purchased has gone down in price.

Additionally, a misstep in the timing of price changes can mean reduced sales overall. Markets with frequent product launches have customers with short attention spans. If the product is at its initial price for too long, people will lose interest and pass it over even when the price does drop. Price skimming strategies are popular in the luxury car market and in consumer electronics and books. These markets share high rates of new product introduction and high costs to develop new products, making skimming an attractive approach for them.

Premium – High Price, High Quality

A premium pricing strategy relies on differentiation and a high perceived quality to command a higher price than that of competitors. This approach to pricing helps firms squeeze more margin out of each sale. Because the price is tied to the perceived quality and not the costs of the product or service, the potential for higher margins is much greater.

NOTE

Because it is nearly impossible for new businesses to compete on price, a premium pricing strategy is usually the most sustainable choice for startups.

Penetration – Low Price, High Quality

A penetration pricing strategy is a perfect example of the strategic use of pricing to make a quick grab for market share. This is another example of incommensurate pricing; however, unlike price skimming, which favors the seller, penetration pricing favors the buyer. The goal is to entice customers by offering a product that is of equal or higher quality than others in the market but is sold at a lower price. Once the objective is accomplished—a new slice of market share has been claimed—the price can rise to become more commensurate with the quality of the product.

This strategy is not without challenges. Offering a quality product at a reduced price eats into margins and is unsustainable in the long term. This means that the penetration process must be monitored closely. Additionally, too low of a price can have the unintended consequence of reducing the value perception of your brand. Although you may rapidly acquire market share, once the penetration pricing period is over it can be tough to recover from the "budget brand" perception. Finally, customers don't like it when they are asked to pay higher prices. The ground that was gained by the penetration pricing can be lost when dissatisfied customers look elsewhere.

Economy – Low Price, Low Quality

Economy pricing is a sustainable, long-term strategy for numerous businesses. It can also spell disaster for businesses that aren't prepared to compete exclusively on price. Economy pricing works best when the business in question can leverage some competitive advantage to dramatically bring down their costs. Leveraging the economy of scale (the ability of large organizations to spread out costs over more units, effectively bringing costs down), a lean supply chain, or advanced processes and techniques are all examples of cost-slashing competitive edge. In this way, an economy pricing strategy can be used to dissuade new market entrants.

The downside to economy pricing is that being perceived as a "budget brand" can be a tough stigma to shake for a growth-oriented company. That is, if the company has the resources to keep costs low enough to maintain a sustainable economy pricing strategy. A very real risk of attempting an economy pricing strategy is finding out that your company doesn't, in fact, have the resources needed to pull it off.

Also, customers who are looking for the best deals and the lowest prices are loyal to the savings, not to the brand. They are fickle and will always be chasing a better deal and as a result will only respond to the price aspects of your brand. Differentiation is difficult for brands that execute economy pricing strategies. Because startups are rarely able to compete on price alone, an economy pricing strategy is not usually a winning proposition for new ventures.

None of the abovementioned price-versus-quality pricing strategies is a silver bullet. Each has associated challenges, and each has strengths or weaknesses when used with various business models. Also keep in mind that your pricing strategy can't be a perfect fit for every customer. Pick the one that makes the most sense for your product or service, your market, your industry, and your business model.

The prices you set at the outset of your venture are not written in stone. Markets and industries change. Competition forces changes in pricing, as do the costs of materials, supplies, and labor. Additionally, products and services mature, new opportunities within a market present themselves, and business strategies shift; your prices must also change as appropriate.

Chapter Recap

» Products and services must solve a problem for consumers. The success of a venture's offering is directly tied to how that product or service solves a customer problem.

» Customer problems don't have to be "pain points." Products and services that accentuate the passions of customers can also effectively solve problems for those customers in powerful ways.

» The process of establishing pricing must be a strategic one. A price floor is the lowest possible price you could charge for a product or service and still make a profit. A price ceiling is the maximum price that anyone would be willing to pay. Your optimal price falls somewhere between the two.

» There are four basic ways to calculate prices: markup pricing, break-even pricing, going-rate pricing, and perceived-value pricing.

» The price/quality matrix is a helpful tool for mapping out your pricing strategy. It uses four quadrants to compare price and perceived quality, with each quadrant representing a method of achieving a different set of strategic market positioning goals.

» Skimming is a pricing method that starts off with a higher price that declines over time; it is used to recoup high development costs and tap into multiple purchasing segments. A premium pricing strategy pairs a high price and a high perceived quality to drive a higher margin. A penetration strategy involves setting a low price as compared to the perceived quality of your offering, in an attempt to entice customers and gain a large amount of market share in a short amount of time. An economy pricing strategy is used when a company is able to compete exclusively on price and offer products or services that are similar to those of their competition.

» The conditions that make one price more favorable than another are always changing, and as a result, a venture's pricing strategy is something that should be monitored and course-corrected as needed—prices are not set in stone.

PART III

YOUR VALUE PROPOSITION

| 6 |
Markets and Customers

Chapter Overview

» Who is your target customer?
» How to use a customer avatar to uncover your target customer
» Researching your target market
» How to segment your target market to get the most out of your marketing dollars

The market for a product is everyone who needs it, is willing and able to pay for it, and is reachable by your marketing efforts. For some products, the total number of people who meet these criteria may be enormous. In such a case, you must segment the market into smaller and smaller niches until you have an area you can dominate. Otherwise, you will be in direct competition with larger, more established companies with whom you are ill-equipped to compete. When every dollar spent to reach your customer needs to go as far as possible, your approach must be laser-focused and very selective. This of course raises the question: how do you identify the people who will become your customers? How do you identify your target market?

Who Should You Be Targeting?

When your product or service is built around solving a problem that people face, you're already starting from a good foundation—work backward from there. The goal is to create a *customer avatar*, or a persona that represents your perfect customer. Once this persona is complete and detailed, it will form the basis of your marketing efforts.

A customer avatar is like a template. The characteristics of your "perfect customer" inform where you look for customers and what you say to the people that your search yields. People who fit the template are a good fit for your product or service. When it comes to purchasing, people who don't fit the template are a "maybe" at best. It may make sense at first to try to reach (and sell to) as many people as possible regardless of whether or not they fit your customer avatar, but if you go down that road you will quickly find that it is expensive and discouraging. Reaching 500 people who have a burning need for the solution your product or service provides is always preferable to reaching 5,000 who don't resonate with the problem you have a solution for. An effective customer avatar is instrumental in finding the first 500 people. You can worry about the next 500 later.

Your customer avatar is *not* a substitute for the detailed research you will do for the Market Analysis portion of your business plan (see chapter 16). Rather, it's a way of stimulating your thinking about who your customer is and why they need your product.

Use the following questions to shape the way you think about and uncover information regarding your target market.

» **Who has the problem that my product or service solves?**
You built your product or service around solving a problem. Who has that problem? The more aware these people are of their problem, the better. Express your answer not in a literal spreadsheet of names and contact information but in a list of traits such as gender, age, disposable income, and other characteristics that are relevant to building your customer avatar.

» **Who has already spent money on this or similar products or services?**
Let's get this out of the way right now. You have competitors. No matter how new or innovative your product or service may be, *you have competitors.* We discuss the nature of competition, how to measure it, and how to think about it in the next chapter, but for now, know that you have competitors and that your potential customers are already spending money with them.

A Note on Competition
Frankly, your biggest fear should be that you truly have no competition. Far from indicating a green field that only you can exploit, it probably means there is no market for your product. Be particularly worried if other firms have tried to enter your market and failed.

Rather than being afraid of competitors, use them for the wealth of knowledge and insight they provide. In addition to keeping an eye out for abandoned, failed, and discontinued product lines that may have something in common with your offering, keep tabs on who your successful competitors are. Keep an *especially* close eye on the ways that you differentiate your offering. Remember, your new venture will be unable to compete directly with an entrenched competitor in a very broad market. The place where startups make their mark is by solving customer problems in a niche or targeted environment.

The people who spend money on competing products are demonstrating a need for a solution to their problem. They are also demonstrating that they are willing and able to pay for this solution. The characteristics that define these people are helpful in constructing your own customer avatar.

Q: What if there are numerous products that are similar to mine in one way or another that have been abandoned by other companies?

Answer: That's not a good sign. If the core of your business is something that has been done before and had little or limited success, it may be time to head back to the drawing board. On the other hand, if you can confidently say that what sets your product or service apart is the basis for why it won't fail, then it may be a real opportunity. If this is the case, tread with care.

Why should people pick you? The role of differentiation in the success of a new venture is a common theme throughout this book. Countless examples reinforcing this focus exist in the world of entrepreneurship, but a sometimes-overlooked benefit of differentiation is that the very act of asserting why someone should choose you over your competition means drilling down an aspect of your customer avatar.

It is easy for new entrepreneurs to overestimate their reach and assume that *everyone* will want what they are selling. Take a step back. Is your passion and experience informing your decision-making process, or are you relying on the feedback of real people you intend to target? It may be humbling to admit, but starting with the assumption that you *don't* know how your potential customers think and feel will ultimately encourage you to uncover the most helpful information to guide the success of your venture.

Quick Case: The prolific and influential direct marketer Gary Halbert had a question he would pose to his copywriting students. In the hypothetical scenario, Mr. Halbert and a student were running competing burger carts. He allowed the student to have as many advantages as they could think of, if they would grant him only one. Students would pick advantages such as premium ingredients, busy locations, or flashy signs and expensive carts. Confident that his hypothetical cart would beat the competition's every time, Halbert would select only one advantage—a starving crowd![9]

Building Your Customer Avatar

Ultimately, your customer avatar should come to life complete with a name, face, and backstory. It may feel silly to talk about a made-up persona as if he or she is a person in the room, but the more realistic your avatar is, the more prepared you will be to craft a stronger connection. And the better you are at solving the problems your avatar faces, the better you will be at solving them for your customers in the real world. Plus, limiting your customer avatar to a single person or a couple of distinct people means that you won't go overboard trying to cram every statistic and demographic into your target audience. In this case, less is more as long as that "less" is focused.

Let's take a look at the characteristics you should define when building your own customer avatar, and we'll run through an example to help you build it using the downloadable PDF included in the digital assets that come with this book. Your customer avatar should include the following aspects of your ideal customer:

» Demographics	» Behaviors
» Interests	» Product-related characteristics

Demographics

Demographics are personal characteristics. They include physical attributes such as age, gender, and ethnicity as well as lifestyle and personal attributes such as education, income, number of children, and home ownership.

Psychographics

Psychographics encompass your customers' interests—the ways that your customer avatar (and by extension your "perfect customer") spends his or her time. Interests include lifestyle choices, entertainment interests, relationship and family habits, hobbies, sports, and cuisine.

Behaviors

Behaviors are interests and habits that are exhibited as trends or tendencies. Behaviors are of particular interest to marketers because they often represent patterns and can therefore be predicted with some accuracy.

Behaviors include financial literacy, spending and purchase behaviors, travel habits, and digital fluency.

Product-Related Characteristics

An avatar's product-related characteristics are the ways in which your product or service is relevant to all the other parts of your customer avatar. How does your offering solve their problem? How does your customer avatar feel about the past, present, and future with no solution to their problem? What about when they become aware of your solution? What key triggers will push your customer avatar toward choosing your solution? Will they have used other solutions in the past? How do they feel right before purchasing? What about right after? What about thirty days after?

By the end of the customer avatar creation process, you have constructed a template that informs you on key aspects of the people you should be targeting. Use this profile to find them on social media, construct better messaging, refine your products, and make better advertising and marketing decisions in general.

Don't forget to take advantage of the Digital Assets included with your purchase of this book. Among other supplemental material, you will find resources like a structured customer avatar cheat sheet. Access this cheat sheet and all Digital Asset files for this title at: go.quickstartguides.com/startingbusiness.

The following is a functional example of a customer avatar for a customer profile that an upscale yoga studio might employ.

Meet Amy Avatar.

Amy is 35+ years of age, is married, lives in Northern California, and has two school-age children. Her household income is over $100K and she has a part-time job while her children are at school and her husband is at work.

Amy is busy and looking for time to herself. She also wants to connect with other moms in a casual setting. Amy is interested in health and fitness but puts her family first. With her responsibilities as a mother and at her part-time job, she isn't interested in spending a lot of her personal time working out intensely. She spends her time on Pinterest, Instagram, and Twitter. Amy is okay with spending more money on products if they make her day easier or if they are of higher quality, but she budgets and considers herself frugal and a savvy shopper.

Amy is interested in healthy food for her family but does not subscribe to a restrictive diet. She is also not interested in traveling too far out of her way to participate in hobbies or other regular activities. She has a high level of digital fluency and relies on her smart devices to make her life easier.

Learning About Your Customers

As I've said (and will say again and again), exploration of your target market and your customers *must* reflect feedback and insight, not guesses and conjecture. But where do you start? No doubt this information can't all be gathered with a simple internet search. However, that's not a bad place to start.

Researching Your Target Market Online

Industry association reports, trade publications, white papers, and case studies are all often available online. These are preferable to blogs and magazine articles, but if the latter cite primary sources, they may be good resources. Some will be freely accessible to the public while others are available only to association members. Additionally, government agencies, small business associations, and other institutional sources may offer industry-specific data. A free library card will grant you access to a plethora of resources, including statistical or financial databases. If your local library doesn't have the reach, try a community college in the area.

Another helpful general-purpose online tool is Google's free data-crunching tool called Google Trends.[10] Trends is part of the Google suite of applications and measures search volume to produce sentiment indicators, interest over time, and interest-by-region information. Other free resources from Google include Consumer Barometer[11] and Public Data.[12] Consumer Barometer focuses on digital products and the role they play in the lives of consumers, and Google Public Data is a searchable, highly visual repository of the publicly available results of research projects, studies, and other insights. As an authoritative source, the US Census Bureau offers a wealth of information about different geographical areas across the country. To explore this data visually, *The New York Times* offers an outstanding tool that reflects insight from the most recent census.[13]

Other popular statistical databases aren't hard to find. The Pew Research Center's massive database[14] is available online for free. For a mix of free and paid statistical information, Statista[15] is a powerful solution. There is no shortage of information in the twenty-first century. Purpose-built online research tools exist as well. For example, ratings and customer-insight mainstay Nielsen offers My Best Segment,[16] an online customer insight portal.

Researching Your Target Market on Social Media

For the socially savvy entrepreneur, social ad buying programs offer interesting insight into trends and interrelated customer attributes. These insights can be accessed and leveraged without committing any advertising dollars if you so choose.

One of the best examples of this tactic in action is Facebook's Ads Manager. Because Facebook derives its revenue from ads, and because Facebook's users volunteer unprecedented amounts of behavioral and demographic data, the social network used by over one billion active users has developed an impressively sophisticated and powerful advertising service. This book is not about the ins and outs of using social advertising, but we'll take a brief look at the use of social platform ad planning as a tool to uncover information about your target market.

What Facebook and other social networks offer their advertisers is insight and—more importantly—laser-focused ad targeting options. By constructing your ad targeting parameters to reflect your target market, Facebook will give you relevant statistics regarding the size and relative composition of your target customers. It is important to keep in mind that these numbers only reflect Facebook users who represent the parameters that you have selected and that they should be taken with a grain of salt. Regardless of the limitations of using social targeting software, it can be a helpful first look at the relevant target market based on a set of very specific targeting parameters.

Researching Your Target Market in Person

What's the best way to find out more about what people in your target market really think? Ask them! The worst they can do is decline to participate. Surveys that are conducted face to face have the potential to uncover unique insight from the very people to whom you want to sell your products. This doesn't have to be a complicated process, either—the best way to get started is to get out and pound the pavement. Use your customer avatar to make a plan, and put yourself where your avatar would hang out.

A tech-enabled alternative to conducting surveys in person is to carry them out digitally. You may have to pay a small consideration to reach respondents, but you will be able to reach many more in the same amount of time, and the resulting data is easy to process digitally. Companies like SurveyMonkey and Fieldboom make constructing and administering online surveys fast and easy, and in some cases they will actively work to help put your surveys in front of people who match your targeting profile.

Thinking outside the box, there is a whole world of digital consumer insight tools. When constructed in a compelling and engaging way, social quizzes can be fun for respondents while providing you with excellent customer insight. There are services that easily set up giveaways, promotions, or data-gathering campaigns that emulate the look and feel of a game show.

Whatever method(s) you choose—and it is a good idea to use as many methods as is economically feasible—ensure that you are *really* getting insight from people in your target market. It can be all too easy to incentivize survey respondents who simply provide their feedback for the prize at the end but don't represent someone whose opinion has value to your efforts.

Segmenting Your Market

Market segmentation is the process of dividing a large, homogenous market into smaller subdivisions or niches that group customers together based on shared characteristics. Whereas the overall market is so broad as to include a wide range of different customers, segmentation picks out groups of customers based on their differences. Market segmentation is critically important because no new company is large enough or well enough resourced to fulfill the diverse needs of an entire market. Instead, they segment the market into smaller sections and strategically target the highest-impact segments. These segments could be high impact because they have a specific problem (incentivizing them to seek solutions), because they have sufficient disposable income to purchase a specific product or service, or because of the geographic area where they are located.

Market segmentation must address the following questions:

» **Can the segment be clearly identified?**
If a segment can't be clearly identified, then it might not be a segment at all. Market segmentation is a strategic process, and if a strategy is based on nebulous information, it will waste resources at best and totally derail efforts at worst. You must be able to say "Yes, that customer is in our segment" or "No, that customer is not in our segment" with confidence. It may seem counterintuitive to point out the customers that you will not target, but this reduction in scope is designed to put your resources to best use.

» **What is the segment's reachable size?**
Understanding the effective size of a market segment helps decision makers compare different segments. The size of a segment can determine whether or not it is worth attempting to reach, or whether or not it can be served in an effective way.

» **Can I develop a marketing plan to reach the segment effectively?**
A segment that is prohibitively difficult to reach effectively may not be a good one to target. The same goes for a segment that your business doesn't *understand* how to reach.

Depending on where your product or service fits into the industry value chain, your customer may not be the end user. For example, a commercial bakery that sells breads, cakes, and muffins to stores who then sell those baked goods to their own customers has a customer who is not the end user. The end user is the store's customer—the person who buys and takes home the baked goods. The bakery's customers are the stores.

» **Is the segment a good fit for my company and its resources?**
Is this a market segment that makes sense for the brand? Is it a market segment that is in line with your mission and vision? Does it fit with your strategy? Can you reach the segment with the resources you have available, and will it be profitable enough to meet your financial goals? Does the segment align with your firm's values? Could there be backlash on social media, etc., for working with this group? These are all important questions with no easy, quantifiable answers.

These four characteristics of segmentation—ease of identification, size measurability, accessibility, and fitness—are present in all segmenting efforts, no matter which segmentation method is used, and apply to both B2C and B2B customers, or business-to-consumer and business-to-business customers, respectively.

A business that has other businesses as customers is known as a B2B business, which stands for business-to-business (or sometimes brand-to-brand). A business that has consumers as customers is known as a B2C business, for business-to-consumer (or "brand-to-consumer"). Both B2B and B2C firms have the same task of identifying and segmenting their customers, though the criteria they select is different by necessity. But not all customers are created equal. Just as the market is segmented, so are the customers that your business targets. This allows you to focus your efforts and tailor messaging and product/service offerings to the specific needs of each customer segment.

Quick Case: Millennials—people who came of age during the '90s—initially proved to be a tough nut for marketers to crack. Did they act younger than their age or were they mature as a group? Were they frugal or did they spend their money freely? Marketers quickly learned that traditional methods didn't gain much traction with millennial consumers, who did not spend frivolously and did not place as high a value on consumer goods as their parents had.

Nowhere was this clearer, or more public, than with the clumsily executed 2017 *Live for Now* campaign from PepsiCo. The ad was a short film that featured a well-known celebrity and popular music with "millennial themes" of social justice and activism. It may have seemed like a smash hit to those in the boardroom, but marketers missed the mark in almost every measurable way, and the ad was pulled just a day after its release due to tremendous criticism.

Audiences accused PepsiCo of pandering to millennials; viewers pointed out that the portrayals of social activism not only appeared contrived and shallow, but that the overt for-profit approach in fact trivialized important social issues that had real impacts on real people. The intended millennial audience further compounded the problem for PepsiCo through use of their social media savvy to draw further attention to what they considered a tone-deaf gaffe on the part of PepsiCo. In a very high-profile way, PepsiCo demonstrated that they were no closer to understanding millennial audiences than they had been a decade ago, and indeed may have lost significant market share and brand currency with the intended audience as a result.

Deep Dive: Market Segmentation

From a product perspective, there are two types of businesses: those who sell directly to the end user (business–to–consumer, or B2C) and those who sell to other businesses (business-to-business, B2B). Segmentation follows the same principles for both, but is slightly different in practice.

B2C Customer Segmentation

There are four key methods of business to consumer segmentation:

fig. 10

Behavioral Segmentation	**Demographic Segmentation**
• Segmentation by customer behavior	• Segmentation by shared personal characteristics such as age or gender
Psychographic Segmentation	**Geographic Segmentation**
• Segmentation based on emotions, values, and lifestyle characteristics	• Segmentation based on geographical differences

Let's take a closer look at each of these segmentation methods.

Behavioral Segmentation

Segmenting customers into groups based on how they act as consumers while making purchasing decisions is known as behavioral segmentation. This type of segmentation is designed to understand, predict, and target the following:

» The purchasing habits of your customers
» The usage habits of your customers
» The spending habits of your customers

Effective behavioral segmentation helps businesses understand the ways in which their product or service meets (or doesn't meet) the needs of different behavioral segments. Additionally, businesses can tailor their marketing efforts to reach customers at times when they are most likely to purchase. Behavioral data doesn't exist independently of other customer data; it is better described as an extension of existing segmentation data and can often correlate to demographic data. Common behaviors to track include the following:

- » Purchasing behavior
- » Occasion/timing (what triggers a purchase?)
- » Usage rate
- » Benefits sought
- » Loyalty
- » Status (first-time buyer, repeat buyer, etc.)

Of course, this data shouldn't be collected for the sake of collecting data—behavior-based data should be collected with a concrete goal in mind.

If a company is looking to increase their regular customer base, the goal of data collection may be to identify the best way to reach customers who purchase infrequently or who make only one purchase and never return. What about customer loyalty? Tracking the behavior of loyal customers can help decision makers understand why those customers became loyal in the first place. Armed with insight, the process of growing a loyal following is made easier.

Behavior segmentation provides unique insight, but it isn't foolproof. Gathering behavioral data risks providing decision makers with "false positives" in the sense that one customer may exhibit the same behavior as another but have different motivations.

Demographic Segmentation

Demographic segmentation is segmentation based on the personal attributes of your customers. These attributes include age, gender, income level, and occupation, to name a few. While a market will, of course, include a variety of people with different and unique needs, grouping these people together based on similar characteristics that are relevant to the business helps companies get the most out of their marketing efforts.

A jeweler that sells premium men's watches is interested in not only a male market segment, but men who make enough money to afford a premium watch. A company that sells retirement planning products is less interested in the gender mix of their market, but very interested in segmenting the market based on age, income, and marital status.

Demographic segmentation is easy to implement and is a good starting point for marketing efforts. That being said, demographic segmentation makes a lot of assumptions. Assuming that broad swaths of the population think and feel the same based on age, gender, or socioeconomic status has only so much application. To increase the effectiveness of marketing efforts, demographic data is usually best paired with another form of segmentation data to build robust and reliable market segments.

Psychographic Segmentation

Psychographic segmentation divides a market into segments based on emotional, values-based, or interest-based characteristics. This classifies consumers within a market into groups based on the way they think and the way they want to live. Psychographic segmentation is based on five general personal characteristics:

» Lifestyle
» Social status
» Activities, interests, and opinions (AIO)
» Values, attitudes, and beliefs
» Personality traits

Together, these various factors come together to create a customer profile.

A company that produces bottled soft drinks and juices is looking to find a new segment to sell their premium juices to. A health-and-wellness-minded professional (lifestyle, values, and attitude) who commutes and regularly visits the gym (AIO) wants a convenient, healthy juice blend that signals to others that he or she takes health and wellness seriously (social status).

While demographic segmentation makes sweeping generalizations and assumptions, psychographic segmentation narrows the focus of marketing efforts. For our beverage manufacturer from the example above, demographic segmentation may narrow the field to working professionals that make more than $65,000 per year. Some may be interested in health and wellness products, some may not. In the case of the company's psychographic segment, the average member of that segment is much more likely to be interested in health and wellness products. Additionally, the increased level of insight allows the juice manufacturer to better understand their customers' pain points and produce products that are a better fit and potentially more differentiated from those of the competition.

The downside here is that psychographic information is much harder to gather than demographic data. Not only is the process time-consuming, but the data that it yields is almost entirely qualitative. Quantitative data—like the data that comes from the demographic segmentation process—is easy to sort and endlessly model, but qualitative data can be a little trickier to handle and understand in a meaningful way. Segmentation by psychographic profiles also runs into the same stumbling block that any attempt to sort and classify people runs into: everyone is different. Despite the increased level of detail and complexity, the simple fact is that two people who have the same values, lifestyle, and interests may not make the same purchasing decisions.

Geographic Segmentation

Geographic segmentation is a broad method of segmentation that groups consumers together based on their physical location. The size of the geographic region that identifies each segment varies based on the individual needs of each business, but in most cases geographic segment data is very easy and inexpensive to collect. This information is often used in conjunction with other segmentation data to augment and focus marketing efforts.

Small businesses that offer on-site services, for example, have an effective range. Consumers outside of this range cannot be serviced cost-effectively or to the same standard as others. A good segmentation starting point for that business is to restrict marketing activities to consumers within that range. Consider seasonal or outdoor products. Winter wear, bathing suits, and outdoor equipment aren't going to be a good fit for all geographic areas—a good starting point for market segment definition.

Sometimes the line between geographic data and demographic data blurs. Some regions have a higher concentration of people who share similar characteristics such as age, ethnicity, or affluence. Also consider geographic segments that are part of a business strategy, such as a move into a new city or an attempt to claim market share from another established business that has a defined territory.

Which Method Works Best?

There is no right or wrong answer. Many segmentation approaches use multiple methods to paint a picture that is not only helpful and strategic, but also relevant to the product and the business model. The best method of segmentation is the one that makes the most sense for your business model and your product/service. Resource restrictions play a major role as well. Every business would love to have extensive behavioral and psychographic profiles to better segment their markets and build better products/services; however, the costs and complexity of gathering that kind of information are prohibitive for many young ventures.

Methods of B2C Customer Segmentation

BEHAVIORAL	DEMOGRAPHIC	PSYCHOGRAPHIC	GEOGRAPHIC
Segments customers based on behavioral traits	Segments customers based on shared characteristics	Segments customers based on values and lifestyles	Segments customers based on physical location
Helps firms understand how, when, why, and how often customers purchase	Uses information such as age, gender, ethnicity, and annual income	Uses key personality factors	Broad segmentation for seasonality or regional restrictions
Insight is used to reach customers when they are most likely to purchase	Inexpensive to gather and easy to implement	Accurate, detailed, and much more predictive/effective	Best used in conjunction with other methods of segmentation
Can be costly to gather, and not everyone who purchases does so for the same reasons	Assumes that people who are all the same age, gender, etc. think or feel the same way	Data is costly and difficult to gather and interpret	Everyone in the same region does not have the same needs

GRAPHIC

fig. 11

EXAMPLE

Let's take two yoga studios located in the same town. Both are using geographic segmentation, as it's unlikely that customers will drive more than ten or fifteen miles for a yoga class. However, using demographic and psychographic segmentation, they can appeal to different customers and both be successful—even if they are next door to each other.

Studio A wants to focus on women who are either new to yoga or want to get in shape and meet new people similar to themselves. Their customer avatar is a 35-year-old mother of two elementary-school-age children who is very busy and doesn't have a lot of time for herself. Her problem is trying to stay in shape with limited time. She is also feeling a little isolated and would like to meet other moms for support and socializing.

The resulting customer segmentation might look like this:

» Women between the ages of 25 and 45
» Average of two children aged 2 to 10
» Family income over $70,000/year (yoga classes are relatively expensive and appeal to a more affluent clientele with disposable income)
» Interested in being healthy and attractive
» Interested in meeting other moms

This studio might focus on daytime classes with special Mommy & Me yoga, gentle/yin yoga, and intro classes, and vegan lunchtime meet-and-greets or other social events.

Studio B has an entirely different customer avatar. Their ideal customers are hardcore fitness enthusiasts who like to compete at sports and stay in peak condition. They are high-achieving professionals interested in mindfulness and Eastern philosophy. While Studio A's customer avatar may feature Trader Joe's as a brand that their ideal customer would patronize, Studio B's customer avatar would feature Whole Foods. The resulting customer segmentation for Studio B is completely different:

» Men or women, ages 18 to 60
» Married or single
» Family income over $100,000/year
» Interested in peak fitness and competition

This studio might offer hot/power yoga, early morning boot camps, lots of evening classes to accommodate busy schedules, and power juice cleansing happy hours.

This is not to say there won't be customers to whom both studios appeal, or who switch from one to another, or who fall completely outside their target demographics. The point is that these two studios are offering the same basic product (yoga classes), but for entirely different customer segments.

B2B Customer Segmentation

As we covered earlier in this chapter, businesses that have other businesses as their customers are referred to as B2B businesses. Instead of the four general segmentation methods used by B2C firms, B2B firms use a mix of three key segmentation methods:

» **Firmographic Segmentation**
Firmographic segmentation is based on firm characteristics such as size or industry—demographic segmentation for businesses.

» **Tiering**
Tiering segmentation organizes customers based on their fitness for the goals of your firm, such as CLV (customer lifetime value), or short-term revenue goals.

» **Needs-Based Segmentation**
This method organizes and classifies customers based on their need profile, such as a need for a low-cost solution or a need for a local supplier rather than one that is based far away.

Let's take a closer look at these segmentation methods.

Firmographic Segmentation

Firmographic segmentation is demographic segmentation for business customers. It segments business customers into groups based on shared qualities. Instead of age, gender, or income, firmographic data looks at such qualities as annual revenue, number of employees, or location. Firmographic data is easy and inexpensive to collect but it is vulnerable to the same shortcomings that plague demographic data for B2C businesses. Just as we can't assume that every member of a demographic group thinks or feels the same way, we can't assume that all businesses that have been opened in the last two years, or that have fewer than twenty-five employees, have the same needs.

Let's say your venture sells enterprise-level shipping and inventory management software solutions. The cost and scope of your product means that companies with less than $25 million annual revenue or fewer than 200 employees will not see your product as a need or be able to afford it. Obviously, your product is only applicable to companies that make and ship physical products. These two firmographic segmentations provide a good starting point for understanding your addressable market.

Tiering

Tiering is a segmentation method that classifies your business customers into different segments known as tiers. These tiers are organized by how valuable the customer is to the business, often in terms of the metric "customer lifetime value" (CLV). Tiering is generally combined with firmographic data to home in on target segments. If a graphical representation of customers who are segmented based on tiers looks like a pyramid with a narrower focus yielding a smaller pool of more and more valuable customers, then the effort to reach and sell to those customers is an inverted pyramid. The more valuable the customer is, the more effort is devoted to closing a sale with that customer.

fig. 12

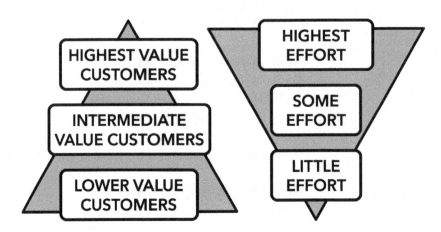

If you have ever heard of the Pareto principle—that 80 percent of your revenue will come from 20 percent of your customers—then you understand the thought process behind tiering. The goal is to identify those high-CLV customers, then focus marketing efforts on those businesses.

Needs-Based Segmentation

As the name implies, this form of segmentation involves classifying your business customers by their needs. Unlike readily available firmographic data, identifying the diverse needs of different companies can be a real challenge. On the other hand, there is no better customer than one who needs what you are selling. The process of identifying the needs of businesses is simplified in the digital age with the rising popularity and efficacy of content marketing and other user-intent-based advertising such as pay-per-click advertising and search engine result page advertising.

Which Method Works Best?

There is no one segmentation method that is best for each market—that's why there is more than one. When determining how to segment your customers, the best solution is the one that makes the most sense for your business, your market, and your industry. That best solution could be a mix of segmentation methods, such as using firmographic data to exclude companies that are too small, too large, too far away, etc., and then segmenting those businesses that fit the bill into tiers based on potential CLV.

Methods of B2B Customer Segmentation

fig. 13

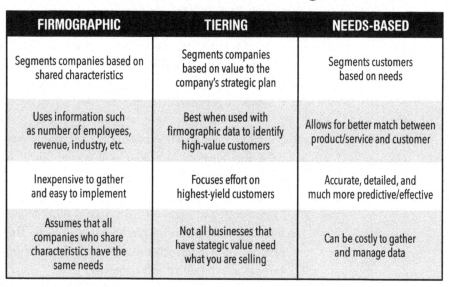

FIRMOGRAPHIC	TIERING	NEEDS-BASED
Segments companies based on shared characteristics	Segments companies based on value to the company's strategic plan	Segments customers based on needs
Uses information such as number of employees, revenue, industry, etc.	Best when used with firmographic data to identify high-value customers	Allows for better match between product/service and customer
Inexpensive to gather and easy to implement	Focuses effort on highest-yield customers	Accurate, detailed, and much more predictive/effective
Assumes that all companies who share characteristics have the same needs	Not all businesses that have stategic value need what you are selling	Can be costly to gather and manage data

Chapter Recap

» The market for a particular good or service is often far too large and far too diverse for a new venture to effectively target everyone all at once. It is necessary to dial in your efforts and focus on a core group of target customers.

» A good way to define your target customers is through the use of a customer avatar. By building your customer avatar, you are constructing a persona that is used to identify your target customers out of a larger market segment.

» Your customer avatar is based on a set of demographics, interests, behaviors, and product-related characteristics that pick your perfect customer out of the crowd.

» When constructing your customer avatar, the attributes you choose must be based on insight, research, and facts. This fact-finding process often starts with numerous online resources and ends with in-person interviews and surveys.

» There are numerous ways to segment markets and it is important to use the segmentation method(s) that make sense for you. A B2C business (one that sells to consumers) can segment customers based on their behavior, demographic characteristics, psychographic characteristics, where they are located geographically, or with a combination of methods. A B2B business (one that sells to other businesses) can segment customers based on the characteristics of their business (firmographics), into tiers based on their potential value to the business, and segment them based on their organizational needs.

| 7 |

Industries and Competitors

Chapter Overview

> » Understanding your industry helps identify your competitors
> » The difference between direct and indirect competition
> » How the forces of competition shape industries and the firms within them

---

Your *market* consists of the people who will buy your product or service. Your *industry* consists of the other organizations with whom you compete. As I said last chapter, you do have competitors. It doesn't matter how new or unique your product or service is, you have competitors. A good way to think of it is to look at what your target customers are doing right now *without* the benefit of your new product or service. Even if the answer is "nothing," that is still a barrier you will have to overcome.

In this chapter we examine the differences between direct and indirect competitors, the nature of competition, and the competitive forces that shape industries and the companies within them. But first, which industry are you in?

Which Industry Are You In?

The nature of new ventures and new products/services means that sometimes entrepreneurs can struggle to label themselves as part of a specific industry. If this describes you, ask yourself the following questions:

> » Who are my competitors?
> » Who is providing similar products or services?
> » Who has a similar process or business model?

Regardless of how you feel about being judged by the company you keep, the ways in which your competitors define themselves can ultimately help you better define the industry your venture belongs to. Industry segments are classified by SIC or NAICS codes.

» **SIC:** SIC stands for Standard Industrial Classification. The SIC system is used for classifying industries according to a four-digit code. It was established in the United States in 1937 and encompasses the majority of economic industrial sectors. Due to concerns that the system was antiquated and inaccurate, it was overhauled in 1997 to become the NAICS classification system.

» **NAICS:** The North American Industry Classification System is a joint industrial classification system between the United States, Canada, and Mexico. Developed in 1997, the NAICS system was designed to replace the aging SIC system. Its updates have reflected the change in economic foci across the continent, and as a result it is more inclusive of the changing service, tech, and information sectors than its predecessor.

Since the SIC system is all but defunct, we'll take a brief look at the modern update. The NAICS code structure is a hierarchical classification system that uses a two- through six-digit designation to classify various economic sectors, industries, and individual businesses. As the number of digits in the NAICS code increases, the focus of the classification becomes narrower, meaning that a six-digit code is much more detailed than a three- or four-digit code.

» The first two digits designate an economic sector.
» The third digit designates the subsector.
» The fourth digit designates the industry group.
» The fifth digit designates the NAICS industry.
» The sixth digit designates the national industry.

There is no formal NAICS assignment process. The entire directory of codes is made available online from the US Census Bureau,[17] and firms can search the database to find and select the code that most closely describes their business. For example, if you are the proprietor of a fast-casual restaurant with on-premises seating and the option to take food and beverages to go, your NAICS code would be 722513, Limited-Service Restaurants.

» 72   Accommodation and Food Service
» 7225   Restaurants and Other Eating Places
» 722513   Limited-Service Restaurants

What's interesting here is that the NAICS designation 722513 doesn't only include fast-casual restaurants. Also included under this designation are carryout restaurants, delicatessens, limited-service family restaurants, sandwich shops, and pizza shops, among others. This list is essentially a summary of your venture's direct competitors.

What about some of the high-profile tech companies that have less-than-conventional business models? Uber and Lyft call their services "ridesharing," but there is no ridesharing industry group/NAICS industry. The generally accepted designation for those services is 485990, Other Transit and Ground Passenger Transportation. What about the "homesharing" service Airbnb? The closest designation is 721310, Rooming and Boarding Houses. What about the tech behemoth Alphabet, Google's parent company? Google has a variety of products and services that cast a wide net. The closest NAICS code is 519130, Internet Publishing and Broadcasting and Web Search Portals. The NAICS system is reviewed on a five-year basis to ensure that classifications are regularly revised to keep pace with the changing economy, but at technology's current rate of change the system can barely keep up.

So what's the big deal? Why should a new venture bother to determine what NAICS code is the best fit? In addition to helping you ensure that your research is comparing apples to apples, NAICS codes are used by insurance companies to compute premiums and by the IRS as benchmarks. A company with a tax profile that is wildly different from others with the same NAICS code will raise a red flag or two and will result in increased scrutiny, or even an audit.

Direct and Indirect Competitors – The Difference

As the name implies, *direct competitors* are those who compete with you in a one-to-one capacity. They offer essentially the same solution to a customer's problem that you do. *Indirect competitors* offer alternative solutions to the same problem. Their products could be very similar to yours or not similar at all. The important part is that a customer could choose them as an alternative to you.

Two pizza shops in the same neighborhood are *direct competitors*. They both offer a solution to their customers' problems—hungry people need food—but more than that, they offer the same solution. Pizza isn't the only thing hungry people can eat, though. If there is also a sandwich shop and a sushi bar in the same neighborhood, then those establishments are *indirect competitors* of the pizza shops. They offer a solution to the same problem, but their solution is different. You also have to account for *substitute products*. What about grocery stores? They too sell a solution to the problem that hungry people face. A family that chooses to eat a home-cooked meal made from ingredients purchased at a grocery store, or a dieter who skips lunch, have both chosen a competing offer as a solution to their problem instead of purchasing a pizza.

Another way to think of direct and indirect competition is that direct competitors compete by offering the same or similar products, and indirect competitors compete by offering different things to the same market. The competition that exists between different industrial actors is just one kind of competitive pressure that is felt by companies, however. The pressures that customers, suppliers, and substitute products exert on an industry are very real and very powerful competitive forces that are often overlooked. A deep dive into Porter's Five Forces model, a helpful framework for understanding the relationships between various forms of competition within an industry, follows this section.

A Note on Differentiation

When you constructed your customer avatar in the previous chapter, I encouraged you to start with the problem you were solving for customers, which is the essence of why they will consider buying your product at all. Now that you have identified your industry and competitors, you need to think long and hard about how you are differentiating your product from what they are offering.

Recall our discussion of features versus benefits—customers buy benefits, not features, so be sure you are differentiating your product on that basis. Also remember that it's very hard to get customers to change their behavior and buy a new product, so your points of differentiation need to be compelling to your target market segment.

Quick Case: Beer is an adult beverage that is popular all around the world, to understate the obvious. Although the overall market is huge, there are also an enormous number of competitors, many of whom are gargantuan multinational corporations with billions in annual sales. Nonetheless, smaller craft breweries are able to enter the market and thrive. Some do so by segmenting their market geographically and staying local, but the ones who become national brands do so by differentiating their products from the larger competitors in ways that are meaningful to their target customers and are not easily imitable by their larger competitors. Some common points of differentiation:

> » *Authenticity* – Craft breweries tout their local roots and ties to the community in many different ways
>
> » *Quality* – Fresh, local ingredients, longer and more complicated brewing and aging processes, and highly skilled brewmasters
>
> » *Specialized Niches* – Smaller craft breweries can experiment with unique or seasonal ingredients to produce an endless variety of interesting and one-of-a-kind products

Deep Dive: Porter's Five Forces Model

No discussion of competition would be complete without a mention of **Porter's Five Forces model.** Porter's Five Forces is a conceptual framework designed to help business decision makers better understand the ways in which the pressures of competition influence an industry or industry sector. First introduced in 1979 by influential business and economics professor Michael Porter, this framework is a straightforward and time-tested tool.

NOTE

It is true that no two industries will have the exact same characteristics, but there are some underlying drivers present in each industry or economic sector in some form. The forces that a Five Forces analysis takes into account are present in every industry—the goal is not to uncover *which* forces of competition exist, but to *what degree* they interact with one another, and how these interactions shape a given industry.

The application of a Five Forces analysis yields the following insights:

» The intensity of competition within an industry
» The attractiveness/fitness of an industry for a venture or business model
» The profitability potential of an industry
» Key elements of an organizational strategy
» Ease of entry into an industry

Rivalry Among Competitors

At the center of the Porter's Five Forces model is the competitive force that exists between companies that offer competing products or services. Competition within an industry is the direct and indirect competition that most people think of when they hear the word. It is the jockeying for position and back-and-forth claim and relinquishment of market share.

The intensity of the rivalry that exists between competitors translates into the amount of control each industry actor (business entity) has.

The higher the intensity of the direct competition between industry actors, the more pressure each feels and the less control each can exert as a result. Suppliers and customers alike can simply move on to a competitor if your deal isn't a perfect fit, which means a considerable amount of resources and strategy are committed to responding to the pressures of direct competition.

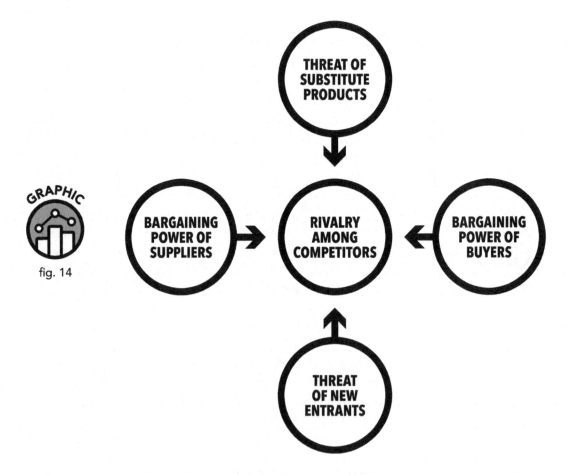

fig. 14

NOTE

A high-competition industry may not always be one that is crowded with industry actors. High competitor rivalry exists when there are numerous similar product or service offerings—these circumstances can exist between only a few business entities or between many.

On the other hand, if the intensity of competition is low, then each industry actor feels less pressure from direct competition and subsequently is able to exert more control over pricing, distribution, and ultimately their bottom line. With less pressure from competition, business entities have a higher degree of control over improving their bottom line and more room to maneuver when it comes to strategy.

The theme of differentiation is a common thread throughout this book, and—this cannot be overstressed—the interplay between industry actors in high- and low-competition environments highlights the crucial need for ventures to differentiate themselves from their competitors.

Potential of New Entrants into the Industry

If the rivalry between current industry actors applies pressure to firms, then it should be no surprise that the possibility of new entrants is a source of competitive pressure as well. The threat of new industry entrants is directly impacted by that industry's *barriers to entry*. An industry with low barriers to entry is one that is accessible to new firms with relatively low effort and cost. In an industry with low barriers to entry, there is a constant threat of new entrants who will increase the intensity of competition between industry actors by introducing competing products or services.

On the other hand, an industry with high barriers to entry is one that is not readily accessible by new or existing firms without a significant investment of resources. Once that resource hurdle has been cleared, these firms can enjoy relatively lower levels of comparative pressure from the threat of new entrants, and these industries generally have lower levels of competition between industry actors as a result.

Barriers to entry are diverse and often specific to the nature of a given industry. Common barriers to entry include the following:

- Economies of scale or scope
- High product differentiation
- High capital requirements
- Other cost disadvantages
- Restricted access to distribution channels
- Intense competition due to a shrinking industry
- Prohibitive government policy

Power of Suppliers

The power that suppliers exert on industry actors (their customers) is a pressure that new ventures quickly become acquainted with. The connection between the amount of power that suppliers can exert and the way it impacts the competitive profile of an industrial sector, however, is often overlooked.

Entrepreneurs often think of their supply chain in linear terms—as a direct line. Nothing could be further from the truth. It is much more accurate to think of your supply chain as a single part of a supply network—a web instead of a chain—and not to forget that your suppliers experience their own competitive pressures, as do their own partners and suppliers, and so on.

What the power of suppliers translates into for industry actors is the ease with which suppliers can drive up the price of goods and services. This power is accentuated when there are a small number of suppliers that provide an essential or unique product or service that industry actors rely on. Remember, your suppliers are industry actors in their own industries. When there is low competition within their industries, they gain the power to make a greater impact on their bottom line. Unfortunately for you, that means higher supplier costs of goods and services!

Think of it this way; the more a firm—or a group of firms—relies on a single supplier, the more power that supplier has.

Power of Customers

In an industry where firms have a high amount of power, prices are driven up. When power is in the hands of the customers, prices are driven down. If a firm has just a few very important customers, those customers have a high degree of power over that firm with regard to prices. Conversely, an industry that has a large, diverse customer base is one where the customers have a relatively low amount of power. Just as the power that suppliers hold is not thought of as a competitive pressure, the pressure that customers put on a firm is also often overlooked as a competitive force by many entrepreneurs.

Threat of Substitute Products

The threat of substitute products or services also puts pressure on a firm. Substitute products and services are those that can be used in place of those that are offered by an industry actor.

The question of substitute products is especially relevant in the case of startups that are introducing products or services to the market that are completely new or unique. Think about what customers are using instead of your new product—even if they aren't using anything. In the case of new services, are your customers simply doing it themselves?

"Nothing" as a substitute product can present a real challenge for new ventures. If "nothing" is performing fine and not costing your customers anything, then changing their behavior becomes very difficult. The same goes for services that may be substituted by customers simply doing it themselves. It may seem like an absurd thing to say, but the tradeoffs your product or service provides have to be very favorable compared to "nothing."

Chapter Recap

» Industries are categorized and classified by a standardized system known as the North American Industry Classification System (NAICS). It is a hierarchal system that uses two- through six-digit codes to classify industries.

» Direct competitors are other firms that offer products that could be substituted for your own. Indirect competitors offer different products, but they fulfill the same need. Direct competitors are competing for your customers and indirect competitors are competing for your market.

» Competitive pressure forces firms to be reactive instead of proactive, meaning that they have less control over improving their bottom line and growing.

» Porter's Five Forces framework outlines the five forces of competition that are present in every industry. In addition to the competition between direct and indirect competitors for market share, firms also experience varying degrees of competitive pressure from the power that customers can exert, the power that suppliers can exert, the threat of new entrants, and the threat of substitute products.

| 8 |
Your Value Proposition

Chapter Overview
- » A brief look at strategic positioning
- » Your value proposition: who is your target customer, and how are you different from your competition?

Your venture's value proposition represents an inflection point in the planning process. This is the part where the rubber meets the road. You are now armed with a deep understanding of your customers and your competition. The question now—Can this opportunity really develop into a healthy business?

Strategic Positioning

Astute students of strategic management will have realized by now that the previous two chapters have been addressing the core elements of strategic positioning. There are four generic strategies along with a fifth hybrid strategy and each can be identified by the economic proposition it provides to the customer and by the breadth of its target market. When compared, these strategies form a matrix, as shown in Figure 15.

fig. 15

Competitive Advantage	
LOW-COST LEADERSHIP	**DIFFERENTIATION**
Cost Leadership	Differentiation
Focused Cost Leadership	Focused Differentiation

Let's examine each in greater detail, moving clockwise from the top left.

Cost Leadership

As the name implies, the objective of a cost leadership strategy is to beat your competition on cost to a broad market. This strategy involves maintaining a competitive price and a product of acceptable quality while simultaneously reducing production costs. What makes this strategy tough to master is the constant need to manage and reduce production costs, and not just across one product or service family, but across an entire organization's offerings. The allure of this strategy is, of course, that when one firm gets it right, they are difficult to unseat.

Cost leadership strategies can be seen with brands such as the speedy oil change service Jiffy Lube, fast food giant McDonald's, and super-retailer Walmart—all brands that are great at what they do.

Differentiation

Generally speaking, a differentiation strategy is designed to convince your customers to pay a premium price for a product or service that solves their problem in unique and compelling ways. Differentiation strategies target a broad market and—as we have discussed in this text—allow firms using a differentiation strategy to compete on uniqueness and features rather than price.

Examples of brands successfully implementing a differentiation strategy include natural grocery retailer Whole Foods, fast-casual Chipotle, and tech giant Apple. In each of these examples, the firm in question is not the least expensive offering, but is a strong contender in its industry based on a differentiated approach.

Focused Differentiation

Rather than approaching a broad market with a differentiated offering, a strategy of focused differentiation focuses on a very narrow portion of the total market, and firms that use this strategy tailor their offerings to match. This narrow market could be a certain limited demographic or a single sales channel such as internet-only sales. A focused differentiation strategy often targets an underserved minority within a broader market. This minority is often easier to win over as customers—their problem isn't adequately being solved and they have been passed over by larger competitors.

Examples of a focused differentiation strategy in action include luxury car manufacturer Rolls Royce, children's make-your-own-friend Build-A-Bear Workshop, and eclectic culture retailer ThinkGeek.

Focused Cost Leadership

A focused cost leadership strategy is built around cost leadership in a narrow market segment or sales channel. As in the broad cost leadership category, a focused cost leader may not be the lowest price option in the industry, but it will be the lowest price in relation to the limited target market.

Examples include teen/tween jewelry and clothing retailer Claire's, discount retailer Dollar General, and one-night DVD/Blu-ray rental kiosk company Redbox. In the case of Redbox, there are numerous less expensive ways to view movies, but the placement of Redbox kiosks and their target market of customers who prefer the DVD experience mean that their one-night rental price is attractive. This price can be achieved because Redbox is designed as a self-serve movie vending machine—no need for retail space, cashiers, or other overhead costs.

We have already discussed why it is very difficult for startups to compete on price. There is a simple reason for this—their costs are generally much higher than those of their larger, more entrenched competition. Thinking back to our craft beer example in the last chapter, notice that none of the listed points of differentiation—authenticity, quality, and specialized niches—are attempting to compete on price. In fact (remember our section on pricing strategy), their higher price is a signal to their customers of high quality. Similarly, any discussion concerning competition advocates for focusing on a narrow market niche to start with. By creating a very specific customer avatar rather than trying to be all things to all people, startups focus their efforts and put their limited resources to maximum effect.

Considering all of this information, the ideal strategic positioning for most new ventures falls solidly in the bottom right quadrant of the strategic positioning matrix in Figure 15: focused differentiation. To be a successful focused differentiator, a startup will require a very well-formulated value proposition.

Your value proposition is the answer to two fundamental questions:

» Who is your target customer?
» How are you different from your competition?

Your value proposition will make or break your venture. Cool technology, a foolproof financial model, a can't-miss social media strategy, etc., are irrelevant if you haven't nailed the two core questions that make up your value proposition. The specifics of actually constructing a concise value proposition and committing it to paper are covered in chapter 16, but for now suffice it to say that regardless of how well your value proposition reads, you *must* have a solid understanding of what it is and how it will impact your business before committing significant time and resources to your venture.

Exploring the Fifth Quadrant

By definition, there cannot be such a thing as a "fifth quadrant." However, the four approaches that are identified in the strategic positioning matrix give rise to a fifth state: the state of "in between." But just as there cannot be a fifth quadrant, there cannot be a strategy that is both broad and targeted. The differences between cost leadership and differentiation are also mutually exclusive. By focusing on differentiation, your firm will incur costs that are inimical to a successful cost leadership strategy. The strategic positioning matrix is yet another insight from Michael Porter, and he cautioned against firms attempting to position themselves using multiple strategies. By making their own "quadrants" and tackling a strategy that is both broad and narrow (or focused on cost leadership *and* differentiation) these firms are "caught in the middle" and see greatly diminished returns compared to what they would see using a single focused strategy.

Q: Can a "hybrid" strategy ever work?

Answer: Since the 1980 and 1985 releases of Porter's books *Competitive Strategy* and *Competitive Advantage*, respectively, critics of the single-mindedness of his methods have emerged. In the *Journal of Business Strategy*, Danny Miller (one such critic) writes:

There are a number of dangers associated with the exclusive pursuit of a single generic strategy, be it cost leadership or any variety of differentiation approaches. Strategic specialization may leave serious gaps or weaknesses in product offerings, ignore important customer needs, be easy for rivals to counter, and, in the long run, cause inflexibility and narrow an organization's vision.[18]

These criticisms may well be true of some established firms in some industries. It is certainly true that a business that exhibits any of the weaknesses Miller specifies has trouble on the horizon; however, the startup that has the resources to devote to imagining their own hybrid strategy is a rare one indeed. Based on what we have covered so far, it should be abundantly clear that, by and large, new ventures have the highest chances of success by selecting and adhering to a strategy of focused differentiation when starting out.

What Is the Value of Your Value Proposition?

The value of your value proposition can't be overstated. In your business plan, your value proposition takes the form of a literal statement that answers those two questions from the beginning of this chapter—who your target customer is and how you are different from your competition. But the *real* form your value proposition takes is in the fabric of your venture, in the way your operations are designed to solve your customers' problems, and in the ways you are different from your competition. In short, your value proposition *is* your venture.

It is not uncommon for entrepreneurs to conflate a value proposition with a mission statement, tagline, or positioning statement. Each of those items certainly has a place, but it is important to remember that they are developed *after* a solid value proposition. Without an underlying value proposition, there is no mission for a venture. Without a target customer there is no tagline, and with no key understanding of differentiation from competitors there cannot be a positioning statement.

Quick Case: *The Demise of Vine* – Few apps grew as fast and crashed as quickly as the short-form video sharing service Vine. Launched in 2013, Vine peaked a year later with hundreds of millions of users. By 2016, owner Twitter announced they were shutting it down. So, what happened? Many stories have been written about the reasons for Vine's demise, but the answer boils down to the elements of their value proposition—they weren't solving a significant problem for their customers and they didn't have any protection against larger competitors offering similar services.

» *Customer problem:* Vine customers wanted to be able to exchange short, highly consumable, creative videos via a social network platform. Initially, Vine's trademark six-second constraint seemed fun and encouraged creativity in producing content. However, having a platform that accepted only six-second videos was too limiting for Vine to ever become a major social network. After a brief period of popularity, interest in the platform waned, exacerbated by intense competition that lured creators to produce content elsewhere.

» *Competition:* Both new and entrenched competitors saw the skyrocketing popularity of Vine and immediately enhanced their own video offerings. Most also supported longer-form videos, text, and still photos, along with better compensation programs for content creators. With Instagram, Snapchat, Facebook, and YouTube as tenacious competitors, it didn't take long for Vine to shut down.

Chapter Recap

» No venture can be everything to everyone, and it is the rare startup that can compete on price. This means it is essential that your venture adhere to a defined strategic position and clearly define its target customer.

» Your value proposition is a make-or-break factor of your venture. It is the why of your startup, and it is the answer to two questions: who is your target customer, and how are you different from your competition?

» A value proposition is not a tagline or a mission statement. A tagline is an element of your brand's marketing collateral, and a mission statement is derived from your value proposition.

PART IV

YOUR BUSINESS MODEL

| 9 |
Operations

Chapter Overview

» Exploring your venture's value chain
» A strategic look at outsourcing, including what to outsource and how to choose what goes out the door

Business operations consist of all of the activities, systems, and processes that a business utilizes to keep it running on a daily basis. The definition, like the term, must ultimately be vague. The operations required to keep a hospital running, for example, are quite different from the processes an auto mechanic relies on to keep their shop in running order. Although you can be as granular as you'd like when defining operational roles and responsibilities, ultimately operations revolve around the delivery of value to customers.

Value is the reason any company—big or small—exists. It is also the economic *how* and *why* of a venture's success. We know that the amount of money a company is left with once they have collected their revenues and deducted their costs is that company's margin of profit. This is the amount that "goes in the bank," so to speak. In his 1985 book *Competitive Advantage*, Michael Porter suggested a different, value-centric way to describe a firm's profit margin:

fig. 16

VALUE CREATED AND CAPTURED − THE COST OF CREATING THAT VALUE = PROFIT MARGIN

This high-level formula is foundational to understanding the concept of a value chain, and to mapping and interpreting your own venture's value chain. Additionally, because value and profit are so closely aligned, it behooves entrepreneurs to study their ventures from a value-centric viewpoint.

The Value Chain

All organizations have a ***value chain*** regardless of whether or not they take the time to identify and explore it. Simply put, a value chain is the journey that your "raw materials" take through your operational systems and processes to become something that your customers will buy. What constitutes your raw materials depends entirely on the nature of your business—in the case of a manufacturer, their raw materials really are raw materials.

At a high level, the value chain for a manufacturer is easy to understand. For example, a company that produces classic furniture takes in raw materials in the form of wood, fastening hardware, and upholstering fabrics. Individually, those components don't have much value for someone who needs a chair. The manufacturer processes the wood, joins the parts, upholsters the chair, and finishes it into a useful piece of furniture.

At each stage of this process—shaping the wood, fastening the components, etc.—value is added to the finished product. A chair isn't finished if it isn't upholstered, in the same way that it isn't valuable without having the legs fastened to the seat. Individually these activities don't produce a valuable finished chair, but without them a chair isn't finished (or valuable).

A coffee shop uses the inputs of coffee beans and cups to brew cups of coffee. A grocery store receives products as inputs. By unloading, stocking, and displaying these items, they are delivering value to their shoppers. When those shoppers purchase, they represent outputs.

What about businesses that are built around less tangible products? Or businesses that don't manufacture goods? These businesses have value chains as well, but they are not directly analogous to the manufacturing model. What they do have in common are raw materials—inputs—that are transformed into valuable finished goods—outputs—by processes that add value every step of the way.

Take the popular food-ordering app Grubhub. While it may seem as though the app's users are its customers, in truth the app's revenue-generating customers are the restaurants it partners with—Grubhub charges partner restaurants a transaction fee. In the case of Grubhub, the app takes hungry diners looking to order ahead or take their food to go (inputs) and delivers them to their customers—the partner restaurants—as outputs. Here, the design and functionality of the app is the "process" that converts inputs to outputs.

Grubhub's partner restaurants are the revenue-generating customers of the business, but the hungry people who use the app are *also* Grubhub's customers. If Grubhub can't offer app users a variety of choices, the restaurant they were looking for, fast results, or a smooth experience, then those users will look elsewhere. For a business like Grubhub this threat is additionally real: how were users placing orders with their favorite restaurants before Grubhub? If Grubhub fails to deliver an excellent experience for users, those users can simply place their order via a quick phone call (and Grubhub will lose their transaction fee).

This is also the case with similar app products that have become household names. Uber, Airbnb, and Lyft are all working to cater to two sets of customers. On one hand, Uber has to deliver value to commuters and travelers looking for a ride. On the other, they have to make driving for Uber a lucrative and desirable profession. The app's value chain has two sets of inputs and two sets of outputs to deliver.

MY TAKE

I often see startups billing themselves as "the Uber of [insert industry here]." What they mean is that they are using a similar model and that the person to whom they are speaking is supposed to think only about the success that Uber has seen. Instead, the first question that should spring to mind is "How are you going to deliver value to two sets of customers?"

Not all apps or tech-enabled services juggle two sets of customers. Music-streaming service Spotify, for example, uses the input of streaming contracts with artists and music labels to deliver the output of an extensive on-demand streaming library. SaaS (software-as-a-service) providers with businesses as customers use engineering, coding, and data maintenance as inputs to produce their various services as outputs.

The bottom line is that no matter what your venture sells, your organization can be expressed in terms of a value chain. Like so many of the other core aspects of your business, managing and improving your value chain is not only essential, it is an ongoing process. Think of it this way: in the case of the furniture manufacturer, the process of assembling and producing a finished chair isn't just the way the company delivers value to customers—it *is* the company.

Evaluating Your Value Chain

In any given market there is, of course, more than just one coffee shop, grocery store, or music streaming app. Simply delivering a cup of coffee, stocking an assortment of produce, or constructing a chair is not enough to build or maintain a competitive advantage. A venture's value chain is an expression of the overarching *how* and *why* that venture is in business to begin with—the value proposition.

Thinking back to chapter 8, remember that a startup's value proposition can be summarized as the answer to two questions:

- Who is your target customer?
- How are you different from your competition?

The execution of your value chain is the day-to-day way that your venture makes that value proposition a reality for your customers. The importance of your value proposition cannot be overstated. If it is built on shaky ground, no amount of process optimization or innovation within your value chain will result in long-term success.

The process of analyzing and evaluating an existing value chain mirrors the process of creating one from scratch—in both cases it is helpful to visually map the process. Value chain mapping and analysis consists of three steps:

1. Activity Analysis
Start by identifying the scope of activities needed to deliver your product or service.

2. Value Analysis
For each activity uncovered in the previous step, identify the ways in which it contributes to the value you provide for your target customers. Look for connections between different activities.

3. Evaluation and Planning
If you are analyzing an existing value chain, examine each activity and look for ways to increase the impact that activity has on the value you deliver. Look for ways to leverage the connections that exist between different activities and identify inefficiencies that can be eliminated due to these connections.

Let's explore the value chain mapping process by analyzing the value chains of an example business—a fast-casual coffee shop with multiple locations in a single region.

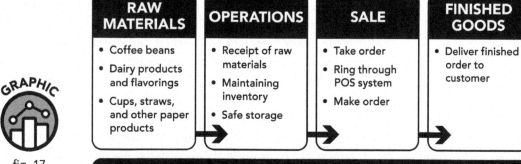

fig. 17

Figure 17 demonstrates the ways in which a coffee shop may deliver value to its customers, from the inputs of coffee beans, dairy products, and cups to the point where the output of fresh coffee is put in the customer's hands (distribution) along with the activities that produce less-tangible results such as service and marketing.

Primary and Secondary Activities

The major activities outlined in Figure 17 are considered *primary activities*, or the activities fundamental to the creation of value to customers. *Support activities* are those that exist at the organizational level, such as procurement, human resources, and research and development. Support activities may not be customer-facing, but that doesn't mean they don't contribute positively to the value that your venture provides. Added to our example coffee shop's primary activities, the support activities are represented horizontally—they are connected to each other through the support they provide.

What to Look For

A value chain analysis is a deep dive into the inner workings of what makes your business tick. Or, if your business hasn't been created yet, a value chain analysis is a way to plan operations with a value-forward approach. The visual tool that the analysis and evaluation process yields is helpful, but the true value of the analysis process is that it forces you to examine which operational components create value and—this is critical—which components *don't* contribute to customer value.

With each activity thoroughly explored, search for connections or common threads between them. These common threads are known as "linkages" and they represent areas where optimization and efficiencies can be exploited. A linkage arises when a value activity that is currently being performed (primary or support) can be performed in a different or new way based on the connection that activity has to another.

When examining these linkages with the objective of creating more value for customers, decision makers can focus on one of two areas: creating a cost advantage or creating a differentiation advantage. In either case, the choice your venture makes must reflect your overarching strategy for success.

Going back to the example of our coffee shop, one of the ways customers receive value is through the offering of ready-to-eat baked goods which are purchased from local suppliers. These inputs are linked to the procurement support activity—contract management with local suppliers is a process step that facilitates the inputs of pastries and baked goods for sale in the shop. To pursue a cost advantage strategy, decision makers could explore more cost-effective sourcing, such as frozen, bulk items. If the coffee shop is pursuing a differentiation advantage strategy, a local baker may be a better choice despite being more expensive.

When business leaders talk about innovation, they are describing methods and tools like the value chain analysis. Through rigorous inspection, creative interpretation, and an eye for detail, entrepreneurs along with their management teams can make informed, strategic decisions to propel their venture forward. Think back to chapter 1 and our discussion of competitive advantage. Exploiting linkages that become apparent in a value chain analysis is one of the sources of competitive advantage that allows firms to improve their differentiation or cost strategy.

Every value chain is different, even for firms in the same industry. When you start to sketch yours out, just focus on the chain of activities that your company undertakes to turn its raw materials into finished products. Don't worry about applying business terms like "operations" and "marketing" until later.

Outsourcing as a Strategy

Once you have determined an overview of your firm's value chain at the high level, you are ready to make decisions about what activities to perform in-house and which to *outsource*. Outsourcing is a critical part of business operations in the twenty-first century, particularly for startups. Outsourcing is cheaper and easier than ever, and using outsourcing dramatically lowers your startup costs, gives you financial and operational flexibility, and allows you to perform critical functions more cheaply and efficiently.

» **Effective outsourcing helps startups focus on core capabilities and cultivate competitive advantage.**

By narrowing the focus and putting the new venture's limited resources to their best effect, the process of outsourcing allows firms to focus on doing what they do best. This concept extends beyond costs and finances and includes intangible capital such as time, effort, and creative energy.

» **Effective outsourcing helps startups survive surprises and negative environments.**

When processes are handled in-house, the direct costs of those processes stay in-house as well. New ventures are often forced to pivot quickly, and pivoting is much harder when carrying the extra weight of in-house processes; in an effective outsourcing scenario these costs are held at arm's length and can be shed when necessary to respond to changing circumstances.

» **Effective outsourcing can reduce lead times and lower costs.**

New ventures are rarely in a position to effectively capitalize on economies of scale (the efficiencies that come with size and volume). By working with other firms that can access these efficiencies, startups can deliver faster while saving money.

» **Effective outsourcing can provide access to expertise and lower the frequency of critical errors.**

In the same way that managing and allocating time, effort, and creative energy are just as important as allocating money, expertise is another intangible resource essential to the success of new ventures. Ideally, gaps in expertise will be filled by members of the founding team, but as businesses and companies change and grow, new expertise gaps may emerge. Working with firms that have expertise and experience in areas where your venture has gaps can also reduce the frequency of critical errors. Leveraging the experience of outsourcing partners is a good first step toward creating your own internal best practices.

Not all activities or processes are good candidates for outsourcing. As with other operational decisions, the decision to outsource is a strategic one. At this point, it may seem as if the concept of your venture's value proposition and the value that you provide to your customers dominates most of your decision-making activities. That's exactly right—it absolutely must be your focus. After analyzing your firm's value chain, examine each activity critically, and be prepared to dive into the tasks and process steps that compose them.

The Outsourcing Decision Matrix

The outsourcing decision matrix is a handy tool designed to help decision makers carry out more informed outsourcing decisions, by comparing the impact of an activity on an organization's operations with its critical role in the organization's value chain (criticality). The outsourcing decision matrix organizes activities into four categories:

- » Retain
- » Outsource
- » Eliminate
- » Form a Strategic Alliance

Criticality is a measure of how important an activity is to creating value. Impact is best described as what would happen to operations if the activity in question were removed. If an activity is a key part of the value chain or is a part of the way your venture delivers value, then it has high criticality. If day-to-day operations would grind to a halt were the activity to be eliminated, then it has a high impact.

» **Retain**
If an activity falls into the top right quadrant of the outsourcing decision matrix (high criticality, high impact) then it is an area where your organization excels. Activities that have a high criticality and a high impact contribute significantly to the way you deliver value to your customers and therefore are not candidates for outsourcing. These activities represent core capabilities; if you were to outsource them, you would be giving away the source of your competitive advantage.

» **Outsource**
Continuing around the matrix clockwise, the bottom right quadrant contains activities that are low criticality, high impact. These activities are prime candidates for outsourcing. A perfect example of a low criticality, high impact activity is payroll and other HR processing. These activities don't directly provide value for your customer. However, if you tried to run your business without them, operations would grind to a halt.

Criticality vs. Impact

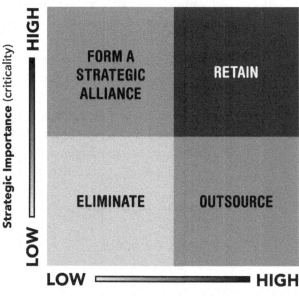

fig. 18

Strategic Importance (criticality) — HIGH / LOW

FORM A STRATEGIC ALLIANCE

RETAIN

ELIMINATE

OUTSOURCE

LOW ▭ HIGH

Impact on Operational Performace (impact)

Specialized HR service firms can usually conduct these activities much more cheaply and easily than you can.

» **Eliminate**
Moving to the bottom left of the matrix, these activities are categorized as "eliminate." They are low criticality, meaning they do not directly contribute to the ways in which the firm delivers value to its customers, and they're low impact, meaning if they were to be eliminated it would not affect operations in a meaningful way.

If you come across activities that neither contribute to producing value for your customers nor have an impact on the success of your operations... why are these activities being carried out? They are consuming resources and providing nothing for your organization or your customers in return. Value chain analysis is a perfect tool for uncovering non-value-adding activities.

» **Form a Strategic Alliance**
The top left quadrant of the outsourcing decision matrix is home to activities that have a low impact on operations but are highly critical to delivering value and generating competitive edge. These activities blur the line between candidates to be outsourced and those that should be retained in-house.

For larger firms, activities such as advertising, warehousing, and distribution can fall into the strategic alliance category. By working closely with a trusted partner, these organizations can free up resources to focus on their core capabilities while keeping a close eye on important activities. For smaller firms, activities that would normally fall into this quadrant are often best outsourced.

On the topic of outsourcing and competitive advantage, recall from chapter 1 that competitive advantage stems from resources, competencies, or capabilities possessed by your company that have the following characteristics:

» Valuable to the customer
» Rare
» Not easily imitated
» Not easily substituted

At this point, you need to decide what your distinctive competencies are, design your business to use these competencies to create competitive advantage, and outsource everything else. The value chain analysis tool and the outsourcing decision matrix are both valuable for helping you qualify the different aspects of your business, but ultimately your new venture will be best served by your staying flexible, seeking out positive change, and focusing on developing the things you do best.

At some point when your venture is further along in its life cycle (see chapter 11) it may make sense to bring those processes and activities back in-house. During the initial stages, however, your new venture's priority is to develop your position, deliver value to your customers, and dial in your sources of competitive advantage.

Chapter Recap

» Profit margin is best described from a value-centric perspective. This viewpoint is summed up in the following equation: Value Created and Captured – the Cost of Creating That Value = Profit Margin.

» All organizations have a value chain. It is the journey that inputs take through operational processes with value added every step of the way. To uncover possible unnecessary processes and potential operational candidates for outsourcing, and to identify critical linkages between primary and support activities, it is important to evaluate your value chain on a regular basis.

» Within a value chain, primary activities are those operational activities that directly add value to inputs and help to produce valuable outputs. Primary activities include inputs (raw materials), operations, distribution, marketing, and service.

» Support (or secondary) activities are those that indirectly add value to an organization's outputs. These activities impact each direct activity. Identifying key linkages between these activities and primary activities helps reduce costs and identify candidates for outsourcing. Support activities include financial and legal, human resources, development, and procurement.

» Effective outsourcing allows new ventures to narrow their focus to the activities that produce value and to focus on what they do best. Outsourcing not only saves new ventures a significant amount of money in costs, but it also increases the business's agility and ability to pivot when necessary.

» A useful outsourcing tool is the outsourcing decision matrix. It compares a process or activity's criticality with its impact and organizes items into one of four categories: retain, eliminate, outsource, or form a strategic alliance.

» It is often in the best interest of a startup to outsource as much as possible. This saves money, keeps operations flexible, and allows new ventures to focus on the activities they do best.

| 10 |
Marketing

Chapter Overview
» Explore the marketing mix, including the 4 Ps of marketing
» Distribution channels and strategic distribution
» The sales cycle

When people hear the word "marketing" they often think only about advertising. It is true that advertising is a large part of the *marketing mix*, but it is only one part. Marketing in general can be seen broadly as the exchange that occurs between an organization and its customers. That exchange can be communication in the form of advertisements (communication from the company to the market) or in the form of customers expressing their preferences, opinions, and feedback (communication from the market to the company). Increasingly, the communication between brands and the customers they serve has shifted from a one-way dictation to a two-way conversation on social media and other platforms.

The marketing exchange consists of physical products as well. Any business student who has heard of the 4 Ps of marketing knows that the product itself, its physical placement within the market, and its price are all essential components of a successful marketing strategy.

Marketing is more critical today than ever before. Consumers are bombarded with information—both real and fake—in addition to often-competing opinions, both informed and uninformed. Another way to think about the role of marketing is to see it as the task of cutting through the chatter and standing out in a positive way to your desired customer group.

The 4 Ps of Marketing

The *4 Ps of marketing* compose what's known as the marketing mix. They are product, price, promotion, and place, and together they form a high-level overview of the considerations that marketers must make when crafting a marketing plan. Far from being focused on advertising or price strategy alone, the marketing mix is yet another example of the focus on strategy and the ways in which decisions made in one part of the business rely on decisions made in another part.

The 4 Ps of Marketing

fig. 19

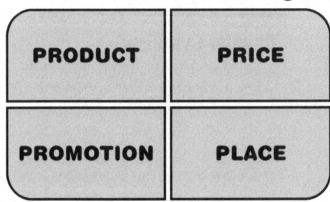

So far, we have already examined two aspects of the marketing mix: product and price. In chapter 5, I explored both the solution-driven nature of successful products and the many facets of a pricing strategy. Keep in mind that your product or service can't be a solution searching for a problem. Successful products are ones that solve a problem for customers. This problem could be a pain point or an as-yet-unrealized barrier to better experiences. Additionally, the pricing of products and services *cannot* be carried out without an underlying strategy.

Since we have focused on product and price in previous chapters, in this chapter we will examine the two remaining p's: promotion and place.

Promotion

An important aspect of the 4 Ps is that they represent the marketing *mix*. The focus that different firms place on different aspects will vary based on the nature of their business, their products, and their customers. Promotion includes all of the advertising, sales promotion, and related public relations efforts associated with a product, and it is represented by the ***promotional mix***. The promotional mix consists of advertising, public relations, personal selling, and sales promotion. The objective for marketers is to find the blend of promotional mix elements that best uses resources while making the biggest impact on the bottom line.

» **Advertising**

Contemporary advertising encompasses a vast array of ways to reach your customers, ranging from sophisticated high-tech solutions such as digital and social advertising to more traditional methods such as print, radio, and out-of-home advertising (billboards, bus stop benches, outdoor advertising, etc.). No matter the form they take, advertisements are characterized by the fact that they are openly sponsored and impersonal. By "openly sponsored" I mean that they are paid for and that the brand paying for them makes no claims to the contrary. By "impersonal" I mean they are not personal selling efforts—advertisements may be specialized to speak to a small group of people, but not just a single person.

Remember customer avatars from chapter 6? A large portion of determining the best advertising and promotion plan is the result of experimentation, measurement, and course correction, but the insights that creating a comprehensive customer avatar produce significantly inform marketing efforts of all kinds. Do your target customers spend time on social media, or not so much? Do your customers watch TV, or do they consume their media in other ways? What magazines do they read, what websites do they visit, what charitable causes or social issues are important to them? This information helps your advertising dollars go farther—there's no point in buying ad space on a website your target customers have never heard of!

» **Public Relations**

Public relations (PR) is the management of the spread of information between an entity—it could be a person, a business, or even an idea—and the public. The key factor that separates PR activities from advertising activities is that PR messages are not sponsored. Public relations messaging is generally referred to as earned media because it is not bought (paid media), which also means that companies do not fully control it (owned media). The objective of PR activities is to shape the conversation surrounding a product or a brand. When successful, news stories, word of mouth, and general "buzz" will reflect a positive impression that is in line with organizational goals. Because these sources are not paid, they often carry more credibility; therefore, positively impacting them can have a tremendous (and cost-effective) effect on the opinions and general interest of potential customers. Press releases, news coverage, articles, goodwill or charitable campaigns, influencers (brand ambassadors), and events are all tools used by savvy publicists.

» **Personal Selling**

Traditional personal selling methods include sales presentations, telephone or video sales pitches, and showrooms or retail spaces. As our world has become increasingly digital, so too have personal selling efforts. Sophisticated email marketing tactics blur the line between advertisements, sales promotion, and personal selling. A new generation of entrepreneurs with increasing social media savvy is transforming the culture of digitally shared experiences into personal selling sessions. Wireless technology combined with fast and easy online payments drives in-app purchases and transforms mobile devices into one-on-one personal selling tools. In short, your personal selling efforts are limited only by your imagination.

» **Sales Promotion**

Sales promotion includes paid and nonpaid media along with non-media messaging and communications that are designed to increase awareness, induce interest, and increase the impact of sales or other promotions. These promotion efforts are generally time sensitive—they are only relevant for the duration of the sale—and are often used in conjunction with other elements of the promotional mix. Coupons, giveaways, sweepstakes, contests, rebates, samples, pop-up shops, and tripwire offers are just a few examples of creative sales promotion tactics.

Getting the Most Out of the Promotional Mix

The promotional mix is not a checklist of four areas where your venture should dedicate as many resources as possible. Instead, matching each of the elements in a way that meets your marketing and sales goals and maximizes each dollar spent will yield the best results. The exact way these elements fit together is entirely dependent on your product and your customer. Even better, when deployed to their best effect, each element of the promotional mix will augment the effects of the others. It is also worth noting that your promotional mix is not set in stone. As your business grows and your objectives change, your promotional mix needs will change as well.

Your promotional efforts are business activities, and, like any other business activities, they should be carried out deliberately, with a strategic mindset and clear objectives.

» **Define Your Goal**

Think SMART when setting goals for your promotional efforts—specific, measurable, achievable, relevant, and time-bound. Effective goal setting is not only a business best practice, but it also avoids "scope creep," or the tendency that projects have to bloat in scope. Setting a goal at the outset of promotional efforts will also simplify the measurement process and make it easier to understand if your efforts were successful or not.

» **Define Your Target Audience**
Different messages resonate with different people based on the problem they have that your product solves for them. Any promotional messaging (indeed *any* communications) that you share with customers must be crystal clear and focused. A garbled message will not only produce lackluster results, but it will obscure the results of your measurement efforts.

» **Test First**
Before committing to a major ad campaign or sales promotion, test your concept. Target a subsection of your audience to see what the response rate is. Test coupons with your email subscribers before taking them public. Use polls and surveys to gain insight, and base decisions on data as often as possible. Don't be too conservative in your tests, however—too small a sample may not yield helpful results one way or another.

» **Measure Everything**
Not every promotional effort is easily measured; this is especially the case with public relations efforts. Try to gather as much information as you can regarding effectiveness to not only help you understand the success of your efforts, but to create a reserve of information that can be used to inform future campaigns.

Use Advertising

Generally speaking, use advertising to introduce new products to your target market or to introduce new features or applications. Use it to persuade your target market to select your offering over those of a competitor by summarizing your value proposition to them—a message that resonates with them and demonstrates how you are different from the competition. Also use advertising to remind your target market that you are open for business, how you solve their problems, and what separates you from the competition.

Keep in mind the medium where the ad will be featured, and don't let your ego get wrapped up in your messages. Your advertising efforts should be designed to speak to your target market and to accomplish your promotion objectives—ads aren't the place to make emotional decisions. Maintain consistency with your brand and keep the message front and center.

Use Public Relations

PR is something that you can't always control. In fact, the credibility it garners stems from the very fact that it is unpaid-for and authentic. Keep an eye out for newsworthy developments as they unfold for your venture and be mindful of the optics of your actions. An unfortunate part of public relations is that sometimes it is necessary to backpedal from public missteps. In the digital age, *everything* has the potential to be amplified.

It takes 20 years to build a reputation and five minutes to ruin it. If you think about that, you'll do things differently.

-WARREN BUFFETT

Use Personal Selling

No matter how clever your advertising, it will always lack the human touch. Yet a focus on personal selling isn't always appropriate for every business or every product. Is a proactive sales force appropriate for your business model? If your products are high-ticket and infrequently purchased, you may need a more hands-on selling approach. Do your competitors use a sales team (internal or otherwise)? If they are selling to similar customers, you may need a sales team of your own. Do your customers come to you, or do you have to go out and find them? The more you have to work to reach your customers in person, the more sophisticated your sales team will have to be.

Use Sales Promotions

Sales promotions are great tools for building relationships with sales partners. They are useful for enticing new customers to try your product and for generating excitement around your products and your brand. Sales promotions may seem straightforward—give your customers your product at a discount—but many of the same strategic factors that impact your pricing decisions come into play when planning and executing sales promotions.

How much of a discount is too much of a discount? Are you running promotions so frequently that your customers are trained only to purchase when your products are on sale? Does the frequency of your sales promotion give your target customers the impression that you are not a premium brand? All of these factors should be considered.

Choosing your methods of promotion is not a stand-alone decision. The attributes of your target customers, details of your pricing strategy, aspects of your distribution strategy, and current stage in the product life cycle all inform the way your promotional material communicates with and convinces customers that what you have for sale is the best solution for the problem(s) they have.

The 4 Ps of marketing may seem product-centric, but they translate easily to the world of service-oriented businesses. A framework with a service-focused twist is the *4 Cs Model*. This customer-forward approach translates the product-centric marketing mix into a high-level overview of similar components for service providers.

fig. 20

PRODUCT ⟶ **C**USTOMER SOLUTION
PRICE ⟶ **C**USTOMER COST
PROMOTION ⟶ **C**USTOMER COMMUNICATION
PLACE ⟶ **C**USTOMER CONVENIENCE

Place

The final P in the traditional marketing mix is place. Place is short for "placement," as in a placement strategy. Placement is all about your channels of distribution—the means by which your products actually get to the customer. This could be in a retail store, directly via a website, via an online marketplace such as Amazon or eBay, or through a wholesaler. Just as your promotion strategy must reflect the characteristics of your customer avatar, your placement strategy must also be customer-focused. Placement is about *where* your products are bought and *how* they are bought.

Earlier, I suggested that to avoid making your core product or service a solution in search of a problem, it is best to start with the problem and work backward from there. Your placement plan is no different. Start with the places where your target customers already spend time and money and work backward into your placement plan from there. Select a distribution strategy that makes sense for connecting your products with your customers.

Distribution Channels and Strategy

A distribution strategy outlines exactly how you plan to get your product/service to your customers and is a summary of a number of different factors. As with any other strategic decision that you make for the future of your venture, the specifics of your distribution strategy should reflect the nature of your product or service, the nature of your business, and your overall business goals. Consider, too, that while the decisions you make now should be made with an eye to the future, your distribution needs may change over the course of the life cycle of your product.

Your analysis of distribution channels begins with an understanding of your industry value chain. Recall from chapter 9 that a value chain is a set of linked value-creating activities that take your product from raw material to finished good. Your industry also has a value chain, and to formulate your distribution strategy, you need to understand where you are located in it. Here is a generic industry value chain:

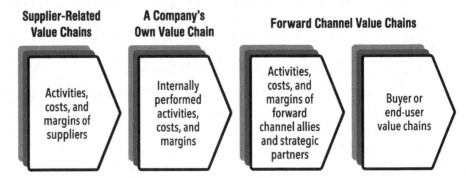

Supplier-Related Value Chains	A Company's Own Value Chain	Forward Channel Value Chains	
Activities, costs, and margins of suppliers	Internally performed activities, costs, and margins	Activities, costs, and margins of forward channel allies and strategic partners	Buyer or end-user value chains

fig. 21

Going back to our coffee shop example from the previous chapter, a national chain store and a local shop have the same buyer—they both sell directly to the consumer via their retail outlets. However, the back end of their value chains may look very different. Whereas the national chain might source their raw materials (coffee beans) directly from the producers (farmers), chances are the local shop will source the same materials through one or more wholesalers.

Sales Channels

The final step in your distribution strategy is your sales channel, the specific method you will use to sell to your customer. Obviously, your place in the industry value chain is an important factor in your sales channel. Selling parts to a manufacturing firm is very different than selling coffee drinks to consumers. There are many different ways to sell things, each requiring different levels of commitment and expertise. Let's take a look at some of the most common ones.

At first glance it may seem as though the best strategy is to access as many sales channels as possible. The more channels, the more revenue opportunities, right? That strategy may work for some business models, but for most startups it is an untenable position. Although more distribution channels may in fact equal more revenue opportunities, those opportunities should only be realized if they can be done so *profitably*. Each channel has costs associated with it. In most cases, the main cost will be the additional marketing and selling resources it will take to reach customers in each channel.

A common pitfall of new ventures could be described as a "build it and they will come" mentality, or the idea that your product or service is so attractive that simply introducing it into the marketplace will generate sales. *This never works!* It does not matter how cool, how sexy, or how tech-enabled your offering is— no one will purchase it unless they fully understand its features and benefits (and that's what effective selling does).

Direct Sales

Selling directly to your customer is a sales strategy that is appealing for many ventures and may seem straightforward on the surface. Who knows your product or service better than you do, and who will be more interested in making sales and thrilling your customers than you will? Additionally, without middlemen, selling direct means capturing a higher margin on sales and having the highest level of control over the final price of your product or service. Nevertheless, a direct sales channel does come with some challenges.

» **Selling Direct with a Sales Team**
A dedicated sales team is a good way to tackle a product or service line with numerous components and/or target markets. Specialized sales teams can target specific segments and will develop a mastery of the sales cycle for their areas of focus. Dedicated sales teams also afford your organization the highest level of control over your communication, promotion, and marketing efforts, both in quality and frequency.

Sales teams require training, however, and it will take time for your salespeople to build the relationships needed to become effective in the target market. Salespeople generally work on salary plus commission, so you'll have to pay them while they develop their territory. You can shorten the learning curve by hiring an experienced sales rep, but experienced salespeople are in high demand in most industries and command top dollar.

» **Direct Sales Online**
Selling directly to customers with an e-commerce site powered by WordPress with the WooCommerce plugin, or with a dedicated e-commerce provider such as Shopify, is an increasingly popular sales method. E-commerce sites can capture sales 24/7 without any direct monitoring. Effective e-commerce sites still require support in the form of maintenance and customer service activities, and there are back-end distribution challenges such as inventory management and wholesaler relations (see below), but the low cost and the ability to scale quickly and sustainably have made online direct sales a staple of modern businesses.

The "build it and they will come" fallacy applies doubly to selling on the web. Just putting up a website will not attract any traffic or generate any sales, no matter how cool your site is. Using the web as a distribution channel necessitates a strong, pervasive, and well-thought-out online marketing presence. Successful e-commerce entrepreneurs often find that they spend over half their time on marketing.

» **Direct Selling via Sales Agents and Manufacturers' Reps**
Many industries benefit from access to outsourced sales reps who function similarly to an internal sales team. These sales reps specialize in a specific field or industry and have a designated territory. They earn a commission when they make a sale. Due to their specialization they require little training, and often they already have a network of existing relationships within their territory. However, your product or service will rarely be the only one that they sell. It is in the best interest of these freelance sales agents to offer a range of products or services, and yours will compete with the agent's other offerings. This means you will need to provide competitive ways to incentivize these agents to give your offering preferential sales effort.

Channel Sales
Instead of selling directly to customers, channel sales strategies employ third parties to sell indirectly. Indirect sales strategies include one or more

intermediaries between the producer and the customer. Channel sales can be an effective way to reduce the costs associated with direct sales strategies.

» **Wholesale Distribution**

Wholesale distribution is a great way to reach a wide market quickly and efficiently. A wholesaler carries inventory from a manufacturer, which it then sells to retailers or resellers (as opposed to a dealer who buys from the manufacturer, then sells directly to the end user). Wholesalers already have relationships within the markets they serve and the sales expertise to move the inventory they purchase. The speed, ability, and reach of an established wholesaler all serve to make up for the discount that will be required to allow the wholesaler to mark up your product to their own customers. This markup eats into your own margins; electing to use a wholesale distribution channel often comes down to the tradeoff of accepting lower margins for the speed and volume that wholesalers can deliver.

Keep in mind that when you use a wholesaler, you are voluntarily removing yourself from direct contact with the end user. When you sell to a wholesaler, they become your customer, and the retailer or reseller is the wholesaler's customer. Being that far removed from the end user means that critical feedback may never make it back to you.

Another concern for new ventures that are looking to work with wholesalers is scale. Wholesalers only make money when they purchase in volume. A new venture may struggle to profitably deliver the volume wholesalers seek.

» **Dealers and Value-Added Retailers**

Dealers purchase inventory directly from a manufacturer, then sell directly to the end user. Value-added retailers (VARs) often assemble different products or services from manufacturers into packages or bundles that reflect specific customer needs. In both cases, unlike working with wholesalers, dealers and VARs work directly with the end user. They have a business imperative to pass along feedback and will often have strong existing relationships with their local customer base.

Unlike wholesalers, who serve as a single point of contact and make their money by purchasing and selling large volumes of inventory, dealers and value-added retailers require individual relationship building—each is a single entity. While some VARs may rely on wholesalers, the majority will require their own relationship and will purchase small amounts of inventory at a time. This issue of scale can mean that your products are at a higher risk of being discontinued. If your product isn't making the margin that a dealer or VAR expected, they will cut it out of their offering in search of a better solution.

VARs work with multiple manufacturers and service providers by necessity, making them part of a horizontal distribution strategy. Some dealers are dedicated to a single brand (think automobile dealers) and are therefore more in line with a vertical distribution strategy. Other dealers focus on a particular product or service—such as cell phones—and sell from a variety of manufacturers. These dealers are part of a more horizontal strategy.

fig. 22

DIRECT SALES		INDIRECT SALES	
INTERNAL SALES TEAM	**SALES AGENTS/ MANUFACTURERS' REPS**	**WHOLESALE**	**DEALERS & VARs**
High level of control over final price and margins (no middleman)	Require minimal amounts of training	Require wholesale pricing	Require wholesale pricing
Produces a high level of control over communication and promotion	Already have an established network of contacts	Can often sell quickly and in higher volume than direct sales	Often require individual contracts instead of a single point of contact
Sales teams can require training and may require time to develop contacts	Require competitive compensation packages to incentivize preferential sales effort	Already have established network of contacts	Purchase smaller amounts of inventory at a time
Sales teams can jeopardize other distribution contracts by undercutting distribution partners Online direct sales sell around the clock and scale affordably	Do not carry inventory: sales are commission based	Reduced level of interaction and feedback that comes from selling directly to the customer or working with the end user	Higher risk of volume inconsistency

Your Sales Plan and the Sales Cycle

A marketing plan is a description of the customers your marketing efforts are trying to reach; your sales plan is the description of the way you will execute sales to those customers. This means that your sales plan will be a part of your overall marketing plan.

The selling process is different for different products. It may be a long process, as is the case with multimillion-dollar enterprise-level software packages. Deals like that can take months or even more than a year to complete. Conversely, a sale can happen in minutes on the sales floor of a retail store.

Your venture's *sales cycle* is the blueprint for the way your sales force actually makes sales. No matter what your sales cycle looks like in practice—we'll get to that in a moment—all successful sales cycles share a set of key traits:

» Goal-oriented	» Clearly defined and measurable
» Focused on the customer	» Predictable and repeatable

In addition to these characteristics, successful sales cycles are responsive to change. This adaptive aspect is crucial to surviving competitive environments and navigating emerging technologies.

The Traditional Sales Cycle

The traditional sales cycle consists of seven steps.

These seven steps may be crunched together into a compressed sales process—as is the case with sales made in retail environments—or may be extended as part of a prolonged sales cycle, such as with a sale of enterprise-level software. It is the goal of effective salespeople to reduce the duration of the sales cycle to its shortest possible length without compromising effectiveness. A shorter sales cycle means that more sales cycles can be initiated (and hopefully completed) within a given time frame.

What constitutes a short sales cycle or a long sales cycle is relative to the standard in a given industry. For a B2B organization that sells enterprise-level software packages, a standard sales cycle could be several months or even a year while the salesperson identifies the customer's need and helps them explore the software. On the other hand, a website such as Amazon may have a sales cycle of a few minutes, composed of a customer searching and reviewing, placing the item in their cart, and checking out.

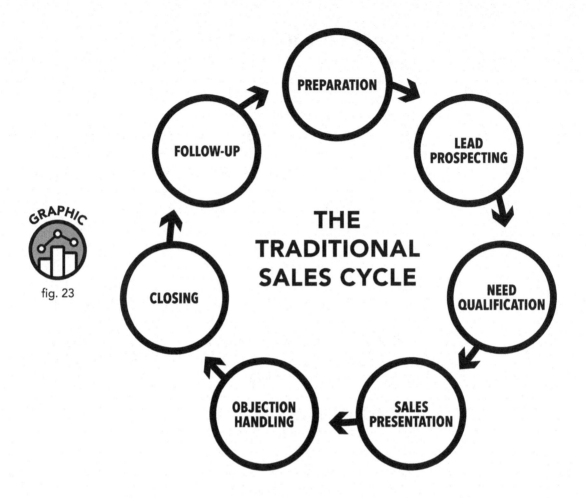

Building Your Sales Cycle

An established sales cycle within an industry is a good starting point for your product, but someone else's sales process isn't going to sell *your* product to *your* customers.

NOTE

Your sales cycle will require a different process for each distribution channel you have selected. Direct sales to end users, for example, will require different process steps than selling your product to customers who are not the end user (such as retailers or wholesalers).

Your sales cycle must be buyer-centric. Walk through the steps of your buyer process and identify each area that can and should be translated into a process step of your sales cycle.

Chapter Recap

» The marketing mix consists of the 4 Ps: product, price, promotion, and place. Each product and organization use a mix of these four elements for the best effect.

» The promotional aspect of the marketing mix is further defined by the promotional mix: advertising, public relations, personal selling, and sales promotion. Like many aspects of starting a new venture, determining your marketing and promotional mixes relies heavily on experimentation and seeing what the competition is doing.

» Sales channels can be divided into two overall groups: direct sales and channel sales. Direct sales methods include direct selling through the use of a sales team, through the use of a website or online presence, or through the use of sales agents and/or manufacturer's reps. Channel sales methods use wholesale distribution, dealers, and value-added retailers (VARs).

» A venture's sales cycle is the blueprint for the way that venture's sales force makes sales. Depending on the customer, the sales cycle may be quite long—in the case of B2B software solutions, for example, a single sale could take well over a year—or quite short, such as a purchase on an e-commerce site.

| 11 |

Planning for Growth and Change

Chapter Overview
» The factors that impact growth
» Planning for (and embracing) change

The idealized growth path of a successful startup looks something like this:

fig. 24

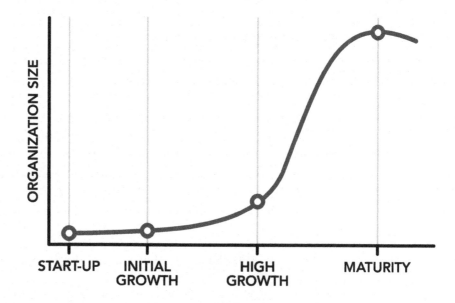

During the *start-up* phase, growth is slow. You're planning and putting resources in place. Perhaps you're beta testing or trying to acquire your first customers. Chances are, you're still working at your day job.

During *initial growth*, you've got your business going and you're making sales, but you're still not making much money and most of your time is spent planning for future growth. You'll still need outside sources of income, but you might be starting to scale back on your other work and/or planning an exit from your current job. It's unlikely that you'll be able to lead your organization through the next phase without devoting your full attention to it.

At some point, if you're successful, you'll have grown the business organically as far as you can, and you'll need outside resources to get you through *high growth*. This might mean raising money, hiring new employees, bringing on professional consultants and managers, etc. This inflection point is known as the "knee of the curve." The infusion of such resources to a startup with a solid foundation can lead to rapid, explosive growth. This is the phase in which you make the transition from a startup to a fully functioning business, which brings about a whole new set of challenges that are beyond the scope of this book. Eventually, the explosive growth levels off and you reach *maturity*.

Q: Will the growth path of my new venture look exactly like this?

Answer: Absolutely not. Your individual story, decisions, funding availability, professional network, and skills—in short, your entrepreneurial thumbprint—will play a major role in shaping the growth path of your venture.

Growing Your Venture

Initially, you grow your business simply by making more sales. However, the time will come when you have to think about growth from a strategic perspective. There are four overarching categories of factors that must be taken into consideration when thinking about the growth of your venture: the general environment in which businesses operate, the industry in which your business operates, your target market, and, finally, your own organization.

Factors from each of these categories can help or hinder the growth of your business, and their collective impact means the difference between achieving growth goals and struggling to develop and grow your business.

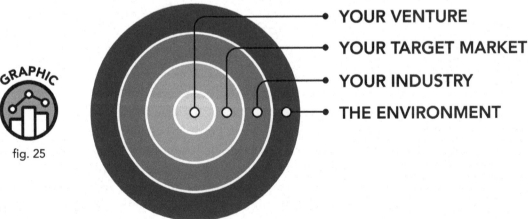

fig. 25

The Environment

In this context the environment isn't the natural environment, but political, economic, societal, and technological trends that shape the environment in which not only your venture but all firms do business. Individually, you have no control over these factors, but they have the potential to exert a high degree of control over the future of your business. This means that it is important to monitor trends and developments in the environment that have the potential to have an impact on your success. Keep the following in mind:

» **Environmental changes can be positive or negative**
Just because an event is outside your control doesn't mean that the impact it has on you will be negative. Technological developments that reduce costs, legislation or regulatory relief, and shifting societal attitudes can contribute positively to the success of your venture. Tracking these developments will put you in the best possible position to capitalize on them—or brace for impact should they change course.

» **Don't ignore environmental trends just because you can't control them**
It is true that you can't control national trends, federal or state-level legislation, or the direction society is heading in, but that doesn't mean you should turn your back on these developments. The closer you watch emerging large-scale trends, the better prepared you can be to capitalize or run for cover.

Your Industry

Recall Porter's Five Forces model from chapter 7. Those elements describe the pressures that are exerted on a firm by competing firms and the nature of the industry itself in the form of barriers to entry, the power of suppliers, and the power of customers. When thinking strategically about the growth of your venture in the context of the industry in which you operate, keep these aspects in mind.

» **How intense is competition?**
A firm that is reacting to competitive pressures does not have room to maneuver. It is difficult to take proactive steps to grow your business when your focus and resources are devoted to responding to developments from competing firms, the threat of new substitute products, and the power exerted by customers and suppliers.

» **What is the industry's pace of innovation?**
An industry that is marked by a fast pace of innovation rewards firms that can keep up and punishes those that can't. If the bulk of your resources are committed to innovation, how much is left over for growth activities?

» **How is intellectual property distributed within the industry?**
It is uncommon that patents or other forms of intellectual property are sources of competitive advantage for startups. When restrictive intellectual property rights are wielded by entrenched firms, they can be used as tools to stifle competition and limit the growth of smaller industry players. Is that a factor in your industry?

» **How volatile is the industry?**
A volatile industry is one that is difficult to predict with any degree of certainty. If the growth of your venture hinges on conditions remaining constant, then things could quickly become derailed in a volatile industry. Additionally, the resources required to insulate your business from industrial volatility may starve growth activities of resources as well.

Your Market

The industry you operate in describes your competitors—your market describes your customers. Whether your customers are consumers or other businesses, they are people, and people change. What may have been true when you were researching your target market may not still be true, and as a result, your value proposition may no longer be a good match for your target market. Or it may still be a good match for the people who are already your customers, but you are unable to reach a broader segment. Whatever the case may be, correctly leveraging your market is essential to the growth of your venture.

» **Is your target market large enough?**
Your product or service may be a perfect fit for your target market, but if that market segment isn't growing—or worse, is shrinking—it will be difficult, if not impossible, to grow your venture as is. If this is the case, the path to growth lies in reaching other customers in other segments, either through new product offerings or through retooling of your current offerings.

» **Are you (still) solving a problem for your customers?**
Customer needs change, new products are released, tastes and preferences come and go—are you still solving a problem for your customers? If not,

then it might be time to go back to the drawing board if you want to give your venture a chance to grow. Additionally, if you failed to correctly identify your target market, you may never have been truly solving a problem for your customers to begin with. If that's the case, you have some work to do uncovering exactly who has the problem that your product or service solves. Remember, don't be a product in search of a problem.

» **Is demand what you expected?**
Low demand can cause a whole host of operational issues, but the big picture is that your venture will struggle to grow if you incorrectly determined demand or if demand is declining.

» **Is your marketing plan successfully reaching your customers?**
A large part of building a winning marketing strategy comes from trial and error. Is demand truly low, or is your marketing plan not reaching enough customers in your target market? Are you still solving a problem for your customers, or are your salespeople not getting through? A good marketing plan will not only reach the people it needs to and convey the needed message, but also scale with your venture as you grow.

Your Venture

Of the growth factors mentioned so far, the only one you truly have control over is your own venture. Sustained growth is a near impossibility if your venture's founding and management team are not in a position to steer the venture down the right path.

» **Are you able to execute your business plan?**
Your business plan represents a road map for your business. Considering the other factors that impact growth, do you have the resources to carry out your business plan? What needs to change before you are able to do so? Here, the value of your business plan as a communication tool cannot be overstated. Members of the founding and management teams, and even suppliers or other strategic partners and stakeholders, must all be on the same page if you are going to execute your plan.

» **Are you maintaining enough organizational agility?**
Considering the range of factors that put up barriers to growth, is your venture ready to adapt? How easy is it for you to change course? This agility isn't just used to avoid negative outcomes, but also to capitalize on opportunities that arise as well. Outsourcing as much as possible is an effective way to prepare your organization to change gears as needed.

» **Are you motivating your team effectively?**
If the people who are going to get the work done aren't there for you, then growth is a challenge. This is true whether your team consists of two people or ten—everyone needs to be able to understand the goal and the method and to believe in the results.

Planning for Change

> *If you're not making mistakes, you're not taking risks, and that means you're not going anywhere. The key is to make mistakes faster than the competition, so you have more chances to learn and win.*
>
> — JOHN W. HOLT JR.

If the above quote doesn't summarize the "fail fast" mentality, I don't know what does. Here are some facts about change:

1. Change is constant.
2. Change is inevitable.
3. Change is good.
4. If you don't agree with the above, entrepreneurship isn't for you!

There simply is no such thing as a static, unchanging startup. Startups by their very nature are in a constant state of flux. You must accept—and embrace—the ever-shifting nature of a new venture or you will not only fail, you'll drive yourself crazy in the process. In the previous section, I outlined some strategic growth paths. I'd be remiss if I didn't also discuss what to do when things don't go as planned (hint: they won't).

There are a variety of factors that can make your plans go awry. Some of them are internal (poor planning, poor execution), and some are external (unexpected competition, changing consumer tastes or political/economic conditions). Even though these things are unexpected, that doesn't mean you can't plan for them. Here are some things to consider:

Practice Sound Risk Management
Have contingency plans with several potential scenarios—planning only for your ideal outcome is shortsighted and risky. Always have several different directions in mind, along with a clear vision of what a pivot would require if necessary. Think about the key assumptions you're making about your business, and outline what you would do if they don't work out

as planned. Higher-than-anticipated costs, faltering demand, or strategic partnerships falling through can all derail even the most robust plans. Additionally, your financial plan should contain a *sensitivity analysis* that takes these risk management aspects into account.

Outsource

As discussed in chapter 9, outsource and contract as much as possible. Staying lean and flexible will allow your venture to survive negative environments and adapt quickly to change. One of the worst things an entrepreneur can do is respond to some initial success by hiring a bunch of staff, renting office space, etc. On the surface those changes may feel like expansions that signify growth, but the reality is that those "investments" become fixed costs that still need to be paid even if the money's not coming in as planned.

Carry Insurance

Specifically, liability and key man insurance. The importance of liability insurance should go without saying, but many startups ignore the value of key man insurance. This type of coverage pays out in the event that a key member of the team dies or becomes disabled. Your founding team has been carefully selected to be a perfect fit; could your venture survive without them? It may be uncomfortable to discuss, but a basic package of business insurance shouldn't be that expensive and can save your business if the worst should happen.

Don't Cut Corners

Take care to address quality and safety at the product development level—whatever that may entail for your product or service. Damage to property, injuries, and loss of life mean lawsuits, bad press, and negative social media campaigns, not to mention the mental anguish that stems from being responsible for hurting others. The effects of cutting corners can sink your business before you really even get going. Have the foresight pay attention to the details and to steer clear of avoidable negativity.

Stay Proactive

It is important to remember that no matter how burdensome the planning process may seem right now, it is always favorable to being reactive in the face of catastrophe. As you develop contingency plans and prepare for the future, build in plans to review your plans and adjust as necessary. Don't wait for a crisis to drive change.

Play Chess, Not Checkers

Think about your next move in all that you do. Here's a fun exercise: Google "chess vs. checkers quote" and see just how many people claim that they were the ones to come up with it. The point is that most people are competing in a simple, linear way (playing a game of checkers) while the smart ones are thinking many moves ahead in a fluid and multidimensional game (playing a game of chess). Make sure you're one of the ones playing chess!

Chapter Recap

» The growth of a venture follows a general path, but the specifics of your circumstances will do more to dictate how the growth of your venture takes shape.

» There are four overarching categories of factors that impact growth: environment, industry, market, and venture. Of the four, you have the highest level of control over your venture.

» The environment describes super-trends and events that take place on the national or societal stage. Industrial factors reflect industrial volatility, the rate of innovation, and the intensity of competition within your industry. Market factors reflect your customers, the size and characteristics of your target market, and the ways you do or don't solve their problems. Venture-level factors include your ability to execute your business plan, the ability of your firm to respond to changing circumstances (both positive and negative), and your ability to keep your team motivated.

» Change is not only inevitable but healthy. Prepare for the potential downsides of change by considering risk management in everything you do, outsourcing as much as possible, staying proactive, and taking the long view by "playing chess, not checkers."

| 12 |

Building Your Team
Management, Staffing, and the Founding Team

Chapter Overview
» The founding team
» How should equity be distributed in your venture?

Another observation that has been attributed to many is that the main assets of most firms walk out the door at the end of the day. Particularly for a startup lacking traditional resources like money, real estate, a plant, and equipment, or even a brand name, the unique skills and abilities of the founding team lie at the heart of its competitive advantage. But you can't go out and pay top salaries to attract the best people, so who are your founding team members going to be? Where do they come from, and why will they work for you? Let's take a closer look.

MY TAKE
Most investors consider the founding team to be far more important than the idea itself. A common turn of phrase in the investment community is *"I'd rather invest in an A team with a B idea than a B team with an A idea,"* or, put more bluntly, *"We bet on the jockey, not on the horse."*

The Founding Team
Starting your own business and carrying one hundred percent of the burden is a lonely and isolating undertaking. Being an entrepreneur is often a thankless job. Long hours, investing revenues back into the business instead of taking a salary, and endlessly networking is less draining when shared among a team. But forming a team comes with its own set of challenges, so when considering the path that is right for your business, keep both the benefits and the detriments in mind.

The benefits of using a team to get your startup off the ground:

» **A team shares in the effort of running a startup.**
Getting a startup off the ground involves managing a wide range of moving pieces, and this task is made much easier when the burden is shared by members of a team.

» **Consensus decisions are better than decisions made by individuals.**
If two heads are better than one, then a decision that has been reached by team consensus is much stronger than one made by an individual. The best teams have a diversity of experience and background, a circumstance that leads to the analysis of issues from every angle and to solutions that may not have been reached by an individual. It goes without saying that you have to be open to hearing different opinions!

» **Team members bring complementary skills to the table.**
Often, an entrepreneur has a narrow focus in a single skill set or technical specialty. There's nothing wrong with that, though it can mean that other areas of the business that fall outside that specialty could be weak. For example, a talented programmer may not be an experienced marketer or salesperson. In that instance, a team member who has strengths in those areas would be a good fit to improve the health of the business.

» **A new venture led by a team has more credibility with investors.**
Keep in mind that, once your business leaves the startup phase and begins courting investors, a complete team will project more soundness and stability than a business that operates under a single decision maker.

» **A team has access to a larger professional network.**
Think about the number of people within your personal and professional network. Imagine if that number was doubled, tripled, or quadrupled. Networking, talking through your business concept with others, and forming mutually beneficial business relationships is much easier when more people are doing the talking.

» **Team members share the burden of fundraising.**
In the same way that many hands make the colossal task of managing a startup lighter work, the burden of fundraising can also be spread across multiple team members.

Despite the significant benefits that having a founding team brings to the effort of getting your startup off the ground, working with a team isn't a silver bullet scenario. Nothing can throw a wrench into the works of a successful startup faster than "people problems." The first question to ask when forming a founding team concerns the formality of the team's formation. A casually formed team may be more comfortable and may have more room to maneuver, but what happens when the business takes off and it is time for founders to start paying themselves? Members of a casually formed founding team have few legal guarantees regarding profit sharing, ownership, and business responsibility.

What this means for founding teams is that the sooner the details of the team's arrangement can be formalized, the better. While it may not be a comfortable conversation for some, having enforceable protections in place is preferable to surprises down the line. The goal of this conversation is to have an open and honest discussion of the attitudes, fears, and aspirations of each of the team members.

The conversations that are required to formalize the founding team require candor, transparency, and honesty from all parties. If prospective team members are unable or unwilling to discuss these aspects, then they may not be a good fit for the business in the long term. Formalizing the relationship between team members protects everyone involved if it is carried out in a fair and equitable manner.

The agreement that results from these conversations generally covers four key issues: ownership, responsibility, decision-making, and operating procedures, though the more facets that are addressed, the more protection that is afforded to each member of the team, and to the business as a whole.

Formalize These Aspects

Because these aspects are so important to ensuring that the formation of your founding team goes smoothly, let's take a deeper dive into each.

Roles and Responsibilities

This portion of the conversation/agreement determines the answers to three questions for each team member:

> » What will this individual do to contribute to the success of the business?

» What sets of activities, processes, and other functions will this individual be responsible for?

» To what extent is this individual responsible for accomplishing their assigned actions and functions?

Despite the fact that founders often fill a number of roles and have broad responsibilities during the early days of a venture, putting specific responsibilities down on paper has a focusing effect on the team. For example, designating Founder A as the venture's development manager doesn't mean that Founder A can't contribute to any other area of the business; it means that Founder A owns development and focuses his or her efforts.

The roles the founding team occupies will change over time. Just as every single other facet of your business should be flexible and responsive to change, so too should these designations.

Decision-Making and Operating Procedures

The roles and responsibilities of each team member should be defined and formalized when you select the members of your founding team. The same goes for the process by which decisions are made.

» **When to put it to a vote**
The decision-making process exists as a series of questions. What decisions can be made by an individual without input from the team? What criteria define when a decision must be put to a vote? And when decisions are put to a vote, does every member of the team have an equal say, or is the vote weighted based on each individual's proportion of equity? What are the procedures for settling an impasse? Who has a deciding vote, or what alternative measures will be taken as tie-breakers?

» **The procedure for removing a team member if necessary**
Despite the extreme discomfort this conversation can produce, removal of a team member is an eventuality that absolutely cannot be left unaddressed. In the instance of uneven team sizes, or teams with a minority opinion, it is possible for the majority of the team to vote out or push out their opponents. Infighting is a quick way to blow your business off course and derail your success. Identify circumstances when, for the good of the business, the ousting of a founder can or should be considered. Failure to

meet critical milestones, misuse of funds, or violation of other agreements are examples of potential conditions that could trigger a vote to remove the offending founder.

» **Other critical considerations**
Are there any other critical concerns that should be taken into account when making decisions that are specific to your business? For example, some industries have a much higher burden of safety, due to their inherently dangerous nature. Instead of leaving these considerations to a case-by-case basis, get them nailed down and understood by all members of the founding team.

» **Define the parameters for normal business functions**
When it comes to hiring and firing, should each founder have a say, or is that not necessary? How about the purchase of routine supplies and equipment? What dollar amount triggers a group decision, and which purchases can be completed by an individual? How should profits be reinvested into the business, or how should they be distributed?

In addition to considerations regarding responsibilities and the decision-making process, keep these other common team-based mistakes in mind:

» **Hiring Team Members Who Have Divergent Goals**
A team that is pulling in opposite directions isn't really much of a team. That's why it is so critical for would-be teams to all be on the same page. Remember that conversation the founding team should have regarding their attitudes, fears, and aspirations? That is the perfect time to get to the bottom of whether or not the entire founding team can operate as a team. Divergent or competing goals between team members are definitely not in the best interest of the business—it is exactly the kind of "people problem" that can grind progress to a halt. This issue often arises concerning decisions about future growth. If some team members are interested in long-term growth while others are more interested in quick financial gains, serious disagreements will soon crop up.

» **Using Only Family and Friends**
Teams benefit from a diversity of experience and opinion. For some entrepreneurs, the people in whom they place the most trust are their family members or longtime friends. There is nothing wrong with that; however, there is a reason that many caution against going into business

with friends, family, or significant others. In a worst-case scenario, your founding team may have to make hard decisions that put the needs of the business over friendships, and that is a situation no one wants to be in. On the other end of the spectrum, the bond of friendship can add a level of implied bias that clouds otherwise uncomplicated decisions.

» **Incorrectly Compensating Team Members with Equity**
The valuation of a new venture is a tricky business. The firm doesn't have a lot of assets, and financials are largely unproven, which means most attempts at valuation are optimistic at best. Tricky valuation translates into potential issues when it comes time to discuss the equity split among founding team members. Take the time to ensure that equity compensation is handled correctly, and view every equity decision through the lens of the two questions "Why?" and "Under what conditions?"

How Big Should My Founding Team Be?

With all of the team-based considerations out of the way, the obvious question remains: how many people should be on my founding team? The answer is less about a number and more about the answer to two questions:

» What key skills are represented within the makeup of my founding team?
» Can my founding team work as a cohesive unit that gets things done?

The answer to neither question includes a number of people. If those bases are covered by two dedicated people, great. If more are needed, then that's something that can be addressed. If a team has a minimum size of two people, then how many founders is too many founders? There is no set upper boundary to the number of founders that can be in a founding team but remember the old saying: too many cooks in the kitchen spoils the soup.

NOTE

The two main questions that entrepreneurs should ask regarding the makeup of their founding team should probably be asked by solo entrepreneurs as well. But instead of thinking about a team, think about the unique mix of skills that you bring to the table and your ability to make progress. Be honest. Are there gaps in your skill mix? Are there weak areas that could benefit from the expertise of a cofounder, partner, or a founding team? If the answer is yes, then you should consider the benefits of using a founding team.

There is no hard and fast rule regarding founding team size, but keep in mind that as the number of founders increases, so too does the chance that a key founder may decide to pull out of the venture. In addition, the more founders there are, the smaller the equity shares for each team member and the more difficult the maintenance of equity sharing—especially if the members of this large team are joining after an initial equity split.

The Ownership Structure of New Ventures

Large, established corporations can attract the best talent with generous and lucrative incentives and cushy perks. Startups don't have that luxury. Instead they rely primarily on sharing equity in the venture. Equity is non-cash compensation that represents an ownership share of a company. Because few ventures are solo operations, this decision can get complicated fast.

At face value, it may seem as though an equal split across the board is the fairest distribution of equity—indeed, it works well for some ventures—but it is rarely the most equitable in the eyes of team members. Often the contributions made by members of the team are not equivalent, or due to their nature may be difficult to compare directly. How do you compare the value of a founding member who has contributed more money than other members to the value of a founding member who has contributed very little money but worked very hard? And should the founding member who originated the concept receive a significantly higher share of equity?

There is no single answer that satisfies all of those questions, and ultimately the answer comes down to the outcome of the conversations that you and your founding team conduct. For many ventures, the "who owns what" conversation is something that no one looks forward to. As conversations go, it requires healthy doses of candor and transparency, is often carried out in several rounds, and requires that emotions be left at the door.

Everyone is going to want a piece of the pie. While those decisions are hashed out, it is *absolutely critical* that everyone keep the long-term success of the venture in mind. Now is the time to weed out anyone primarily interested in making a quick buck.

Equity Distribution

The easiest way distribute equity between the members of a founding team is to simply give each member of the team the same amount of equity, but that rarely occurs. To be honest, an even split is rarely seen by members of the team as the most equitable way to distribute equity in a startup, and they will waste no time pleading their case.

> » *"This company was my idea!"*
> » *"Cofounder X has been working for two months. I have been working for six months!"*
> » *"I didn't take a salary for three months, but during that time cofounder N did!"*
> » *"Cofounder Y's experience doesn't come close to mine!"*
> » *"I have raised thousands of dollars, plus I brought on cofounder Z!"*

As you can see, equity distribution is more of an art than a science. The sheer range of unique circumstances that can and will arise means that no one method of uneven equity distribution is a one-size-fits-all solution. But consider these common methods of determining who gets what:

> » **Ideation**
> Especially popular for technology-based startups, the person or people who contributed most to the venture's value proposition claim a larger portion of its equity. This makes perfect sense in situations where it is reasonable to say that the venture wouldn't exist at all if it weren't for the efforts of some cofounders over others. On the other hand, the value of ideas lies in their execution. Simply having had the idea for the business may not be enough to warrant a higher equity share.

> » **Salary Replacement**
> In some cases, members of the founding team will agree to take a higher share of the startup's equity in lieu of drawing a higher (or any) salary. The motivation to do so is the belief that as the company grows and increases in value, the higher equity share will make up for the lost direct compensation. Equity sharing based on salary replacement is great for the health of a young startup—less money paid in salaries and wages means more to reinvest in the company—and it incentivizes those founding team members who elect to take salary replacement to continue to work hard. The bigger and stronger they build the company, the bigger their payoff. Additionally, salary replacement agreements between founding members send a positive message to investors. If there are members of the team who believe so strongly in this opportunity that they are willing to accept a slashed salary, that is a great sign.

» **Other Contribution Considerations**
Uneven distribution can be based on any number of other considerations related to a team member's contribution to the effort. It is ultimately up to the team as a whole to come to an agreement. Other contribution considerations could include:

» The true market value of each founder's true contribution to the venture
» The opportunity cost that a cofounder has faced
» Active role of each cofounder in attracting and presenting to potential investors
» The amount of seed capital contributed by each cofounder
» Future contributions that will be made by cofounders

Q: Should our team use an equity split calculator?

Answer: An equity calculator is a software program that calculates an equity split based on a number of factors. The makeup of the founding team complete with contributions is plugged into the program and it produces a recommended equity split. While this may seem like a fair and impartial process, it is really only acceptable if everyone on the founding team is behind the results one hundred percent. Additionally, everyone on the founding team will have to work closely together, trust one another, and rely on one another with complete confidence. Is it better to trust solidifying that relationship with a software program or through discussion?

Key Questions Regarding Owner Equity

A full, comprehensive look at the best way to divvy up owner equity is well beyond the scope of this book. As I said at the top of this section, it is an art more than a science, and it depends almost entirely on the conversations your team members have and the conclusions that are reached through the discussion process. That being said, here are a few final questions you may have regarding the equity split process.

» **When is the best time to discuss ownership structures?**
There's no time like the present. Of course, it has been said that when equity split decisions are rushed into that cofounders can be considered equal in the sense that they are equally unhappy. Discussions relating to equity splits should certainly occur before things are too far underway with the venture, but they also should not be rushed. Taking your time and understanding the commitment level, goals, and aspirations of various founding team members will help everyone craft a more equitable agreement.

On the other hand, waiting until it is too late can cause strife that destabilizes and sends a young venture off track. The bottom line? Take your time and do it right, but start thinking about it now.

» **What happens if more members are added to the founding team?**
If more members are added to the founding team after equity ownership has been decided and it is agreed that this new member should receive equity, then the overall equity percentage that each existing member owns will decrease—a venture cannot be owned more than one hundred percent. This is known as *dilution*. Because startups don't have the resources to attract the best talent with high salaries or other direct perks, equity in the venture is often used as an enticement. To avoid issues down the road, a common practice is to reserve a portion of the venture's equity for this purpose.

» **What happens if a founding member wants to leave the team?**
There are a number of reasons why a founding team member may ultimately want to leave the founding team. Exactly what happens next depends on the nature of your agreement. An approach that puts the needs of the venture first—and protects every member of the founding team—is the creation of a vesting schedule.

A vesting schedule dictates a time period over which equity shares are distributed. This is important for ventures no matter how equity is split. A standard vesting schedule will release equity options over a period of five or so years, and this prevents a founder from dumping their shares of the company and leaving the team within the first year.

» **Do We Need a Lawyer?**
During the discussion process where founding team members figure out an equitable split, an experienced startup lawyer can provide helpful counsel, although this is often not strictly necessary. When it comes time to finalize the consensus decision, however, it is a good idea to bring a lawyer with startup experience on board. An experienced startup lawyer can not only help finalize equity split decisions, but can help navigate foundational HR aspects, help ensure regulatory compliance if applicable, help finalize your legal entity classification, and in some cases can even be a helpful ally in the hunt for funding.

Chapter Recap

» Many investors consider the founding team to be more important than the opportunity itself. They often consider their investment a "bet on the jockey, not the horse."

» Starting your business with a team is far superior to starting it alone. Teams can share in the burden of running a startup, contribute to a more robust decision-making process, bring complementary skills to the table, carry more credibility with investors, and have access to a larger professional network than an entrepreneur who is working alone.

» When working out the details of your founding team, ensure that some key aspects are formalized early in the foundation process. It is important to nail down what each member of the founding team will do to contribute to the success of the business; what sets of activities, processes, and other functions each member of the founding team will be responsible for; and the extent to which each founding member is accountable for accomplishing their assignments.

» It is also important to determine the ways in which key decision-making procedures will be carried out by the team, such as establishing which decisions should be put to a vote and which can be handled by individual team members, the procedure for removing a team member should the need arise, and which members should be involved in which business processes as the venture moves forward.

» There is not a specific numerical answer to the question "How big should my founding team be?" The answer should instead reflect the skills you and your team already bring to the table, as well as any gaps that may still exist.

| 13 |
Where Does the Money Come From?

Chapter Overview
  » Understanding funding requirements
  » Understanding funding sources

Here's an idea for a business: if I was paid a nickel for every reader who fast-forwarded to this chapter right away, I'd be doing very well for myself. Every new entrepreneur is worried about money, and they all want to know how to get it and who will fund their new venture. The sources and amounts of funding available to you will depend on where you are in your venture life cycle and how successful you've been so far. Spoiler alert: no one you don't already know is going to give you significant funding to start your business. And if you are one of the readers who jumped right to this chapter, I encourage you to read it, but be sure to read the other ones (they're kind of important too).

How Much Do I Actually Need?

Before tearing your hair out worrying about money, it is essential that you develop a firm understanding of how much you will actually need. The term "firm understanding" is used loosely here; if you are still in the planning stages, then the best you will be able to produce is a good estimate. If you have already made some sales (but your venture hasn't taken off yet) you will have a much better sense of what that estimate will look like.

The exact nature of your startup cost estimation will, of course, depend heavily on the nature of your venture, but here are some of the expenses that are common to nearly all startups:

  » **Connectivity and Web Presence**
    This includes access to high-speed internet, computer, and phone along with your domain name, site hosting, and design elements. The first three you likely already have, and as we touched on in chapter 4, your personal

phone can double as a business phone through the use of services like Google Voice or Grasshopper.

» **Professional Services**
Starting a business can often be done without the assistance of a lawyer, but that doesn't mean it's a great idea to go it alone, especially if you are unsure. The services of an accountant are recommended as well, particularly for taxes and setting up your chart of accounts.

» **Fees**
Make sure you are familiar with regulatory expenses such as licensing fees, operating licenses, and other regulatory considerations.

» **Initial Inventory**
Not every venture will require initial inventory, and some will require more than others. Keep in mind that startups that sell services (as opposed to physical products) still often require on-hand inventory in the form of supplies or other consumables involved in the execution of services.

» **Initial Marketing Expenses**
Initial marketing expenses cover small costs such as business cards as well as more significant expenses such as signage and initial awareness campaigns (and everything in between).

It is not prudent for new ventures to dump all of their initial marketing dollars into one marketing method. A lot of marketing consists of experimentation—until you have historical data that tells you what works, what doesn't, and what you haven't tried yet, it is best not to put all of your eggs in one basket.

The list above encompasses only the broad categories of startup expenses that you can't forget about—it is by no means an exhaustive list.

Understanding Burn

The money that you are putting together at this stage isn't just to cover one-time or infrequent startup expenses such as professional services or licensing fees. The money that your startup relies on in the beginning of its life cycle can also be thought of as padding to combat your venture's *burn rate*. Burn is best described as negative cash flow. A startup's burn rate is the rate at which it is experiencing negative cash flow that eats into the money that has been raised for this very purpose—to combat burn.

Remember, in the initial stages of a startup, sales represent only a trickle of revenue if there are sales at all. If all goes as planned, your startup will reach its break-even point, start turning a profit, and no longer rely on the money that was initially raised. The problem is, that point may not be for a while yet. The exact window between launching and reaching profitability depends heavily on the kind of business a startup is. Internet-based businesses have the potential to reach profitability much faster than brick-and-mortar businesses, for example.

We don't dive into it here in the text, but calculating the break-even point of your venture is covered some of the Digital Assets. Find them at go.quickstartguides.com/startingbusiness.

At the risk of sounding like a broken record, this is another reason a comprehensive business plan is an important part of the venture-planning process: for understanding how much money you will need. A thorough planning process produces as robust an estimate as is possible of the amount of money that will be needed.

Your venture's estimated break-even point, combined with your burn rate, produces your *runway*, or the amount of time you can be in business before your burn rate surpasses the amount of money you have raised. The relationship between the amount of money you have raised, your burn rate, and your runway is complex. Key questions concerning how fast of a burn rate is appropriate (how fast is too fast?), what represents an appropriate runway, and how or when a drive for profitability should be surpassed by a drive for growth can be hotly contested within the entrepreneurial community. To get to the bottom of some of these issues, it might be a good idea to step back and take a look at the big picture.

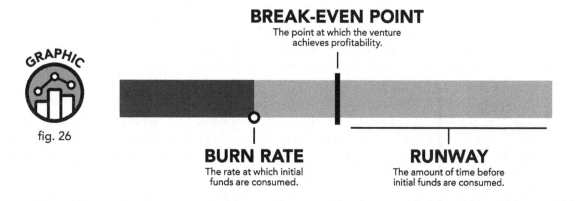

BREAK-EVEN POINT
The point at which the venture achieves profitability.

fig. 26

BURN RATE
The rate at which initial funds are consumed.

RUNWAY
The amount of time before initial funds are consumed.

The Big Picture

The break-even point—the point when your venture actually turns a profit—is the point when you as an entrepreneur can breathe a (small) sigh of relief. By no means does it mean that you can put up your feet and let your business run on autopilot—once your business has reached its break-even point you are faced with an entirely new set of challenges. Until then, the startup capital you put together will have to get you to that point. Working backward from an estimated break-even point, remember that your burn rate doesn't just need to cover basic startup costs such as equipment or inventory—it will also need to cover everyday operations until revenue is sufficient to make those operations self-sustaining.

Entrepreneurs are optimistic, passionate, and hardworking, but that doesn't mean they can see into the future. Planning the amount of money your startup will need without adding in as large a safety margin as possible is not only shortsighted but imprudent. There are many reasons why businesses fail, which is all the more reason that a safety margin should be worked into your financial planning. Shifting customer preferences, economic contractions and downturns, surprise expenses, and fluctuating supplier costs all coalesce into a minefield of potential costs that can derail carefully planned runway and burn rate calculations.

Like many answers to key questions regarding your venture, the answer to the ultimate question *"How much money do I need?"* ends up being *"It depends."* In the next section we'll discuss where the money actually comes from, but if it fails to cover key costs until your venture reaches profitability, it isn't enough. Your funding must cover the following:

» Initial startup costs including equipment, inventory, fees, and initial marketing expenses
» Operations until they become self-sufficient
» Losses up to the point where the venture reaches its break-even point (enough money to cover the burn rate)
» As large a safety margin as possible

When startups die, the official cause of death is always either running out of money or a critical founder bailing. Often the two occur simultaneously. But I think the underlying cause is usually that they've become demoralized. You rarely hear of a startup that's working around the clock doing deals and pumping out new features, and dies because they can't pay their bills and their ISP unplugs their server. Startups rarely die in mid keystroke. So keep typing![19] - PAUL GRAHAM

Where Does the Money Come From?

As your mother always told you, money doesn't grow on trees. For the average person, it is easy to get overwhelmed very quickly with the funding portion of launching their venture. The following section is a simplified summary of different forms of funding that are available to startups of various stages.

NOTE

All funding sources have pros and cons, and not all are appropriate or feasible for all ventures. It is beyond the scope of this book to discuss correct funding strategy, except to note that failing to understand the nature of these funding sources and developing an inappropriate funding plan are common problems that entrepreneurs face.

Bootstrapping

A business that is bootstrapped is one that is funded by the founding team. More than any other form of funding, bootstrapping speaks to the can-do mythos surrounding successful entrepreneurs. When you "pull yourself up by your bootstraps" you are doing something difficult, on your own, with limited or existing resources. Bootstrapping is a minimalist approach to funding, and because that often translates into doing more with less, it can be a driver for creative solutions and ingenious ways to stretch resources. It can also be mundane, such as continuing to work your day job to cover your expenses while you get your business off the ground.

» **Bootstrapping Advantages**

When the money is your own, you maintain direct control. There are no investors or lenders calling and expecting a return on investment. In some cases, this kind of pressure can actually be good. It can force startups to conform to a timeline that prioritizes delivering results and achieving milestones; however, a large factor in the decision to become an entrepreneur is the ability to choose one's own destiny.

Additionally, bootstrapped ventures grow organically. Without large amounts of cash on hand, decision makers must be laser-focused on achieving profitability. This focus comes at the sacrifice of fast growth, but it does mean that the venture is less likely to grow too fast, consuming its runway at an unsustainable rate.

» **Bootstrapping Disadvantages**

The glaring challenge in bootstrapping a startup is the need for personal funds that can be diverted into the business. Although the business may not require outside funding at first, your personal bank account is the source of funding and—as many of us are painfully aware—that money is not bottomless. It is very possible that when bootstrapping your venture, you could go into personal debt.

On the business side of things, bootstrapped ventures are always scrambling for resources. Not just cash, but the advantages that cash can purchase—staff, equipment, inventory, etc. As a result of being cash-choked, bootstrapped ventures grow slowly compared to other funding models, and the lack of resources in critical early stages may lead to a risk-averse culture. When startups recoil from risk they often miss growth opportunities and can lose a healthy appetite for change—something that is absolutely critical for startup success.

Bootstrapped companies can also suffer from inattention. When you have to spend time working other jobs, the time you have to grow your business gets pushed to nights and weekends. At some point, your venture won't be able to grow without your devoting your full time and attention to it.

fig. 27

Bootstrapping
ADVANTAGES

- No loss of control
- Organic growth - the venture will not outgrow its resources

Bootstrapping
DISADVANTAGES

- Pool of funds are only as large as your bank account
- Chronic lack of funds can stymie growth and create a risk-averse culture

Friends, Family, and Fools (FFF)

As one might expect, approaching friends and family for startup funding is a delicate situation that can get messy quickly. Friends and family are self-explanatory funding sources. Fools are something of a joke—the joke being that because startups have a tendency to fail, only a fool would invest his or her hard-earned money in an unproven venture.

» **FFF Financing Advantages**

This type of financing has a much lower threshold of access than other methods covered in this section. While your credit history and personal history certainly should be considered when friends and family loan larger sums of money, elements of personal relationships will often make friends and family more inclined to help and sympathetic to your cause. That is not an excuse to bleed these people dry—they are your friends and family, after all. Don't ask them for more than they can afford to lose, and think of their needs every step of the way.

» **Best Practice**

When soliciting friends and family for funding, don't be shy about demonstrating the amount of your own money that you have already sunk into your venture. Ask for specific amounts of money and tie those funds to specific milestones. Go above and beyond to offer friends and family a formal agreement as well as a handshake deal. Tie debt repayment to the success of your venture, or better yet, offer debt that is convertible into equity. This is an overlap of the work and personal portions of your work-life balance triangle, but that doesn't mean that the work portion should have to damage the personal side of things. As an entrepreneur, always be thinking about the ways that you can grow your social network—you never know who might become a key initial investor in your venture!

On the other hand, giving out equity in exchange for funds, while very common, creates valuation issues and must be done thoughtfully. For example, if you give away 10 percent of the company for a $10,000 investment, you're implicitly valuing your company at $100,000. If you need additional funding later, and you give another 10 percent for $5,000, your company is valued at $50,000. Which is right? Too many competing claims on the assets of a company could scare away potential investors in the future.

» **FFF Financing Disadvantages**

If you have friends or family with deep pockets and substantial business acumen, great! They are the people you should be chatting with first. More often than not, however, personal networks include a mix of different people from a variety of backgrounds. This means that your FFF financing may come from nonprofessional investors who themselves do not come with connections to suppliers, customers, or others within your industry.

Additionally, the money from FFF sources may not come with any more tangible strings than debt or equity funding, but there are invisible strings attached. It can be tough to initiate and maintain conversations regarding money, and there is added pressure not to lose the money of people you care about. This disadvantage should not invalidate FFF financing for your venture—many, many startups couldn't have gotten to where they are without financing from friends and family—but it does mean that prospective entrepreneurs should tread carefully.

fig. 28

Friends, Family, Fools
ADVANTAGES

- Fewest barriers
- Easy access to funds; your friends and family *want* to help

Friends, Family, Fools
DISADVANTAGES

- Financing often comes from nonprofessional investors with little to no connections
- Loss of principal could damage relationships

When considering FFF funding, I always recommend what I call the Thanksgiving Dinner Test. Imagine your business doesn't work out, and you end up losing all of your investor funding. Would that ruin your Thanksgiving dinner, or would your family be okay with it? Is the money you're borrowing immaterial to them, or are you risking their entire life savings? Think carefully about these questions.

Debt Financing

Debt financing is the catchall term for efforts to raise capital that include taking on debt in some form. Common sources of debt financing for startups include commercial banks and startup-specific lenders such as Kabbage.

» **Debt Financing Advantages**
Debt financing methods of raising capital allow ventures to retain control of their business—once the loan application process is complete and your loan is approved, the money is yours to do with it what you will. This process can be completed relatively quickly, and, once approved, the

money doesn't trickle in. It is deposited in one lump sum, which means it can be put to use right away.

» **Debt Financing Disadvantages**
Loan applications often require an extensive operating history, collateral in the form of hard assets, or both. This immediately disqualifies many startups from being able to take advantage of debt financing. The lack of historical data and sufficient collateral are often insurmountable barriers in the application process.

Not only do many startups not qualify for debt financing options, but the road to new-venture success is littered with stories of businesses that struggled to service their debt obligations. This problem is not restricted to new ventures only; large, established corporations can succumb to the cash flow problems that taking on too much debt can create.

Debt Financing
ADVANTAGES

- No loss of control
- Lump sum deposit; funds can be used right away

Debt Financing
DISADVANTAGES

- Minimum operating history required to qualify
- Servicing debt can damage healthy cash flow

fig. 29

Equity Funding

Equity financing is the practice of raising capital through the sale of ownership shares of a venture. It allows startups to raise money without suffering the constriction of debt obligations, but at the expense of sharing or diluting control of their venture.

Angel Equity Financing

Angel investors are independently wealthy investors acting either individually or as a group (known as an angel network). Angel investors are distinct from venture capital investors. They both deal in equity financing, but angel investors are more willing to invest in early-stage startups rather than providing funding to accelerate fast-growth ventures. This desire to "get in on the ground floor" makes angel investment particularly attractive for early-stage ventures.

» **Angel Equity Financing Advantages**
The equity financing that angel investors provide is often advantageous to startups if a satisfactory deal can be reached. Because angel investors can be less concerned with hitting short-term profit targets, they are often willing to work with startups to set them up for long-term success. This may mean only providing just what the venture needs instead of forcing faster, unsustainable growth or working with startups that are still in earlier stages of growth—the kinds of ventures that debt financing institutions and venture capital firms would never touch.

Additionally, despite the fact that angel investment is generally equity investment, not all angel investors insist on active control in the venture. The level of participation an angel investor has depends on numerous factors—the experience and temperament of the investor chief among them—but compared to venture capital equity financing, angel investors are often much less hands-on.

For angel investors who have industry expertise or a history of investing in a particular industry, another advantage they bring to the table comes in the form of guidance and advice. If they are part of an angel network, they may also be able to set up introductions with other investors, mentors, or industry contacts.

» **Angel Equity Financing Disadvantages**
Not everyone can become an angel investor. The SEC requires that individuals who deal with unregistered securities (such as shares in a private company) must meet certain criteria to become an accredited investor. These criteria include income minimums and a minimum net worth. This means that if an angel investor should turn out not to be an accredited investor, your venture could be exposed to disruptive and costly legal consequences.

Q: **What about crowdfunding? Isn't crowdfunding the same as finding numerous unaccredited investors?**

Answer: Not really. Crowdfunding does not have to take place in the form of equity financing and often doesn't. It is common for crowdfunded startups to offer early access, exclusive rewards, or other perks in lieu of equity-sharing arrangements. Legislation is also on the side of helping startups grow through the use of crowdfunding. The Jumpstart Our Business Startups (JOBS) Act of 2012 loosened the burden of SEC reporting on crowdfunded startups—new ventures can raise up to just over $1 million annually without registered securities.

Although many angel investors have some degree of industry experience, their investments may not always constitute "smart money." In the world of investment, smart money is money that comes from a source with a track record of making smart investments. If your venture is the recipient of smart money, congratulations—you demonstrated to the investor that you have what it takes to be successful and inspired their confidence. The other side of the coin, however, is that if the money isn't "smart," the angel investor may not be able to help you make success-based decisions if he or she is a new investor or one with a limited track record. Because angel investors are individual investors and often not professional investors, experience, track record, and expectations can vary wildly from one "angel" to the next.

Considering the advantages and disadvantages, you may be asking yourself how likely it *really* is that your venture can court and successfully close an angel investment deal. Angel investors have traditionally been associated with Silicon Valley tech startups, but today that is largely a misconception. Angel investors exist in a wide range of industries and regions. In fact, a 2017 study by the Angel Capital Association found that 63 percent of angel investors are based outside of the major metropolitan areas of San Francisco, New York, and Boston.[20]

Angel investors look for a winning team, a completed business plan, a risk-conscious founding team, and a business that is built on a solid foundation of integrity (angels who can't trust their startup partners get cold feet quickly). Companies like AngelList[21] and Gust[22] are tools for startups and angel investors to connect with one another. The former is geared toward individuals, and the latter is angel group-oriented.

fig. 30

Angel Equity Funding
ADVANTAGES

- Encourage organic growth
- Allow entreprenuers to retain control while offering guidance

Angel Equity Funding
DISADVANTAGES

- Angel investment may not always constitute as "smart money"
- Experience, track record, and connections can vary from one angel to the next

Corporate Partner Equity Financing

In some strategic partnerships it makes sense for one company to benefit from an equity stake in its partner. From the perspective of a startup, nothing is better than partnering with an established company that can confer instant brand recognition and access to new customers, new partners, and new resources.

In his 2013 title *101 Startup Lessons: An Entrepreneur's Handbook,* author George Deeb outlines a strategic partner equity deal he was part of when National Geographic purchased a 30 percent equity stake in his adventure travel website iExplore. National Geographic was able to leverage the travel-experience-based offerings of an emerging adventure travel website (emerging because the deal took place in the year 2000) as a complement to their natural-world-focused publication. In return, iExplore received a quick boost in recognition by association with the historic publication, along with marketing and promotional support. National Geographic was incentivized to keep iExplore afloat—they had skin in the game to the tune of 30 percent. Critically for iExplore, the initial support that National Geographic provided was able to be parlayed into other investor support during a period of financial uncertainty. If National Geographic believed in this startup, that was good enough for other investors.

The story of National Geographic and iExplore is a good example of an equity-based partnership and how it can be an asset for larger corporations as well as a boon for well-positioned startups. As Deeb elaborates, it is also a cautionary tale. The deal was made before a post 9/11 slump in travel spending, and at a time when iExplore had cash to spend. As sales declined, iExplore found that they needed cash on hand to adequately take advantage of the marketing and promotional considerations they had negotiated as part of the deal. Deeb's synopsis of strategic equity partnerships? The devil is in the details![23]

» **Corporate Partner Equity Financing Advantages**
Established companies have deep pockets, and a well-structured strategic partnership has the potential to completely change a startup's future. The equity stake that changes hands gives the larger, established company a deep incentive to encourage the success of startup partners and integrate them into the completion of strategic objectives.

This focus on the future has other short-term benefits as well. Large corporations are always on the lookout for ways to reduce their tax liability, and an equity financing strategic partnership can be chalked up as a tax-advantageous loss. Corporate partners may apply less pressure to be profitable right away, unlike with debt financing funding options or venture capital firms.

» **Corporate Partner Equity Financing Disadvantages**
The National Geographic and iExplore deal from the previous example is a summary of a summary. The account glosses over numerous back-and-forth meetings, extensive negotiation, and a significant amount of work on the part of the startup. That deal went through, but Deeb makes no mention of other deals that had been proposed and fell through, or how long the process to come to an agreement took. Together, this commitment of resources—specifically time and energy—can be a drain on resource-strapped startups, only to end in a deal that falls through.

Not only is the strategic partnership process a lengthy and bureaucratic one but consider that not every corporation is looking for a startup to take a chance on. Short-term tax benefits aside, your startup has to offer a concrete benefit to a potential corporate partner and demonstrate that not only can you deliver on your end of the bargain, but you can stay in business long enough to do so.

Keep in mind as well that the issue of control is ever-present in equity funding arrangements. Corporate partners will often push to align your priorities with their strategic objectives as a condition of the equity deal and may even ask that they place personnel on your team. Concessions like these can culminate in a greater loss of control than some founding teams anticipated, and for many entrepreneurs can represent too high a cost to pay for the capital they need to grow their venture.

fig. 31

Corp. Partner Equity Financing
ADVANTAGES

- Corporate has deep pockets and lots of resources to set you up for success
- Often low pressure to achieve profitability right out of the gate

Corp. Partner Equity Financing
DISADVANTAGES

- Working out these deals can be a resource of strain on startups
- Corporate partners will often require large amounts of control

Venture Capital Equity Funding

No source of startup funding has captured popular imagination and romanticized the role of the modern entrepreneur more than venture capital. Like angel investment, venture capital comes in the form of private equity. Unlike angel investment, venture capital is normally only accessible by ventures that conform to a general template. Specifically, those who are out of the initial stages of unproven demand, but not at the stage of organizational maturity where growth slows and revenues can level off.

Venture capital firms—the firms looking to invest their money in startups with high growth potential—adhere to a strict set of criteria when selecting which ventures to invest in, and they are known for passing on many more opportunities than they commit to. The startups that do make the cut are expected to produce returns of 30 to 50 percent annually and are expected to cede large portions of equity, so much so that in some instances venture capital has been referred to as "vulture capital." If that sounds harsh, remember that venture capital firms are accepting tremendous levels of risk and writing very large checks.

» **Venture Capital Advantages**

Angel investment funds don't always constitute "smart money," but that is not the case with venture capital. Venture capitalists are choosy—with the amount of money they are committing, they must be. So any startup that secures VC backing also receives an automatic endorsement by association. This endorsement isn't unearned, either. Venture capital firms have deep pockets, extensive connections, and no shortage of guidance for the startups they work with.

In many ways, the reputation of venture capitalists as kingmakers is not undeserved. Some of the biggest names in ultra-successful startups couldn't have gotten to where they are without large infusions of venture capital through multiple rounds of funding. It is worth noting, however, that the vast majority of startups that reach success do so *without* VC funding. According to a report from Empact and Fundable, a grand total of .05 percent of US startups are funded with venture capital. Which is a miniscule number compared to the much larger number of US startups that receive angel investment funds: .91 percent.[24] As you can see, less than 1 percent of businesses receive either angel or VC investing, so think very carefully about whether this is a reasonable and/or desirable goal for you.

» **Venture Capital Disadvantages**

As you may have guessed, the restrictive guidelines that venture capital firms adhere to mean that they pass over most startups. In fact, venture capitalists may be so laser-focused on limiting risk that they only consider new ventures that have already cleared their first round of funding, or only work with startups that require funding to grow rapidly.

At any rate, venture capital firms aren't writing small checks. Many venture capitalists won't touch requests for funds under $2 million—they are used to cutting high-dollar deals that have a high chance of paying out. These big checks also come with big strings. There is no venture capital arrangement that doesn't involve ceding significant amounts of control. Venture capital firms are notorious for stepping in to ensure their return on investment, going so far as to place key people on a startup's board of directors.

What's more, venture capital can dry up in an instant. A firm can decide to pull their support if things aren't going their way, resulting in a hit that many ventures will be unable to recover from. The opposite of micromanagement and oversight can also be true. If another startup your VC is funding begins to flounder or they are simply very busy, your startup may not receive the level of attention that you expect.

fig. 32

Venture Capital Equity Funding
ADVANTAGES

- Venture capital represents "smart money"
- Venture capital firms offer connections, guidance, and resources.

Venture Capital Equity Funding
DISADVANTAGES

- Extremely restrictive–VC firms deny many more startups than they choose to work with
- Often requires ceding large amounts of control

Crowdfunding

Call it a sign of the times, but an increasing number of businesses have called upon the masses in lieu of using what could be considered more traditional funding methods. The startups that have seen tremendous crowdfunding success make it seem as though all your venture needs to do to gather all the money you need is to create a campaign on Kickstarter or Indiegogo and the dollars will start pouring in. As with numerous other examples from the word of entrepreneurship, the high-profile successes eclipse the reality that many, many projects are chalked up as unsuccessful. By Kickstarter's own admission, approximately 36 percent of projects succeed.[25]

There are many reasons for this. Not all businesses, products, or campaigns are appropriate for crowdfunding. Not all campaigns are executed according to crowdfunding best practices. And there is no way to know if the entrepreneurs behind these projects had other issues with their ventures that may have contributed negatively to project success.

» **Crowdfunding Advantages**
The biggest advantage of crowdfunding is the money. The whole idea behind the crowdfunding process is that a lot of small amounts of money can add up quickly. These dollars can be gained in exchange for perks

such as early access, exclusive bonuses, or VIP features. These enticements would normally not work at all on professional investors, but because the average crowdfunding investor is nonprofessional and the sums of money are usually quite small, crowdfunded dollars can often be obtained without sacrificing equity or assuming debt.

The everyday people who commit money to crowdfunded projects aren't just an ocean of microinvestors—they are also regular people. A crowdfunding campaign that fails to meet its goal or that receives lukewarm feedback can be a signal of a product or service that fails to meet a real need. A campaign need not fail to produce insight, however. There is no shortage of people on the internet who would like to offer their opinion, solicited or not. A crowdfunding campaign can act as a dry run or a sort of stress test for a concept, product, or service. Serving as a magnet for input and opinions, your campaign can be a valuable source of feedback.

Crowdfunding success carries different amounts of cachet with different types of investors, but the fact remains that it is an accomplishment to run a successful crowdfunding campaign. If you can pull off one or more crowdfunding successes, that achievement alone confers instant credibility. And, depending on the type of investor or funding you are approaching, it is not out of the question that you could have pulled in more via crowdfunding than you were asking for. All of these aspects contribute positively to your request-for-funding pitch.

» **Crowdfunding Disadvantages**
The JOBS Act of 2012 that made crowdfunding a viable option for startups was a boon for new ventures in that year and for several years thereafter. At this point, the crowdfunding marketplace is crowded with startups who are clamoring for funds. This doesn't mean that crowdfunding is tapped out, but it does mean that ventures that are seeking funding do have to work for it. That work may mean developing high-production-value presentations, waiting until you can increase the valuation of your business, giving more bonuses to your microinvestors, or some combination of all three.

This feeds into the point that not all products or services are appropriate for crowdfunding campaigns. First, crowdfunding is best for projects that require smaller (on average) funding commitments. Second, products that aren't sexy or eye-opening (despite being valuable) don't do well with the nonprofessional investor class. Additionally, if your crowdfunding campaign includes equity sharing, be aware that professional investors may be uncomfortable sharing equity with numerous inexperienced investors.

Crowdfunding is also a poor choice for ventures that need funds *right now*. Fundraising campaigns can take months to produce results, though there have been exceptions.

fig. 33

Crowdfunding ADVANTAGES

- Funding does not come with debt or equity strings
- Crowdfunding campaigns can serve as barometers of customer sentiment

Crowdfunding DISADVANTAGES

- Not all businesses and products are a good fit for crowdfunding
- Fundraising campaigns can take time and must meet their goal to recieve funding

Government Loans

The Small Business Administration (SBA) incentivizes small business growth in the US by offering low-interest loans for qualifying businesses. These loans are available through some banks and credit unions and benefit both the business owner and the lender. For-profit lenders like banks are wary of risk, and this results in their denying many loans. SBA loans, on the other hand, are backed by the Small Business Administration and reduce risk to lenders. If businesses default, the government pays off the balance.

These loans not only benefit new ventures by providing the funds they need at favorable interest rates, but they also often have lower thresholds of acceptance—simply maintaining a good business credit score and adhering to the terms of repayment are often the only major criteria considered outside of your business plan and standing. These loans are designed to get businesses up and running, help them establish credit and purchase equipment, property, or other items with high initial cost. Government-backed loans are not blank checks and they are not handouts.

As with any other debt your business assumes, keep in mind that revenue will have to be diverted to service the debt.

NOTE

The SBA does not administer any loans or debt financing directly. Instead, the agency underwrites loans that are made available from participating for-profit lenders such as banks and credit unions.

Think of Funding in Stages

As noted at the beginning of the prior section, the specific funding path that is best for your venture is a product of the specifics of your business, where your startup is in its life cycle, and the options available to you. It is beyond the scope of this book to outline various funding strategies in detail, but generally speaking, think of funding in stages.

» **Pre-Seed**
This stage of funding comes before your startup is up and running. This money is used to further develop, test, and research your product; to overcome initial industrial barriers to entry (such as regulatory licenses or compliance issues); and to take care of the costs associated with getting started. Often, bootstrapping and funds from friends and family are most appropriate for this stage.

» **Seed**
The seed stage of funding is the point at which your business will need funding to keep it afloat until it is capable of generating its own cash flow, or it is ready for further investments. This funding stage may be lumped in with the pre-seed stage, depending on the funding options available to you and the amount of money you need. SBA-backed microloans, grants if your venture qualifies, and crowdfunding options are often most appropriate for this stage of funding.

» **First-Round Funding**
First-round funding is often the first time a venture opens up equity to entice the investors to provide the funding needed to expand, or to reach a point where the startup can generate its own sustainable cash flow if that wasn't achieved with seed funding. Prior to this point, there often isn't much to a venture to give it the level of equity that can be used as an enticement. This is the stage when many ventures turn to angel investors.

» **Second through Fourth Rounds of Funding**
As the venture grows and looks to expand into new markets, create new products, or extend existing lines, more capital will be required for each of these activities. The venture will have reached the point where it has proven that it can deliver returns, but this is also the point where large infusions of cash will be needed for the business to expand substantially. At this point in a startup's life cycle, it will be in a better position to be attractive to venture capital firms.

» **Additional Funding and Beyond**
As a startup with a track record of success matures, it gains access to larger and more impactful forms of funding. At this stage too, debt financing becomes more and more attractive, assuming the venture has the cash flow to service their obligations.

At this point, "going public" becomes a real possibility as a tool not only to raise capital, but to allow venture capital firms to cash out. Another funding measure is mezzanine funding, a kind of mixed debt and equity high-value loan.

Chapter Recap

» A startup's break-even point is the point at which revenues equal costs and the business can begin to turn a profit. The length of a venture's runway is dependent on the amount of money raised along with the rate at which that money is consumed—the burn rate.

» Bootstrapping has the advantage of having no barriers to access; however, it is reliant on personal sources of cash. FFF funding (friends, family, and fools) is a similar proposition and has the advantage of asking for funding from people who are likely to be interested in your success.

» Debt financing is the catchall term for loans and other forms of debt. Debt financing allows ventures to retain control of operations but requires an operating history and can make a dent in cash flow.

» Angel investing hinges on the strategic value a venture can provide for an existing corporation and can mean ceding a significant amount of operational control.

» Venture capital firms are seeking very particular types of startups, often at specific stages. They have very large amounts of money to invest but will also demand a high level of control over operations to secure the return on their investment.

» Crowdfunding isn't a good fit for every venture—the people who are providing financing are regular people, or nonprofessional investors. This means that "sexy" or eye-opening products resonate best with them, and that a crowdfunding campaign can act to validate demand.

» The Small Business Administration guarantees some loans that are issued by private financial institutions. These loans have low barriers to access but carry the same concerns as any other debt financing.

» The best way to think of funding is in stages. Pre-seed, seed, first-round funding, and successive rounds of funding each have different funding types that are accessible and appropriate for that stage of business growth.

PART V

WRITING YOUR BUSINESS PLAN

| 14 |

Do You *Really* Need a Business Plan?

Chapter Overview
» Why you need a business plan
» Common business plan misconceptions

"Why should I bother writing all this down?"

It's one of the first questions on every entrepreneur's mind when they start their venture. Business plans are much maligned in these days of lean startups, business model canvases, and extremely low financial barriers to entry. Even venture capitalists in certain spaces don't need—or even want—one to fund you.

So why bother at all?

This sort of thinking reflects a fundamental misunderstanding of the business planning process. Business plans are an important part of your strategic planning process *even if no one ever sees it but you.* A well-developed business plan lays out goals, objectives, strategies, and tactics. It documents assumptions and challenges your thinking. It's a discovery tool, a communication tool, and a yardstick all rolled into one. The business plan writing process will focus your efforts and crystallize your thinking, and for most ventures will save you time and money in the long run.

» **Discovery tool**
The process of writing your business plan isn't just busywork. Diving into each of the facets of your opportunity's nuts and bolts provides you with its first real feasibility test. This process uncovers whether or not your idea can develop the legs it needs to stand on its own in the marketplace; that is, is it truly an *opportunity*, or just an interesting thing to think about? It may not be easy to accept if your idea fails the test, but ultimately, walking

away from an opportunity that doesn't make sense even in the planning stages will save a mountain of time, energy, and money.

Writing a business plan forces you to get to the bottom of the aspects of your business that you don't know enough about and uncovers the aspects that you don't know you don't know enough about.

» **Communication tool**
Business plans are used to communicate goals, milestones, and objectives to stakeholders both within the organization and without. The stakeholders everyone thinks of with respect to business plans are investors such as venture capitalists. However, other stakeholders including lenders, suppliers, potential partners, key employees, and even customers could be very interested in reading your plan and understanding your full thinking about your venture.

» **Yardstick**
Business plans are essentially strategic plans for a startup. Strategic plans start with the overall mission of the organization, outline a series of high-level strategies you will use to achieve it, and further break those strategies down into goals, objectives, and specific tasks that follow the SMART criteria outlined at the start of part 2 of this book. A good strategic plan is periodically reviewed to ensure that it is still relevant and that the organization is making appropriate progress toward its goals. Does this sound like a business plan? It should.

Misconceptions About Business Plans

At the outset of the business planning process, formal business plans can seem daunting to new entrepreneurs. It's true—writing an effective plan takes time, effort, and research, but the benefits your venture will reap from having a business plan are well worth it. Not to mention the benefits that you as an entrepreneur will reap by simply rolling up your sleeves and purposefully exploring your opportunity top to bottom, inside and out. Before we get started writing your actual plan, let's separate the fact from the fiction surrounding business plans and the business planning process.

» **I don't need a business plan because I know (read about) someone else who succeeded without one.**
It's not uncommon to meet other entrepreneurs who started their own successful businesses, to know family or friends who became business

owners, or to hear stories about people who found success without the benefit of a business plan—formal or otherwise. Clearly, it's quite possible to run a successful business without a comprehensive business plan. But stories of success often obscure critical aspects of the twists and turns that it took to get to the punch line. By focusing only on the positive upshot of the story, we can overlook the ways in which that entrepreneur's journey could have been easier and more straightforward and consumed fewer resources.

Waiting to decide whether or not you will rent or own, developing your sales and marketing plan *after* opening the doors, and being ambushed by surprise costs from vendors are all expensive, frustrating, and discouraging examples of issues that can be mitigated or avoided outright with comprehensive and deliberate planning. A business plan is not a suit of armor, but an informed and purposeful business planning process can help reduce the number of times you need to wear armor.

» **I don't need a business plan because I am not seeking funding.**
It is true that you won't find any funding without the help of a business plan of some sort, but that doesn't mean that a business plan is solely used as a tool to acquire funding. When you seek funding, your business plan acts as a communication tool and a sales document. It is the main way that you communicate your opportunity and "sell" your audience—convince them that your opportunity is real and that your founding team members are the right people to make it a success.

Acquiring funding is only one use of a business plan, however, and before it is ever scrutinized by readers outside your venture, it should be well circulated among your founding team. This includes founding teams that consist of only one person. Well-defined business plans are effective communication tools that are used to convey goals, objectives, and milestones to managers and founding team members, suppliers, customers, and other potential partners. All without ever asking for funding.

Keep in mind that just because you are not seeking funding right now, this doesn't mean that you won't in the future. It's never too late to start your business plan, but the earlier the better—especially if you intend to seek funding in the future.

» **I don't need a business plan because my business will be changing all the time.**
Your competition, customers, and knowledge base will indeed be changing all the time. It's no secret that successful businesses change to stay ahead of the curve. If your business plan is an expression of your venture, and your venture is always changing, doesn't that mean that your business plan should always be changing too? Yes, it absolutely does. It may seem like a lot of work, especially if you aren't seeking funding right now, but the very nature of strategic planning is that it never ends.

Keeping your business plan up to date to reflect the current state of your venture means that you can continue to reap the benefits of having a business plan. A business plan should be treated as a living document, not something that has been written in stone.

» **Your Business Plan is the Centerpiece of Your Communication Strategy**
When you are presenting your venture to any interested stakeholder, there are various ways to communicate it to them. The business plan forms the centerpiece of each of these ways:

1. The executive summary and elevator pitch (covered in the next chapter)
2. The plan itself (covered in the rest of this chapter)
3. The pitch deck (covered in chapter 15)
4. The due diligence process (covered in chapter 17)

Before you get too far along, you need to have all of these in your toolkit.

Before Writing Your Plan

For many entrepreneurs, the prospect of writing a business plan is not an exciting one, especially if they have never written one before. When writing your plan, keep these key tips in mind:

» **Your business plan is never finished**
Your business plan is a living, strategic document. Do your due diligence, but don't stress over getting your plan *done*. Your business plan will grow and change with your business, but do make sure that you have covered all of the necessary bases.

» **Don't procrastinate**

That's good advice in general, but the sooner you have the details of your plan worked out, the sooner you can move on to the next phases of launching your venture. Plus, it is better to know sooner rather than later whether your value proposition holds water.

» **Don't obsess over writing the best plan in the world**

That doesn't mean write a sloppy, uninformed plan. Write *your* best plan. Stick to the structure outlined in the following pages and take your plan seriously. Don't get caught up in worrying about whether your plan is good enough. Seek out and act on constructive feedback and build on the learning that the plan-writing process encourages. Write the best plan possible and course correct as necessary.

» **Pivot with new learning**

Being open to changing your approach based on new information goes on well past the business planning process. Embrace change and be receptive to it, but don't change just for the sake of changing. Examine new information carefully and critically and be ready to change as needed.

» **Don't write your plan forever**

Writing your business plan is important, but it's not what your venture is all about. Write the best plan you can and be ready to pivot with learning. At some point you need to stop planning and start satisfying the needs of your customers!

Q: Is it smart to save time and outsource the writing of my business plan?

Answer: The short answer is no. Even an expert freelancer or consultant won't know your business in the same intimate way that you do. Additionally, all of the learning and discovery benefits that come from writing your plan will evaporate. As the business owner or member of the founding team you should be the expert in your business—farming this process out doesn't help prepare you to lead your venture to success.

Chapter Recap

» A comprehensive business plan is more than a road map for your venture. It is also a discovery tool, a communication tool, and a yardstick.

» Many first-time entrepreneurs erroneously believe that they don't need a business plan because they know someone who has had success without one, or because they are not actively seeking funding, or because their business will always be changing.

» It is certainly possible to start a successful venture without a business plan, but the journey will be harder and more stressful than it will be for a startup that is informed by a well-constructed and researched business plan.

» Before getting started writing your plan, remember that your business plan is never finished. Don't procrastinate, and don't obsess over writing the best plan in the world. Your plan is a living document that will change and evolve as your business changes and evolves. Be ready to pivot with new learning and don't get bogged down "writing your plan forever." Writing your business plan is important, but at some point you have to put down the pen and get out there!

» The writing of your business plan should not be outsourced. One of the main objectives of the business planning process is that you, the entrepreneur, learn as much as possible about your opportunity.

| 15 |

Introducing Your Venture

Chapter Overview
- » Your business plan
- » The executive summary and pitch deck
- » Your company overview
- » Product/service description

The length and specifics of your business plan will vary, based on things like where you are in the planning process, the age and status of your venture, and whether or not you are seeking funding. That being said, there is a standard business plan format that should be followed not only to ensure that nothing is left out, but also because it is the standard format that audiences will expect.

A standard formal business plan is broken up as follows:

Introducing Your Venture	Executive Summary
	Company Overview
	Product/Service Description
Your Value Proposition	Market Analysis
	Industry Analysis
	Value Proposition
Your Business Model	Operations Overview
	Marketing Overview
	Growth Plan
	Management and Staffing Plan
	Financial Summary
Appendixes	

From here on out we will cover each of these sections in detail.

1 Executive Summary

2 Company Overview

3 Product/Service Description

4 Market Analysis

5 Industry Analysis

6 Value Proposition

7 Operations Overview

8 Marketing Overview

9 Growth Plan

10 Management and Staffing Plan

11 Financial Summary

12 The Appendixes

GRAPHIC

fig. 34

fig. 35

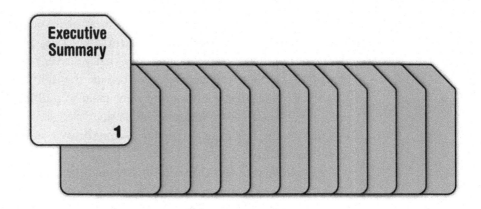

Executive Summary

1

The Executive Summary
→ (length: one page or less)

The Executive Summary is the most important part of your business plan. It is the first part of the plan that your audience will read, and in many cases it may be the *only* part. The Executive Summary portion acts as a summary of your plan, an introduction to your business opportunity, and a reader hook that is designed to pull your audience in. Because the executive summary serves such an important role for the business plan as a whole, it must be well-written and enticing. If your audience isn't interested in what the executive summary has to say, then the chances of their reading the rest of your plan plummet to about zero.

We'll address another important plan summary in this section as well: the elevator pitch. Your elevator pitch is a networking tool and a sort of summary of your summary, designed to be delivered in less than a minute. It may be written down somewhere, but it doesn't accompany your business plan. Instead, keep it in your head and don't hesitate to bring it out at a moment's notice. A well-developed elevator pitch may seem like an afterthought, but nothing could be further from the truth. Networking skills are an entrepreneur's best friend, so treat your elevator pitch with the same consideration you would your executive summary.

Because the executive summary is a summary of the contents of the business plan, it should be written last despite being on the first page. In order for it to be an accurate summary of the contents of the plan, each of the details needs to be compiled first. This also means that developing your elevator pitch can't be done until the executive summary is completed, since your elevator pitch is based on the contents of the executive summary.

No matter what portion of your business plan you are writing, keep in mind that the entire document is essentially a sales pitch. The content is designed to sell the reader on the idea that your venture will be successful, that you have done your research, that you are the right entrepreneur for this opportunity, and that you have the right team to pull it off. Even if no one reads it but you, you're selling yourself on these things! Because your executive summary is the first page that is put in front of your audience, it is central to your sales pitch.

A good way to test this is to review your executive summary *out* of the context of your business plan. Ask yourself: Can my executive summary stand on its own? If it was removed from the business plan, would it make sense? A reader should be able to understand your executive summary without any prior knowledge of your plan. This also means that the executive summary should not directly reference any other part of the plan.

Your plan has to be completely understandable by the average lay reader without any specific expertise in a given industry. That means technical jargon, acronyms, etc., must be kept to a minimum. It also means you need to avoid what I call "MBA speak"—vague generalities and buzzwords that sound good but don't convey any meaning.

What to Include

Your executive summary must answer several basic questions for your audience. Because real estate on the page is limited, use only one or two sentences to answer each question and ensure that you are being as clear and concise as possible. The answer to each of these questions is summarized from the different, pertinent sections of your business plan.

» **What exactly is your product/service?**
The answer to this question is a summary of the information in your Product/Service Description section. Front and center, your readers should completely understand exactly what it is you have for sale. It's important to be specific.

» **What is your market?**
This information is summarized from the Market Analysis section. It tells your reader not only that your product or service *has* a market, but that you have taken the time to gather information about that market.

» **Who is your customer?**
This information is also summarized from your Market Analysis section. It demonstrates to your reader that you know who your customer is and what potential pain points they may have. Your customer avatar will be a big help here.

» **What is your value proposition?**
Summarized from the Value Proposition/Competitive Advantage portion of your business plan, this information is a key selling point. Mainly it should be presented in such a way that it gets the reader excited about your venture.

» **How big can this venture be?**
This is the (realistic) potential scope of your venture. This information is summarized from your Growth Plan and Financial Summary.

» **What is your business model?**
This is summarized from the Company Overview and Operations Overview sections.

» **Can your team pull this off?**
Take a few sentences (summarized from the Management and Staffing Plan section) to highlight the unique qualities of your team and why they are the best choice to make this venture a success.

Use tight, concise language with a positive tone. Read your executive summary out loud. Does it flow, or is it choppy? Put yourself in the place of your audience. Would you be interested in learning more, or would you be inclined to pass? Operate under the assumption that your executive summary will receive five minutes or less of attention. Make every word, and therefore every minute, count.

What Not to Include

It can be easy to want to point to all of the evidence that you have spent time meticulously assembling and checking, or to back up the answer to each of those questions with specific examples. **Don't.** An executive summary is not a place for detailed financial projections, glossy charts and graphs, or extensive market research. It is the place where your business plan is summarized, and your audience's burning questions are answered in brief. Remember, the purpose of your executive summary is to encourage the reader to want to learn more about your plan, not to answer every question they may have in exhaustive detail. That comes during due diligence.

Another aspect of writing your executive summary to keep in mind: avoid excessive jargon. It may be tempting to flex your professional muscles and show off to your audience, but highly specific or obscure language will only frustrate them. Use industry-specific jargon only when absolutely necessary and keep concepts simple and accessible. This isn't because your reader is stupid, but because an executive summary should be crafted for ease of reading and clarity.

Your Elevator Pitch

If your executive summary is a summary of your business plan, then your elevator pitch is a summary of that summary. Elevator pitches are short, succinct, and highly persuasive speeches about a business opportunity.

The term "elevator pitch" comes from the hypothetical idea of being on a long elevator ride with a potential investor. Because she is "trapped" in the car with you for the duration of the ride, she has to listen to your pitch. In theory, if your pitch is strong enough, she will be intrigued and want to hear more, and will give you her card for follow-up when she gets out at her stop. Of course, this scenario has no bearing on reality. No one is forced to listen to your pitch, and any attempt to coerce someone to do anything will only result in resistance.

A better way to think of your pitch is as a networking tool. Imagine you're at an event, and you spot the same investor waiting in line for a glass of wine. You go up to her and introduce yourself as an entrepreneur. She'll probably ask you about your venture. Here is your chance to give a smooth, polished, informative, compelling, and *brief* introduction to your business. She won't have time to discuss it further here, but she may well give you her card for follow-up!

Networking is a critical entrepreneurial skill, and your elevator pitch serves the same purpose as a handshake and a business card for your business opportunity. It can allow you to make the most out of meeting investors or potential talent, and it helps you familiarize yourself with your business at the high level. When planning your elevator pitch, aim for under a minute and practice, practice, practice.

A good template for an elevator pitch is as follows:

> » Your name
> » Company name
> » Product or service
> » Target customers
> » Value proposition or competitive advantage
> » Call to action

Let's look at those in a little more detail.

» **Your name and the name of the venture**
Of course you can't leave this information out, and it should be accompanied with a networking card so that your audience can contact you or follow through on your call to action.

» **Your product or service**
Just like the summary you provide in your executive summary, it should be crystal clear to your audience *exactly what it is you're selling*. If you aren't sure how to pack that information into such a blurb, that's a problem. You need to know your product or service like the back of your hand.

» **Your target customers**
Who are the people who will be buying your product or service? What problem are you solving for them? Ideally, your product is such a good fit for your target customers that your audience will say "That's obvious!" Some people like to lead with this but be careful—people will stop listening and start wondering what your product actually is if you don't tell them pretty quickly.

» **Your value proposition or competitive advantage**
Why is your venture a winning proposition? Just like with your product, if you can't summarize why your business will be healthy and competitive, that's a problem.

» **A call to action**
A call to action is when you transfer the ball into your audience's court. What is the action that you would like them to take after listening to your pitch?

Be realistic about your "ask" at this point. No one is going to be persuaded to invest money in anything based on a twenty-second pitch (sorry, *Shark Tank*). When crafting your call to action, keep the value of your audience's time in the front of your mind. Some kind of follow-up on your part is all you should expect.

Your Pitch Deck

If you are asked to make a presentation to an investor, you will be expected to have a PowerPoint-type presentation known as a pitch deck. The pitch deck is also an abbreviated synopsis of your business plan, but in somewhat greater detail. The added visual component of a pitch deck means that you have a lot of opportunity to make your slides captivating and engaging, but it is important to remember that the *content* of your pitch deck is the most important factor.

Your pitch deck should cover the same basic areas as the executive summary, but in more detail. It should consist of around ten slides. Although you should be prepared to give additional details in your accompanying talk, the slides are still not the place for tables full of numbers, etc. Really slick entrepreneurs anticipate the more specific questions investors will ask and have detailed backup slides with that information ready to pull up upon request.

GRAPHIC

fig. 36

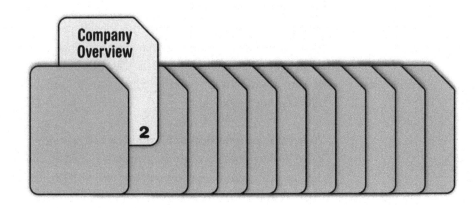

Company Overview
→ (length: approximately two pages)

The company overview is the reader's introduction to your plan. You will provide more details about some of these areas in later sections, but in the beginning of the plan readers will want to see a basic description of your company, what it does, and how it is organized. Again, leave the "MBA speak" and technical jargon out of your text. This section should contain the following elements:

» **The name and status of your company**
Basic information regarding your business and its status.

Q: What if my business doesn't exist yet?

Answer: Be honest about the current state of your business, even if it doesn't yet exist. If that is the case, use this space to discuss the sales that you have already made, the rate at which you have acquired clients so far, etc. Keep in mind that investors such as venture capitalists, banks, and angel investors don't invest in startups. At this point, you're writing the plan for your own use.

» **A description of what your company does, along with core products/services**
The details concerning your product or service will be included in the next section of your business plan, the Product/Service Description. A very brief overview is appropriate for this section.

Nothing is more annoying to readers than to get several pages into the plan without a clear idea of what the company does. You will provide much more detail about this in the next section; however, here you should provide several clear, concise sentences addressing the issue. Avoid vague generalities or technical/business jargon. I've mentioned this several times for a reason—it is a very common, and very annoying, issue with business plans.

» **The history of your company**
Here you will tell the story of how your company came to be and what stage of the development process it is currently in. This is a great opportunity for you to infuse the history of your business with storytelling elements. What challenges did your business overcome to become what it is today? How does the history of your business reflect your entrepreneurial thumbprint? What unique aspects of your vision and perspective are reflected in the story that stars your company? Also keep in mind, while attempting to induce excitement in your audience, that this is not a time to get wordy or waste space. As with all sections of your business plan, keep it concise and to the point.

» **The company's legal form**
Unless there are compelling reasons to set up your venture as a C corporation, you should be considering whether to organize as an S corporation or an LLC. Each of these can be easily converted to a C corp at a later date if necessary. Keep in mind that entrepreneurs who undertake ventures as sole proprietors expose themselves to potentially catastrophic financial ramifications—in the event that their venture is found liable for damages, sole proprietors have no legal entity to shield their personal assets.

» **A summary of the company's management team**
Your business is inherently dependent on the people that make it up. Specifics regarding your management team will be included in the Management and Staffing portion of your plan, but this is a great place to highlight the experience, accomplishments, and other pertinent information related to your management team.

» **The location of your company, along with any other facilities**
This information may not be important unless the location of your firm reflects a strategic decision. For example, some companies are located in certain states to take advantage of tax credits or other incentives, or in certain cities to be in close proximity to shipping or freight-handling hubs. This is the place to mention those strategic decisions. This area should also include information about multiple facilities, whether your company rents or owns those assets, and any plans to expand to new facilities in the near future.

Both the introduction and the following portion are presented here in a broken-out format; however, in your finished plan they should be presented in a paragraph format with one or two sentences for each point.

Next is a section that summarizes the goals, objectives, and exit strategy for your company. This is the portion of your business plan where you spell out the objectives of your company and answer key questions that investors will have regarding your vision for its future. This section should include the following information:

» **A summary of the company's growth prospects**
What are the short-, medium-, and long-term growth prospects for the company? Be realistic. This is not the place to include charts, tables, or financial forms, but your assessment of the company's growth prospects should reflect as much real data as possible.

» **The company's goals and your vision**
What is your vision for the future of your business? What are the key milestones that will mark the completion of these goals?

» **A clearly defined exit strategy**
Investors will be looking for evidence of a clearly defined exit strategy, and you should have one in mind for yourself as well. Outside investors want to understand how and when they will be able to receive a return on their investment, or a "harvest" on the business. This exit strategy often takes place as a *liquidity event* at some point in the foreseeable future, such as selling to a larger firm. A best practice when it comes to exit strategies is to provide two, with one as a contingency plan in case the preferred option ends up not working out.

An exit strategy is still a good idea even if you are not seeking equity funding with your business plan. Keeping an exit strategy in view on the horizon brings discipline to the venture-planning process and helps decision makers keep in mind the fact that every venture has a beginning, a middle, and an end. Even if you are not planning on selling the business, it is necessary to plan for growth and change. Ignoring the fact that your venture has a multi-stage life cycle will eventually lead to its downfall. Always remember, *"Failing to plan is planning to fail."*

» **A summary of your business model**
Provide a brief description of your business model. This information will be covered in detail in later sections of the business plan, but what the reader wants to understand here is specifically how you are going to make money.

This is another area where business plan authors will often gloss over specifics, assuming it's obvious or not important. Nothing could be further from the truth. Similar products can have very different business models. Take apps. What the product is might be obvious, but how you monetize it is not. Some common possibilities:

1. Sell downloads
2. Charge a yearly licensing fee
3. Offer the app for free and sell ads or other in-app purchases
4. Offer the app for free, but require paid upgrades to "unlock" popular features (a "freemium" model)

There are many others as well. Be very clear in this section about exactly how you make money.

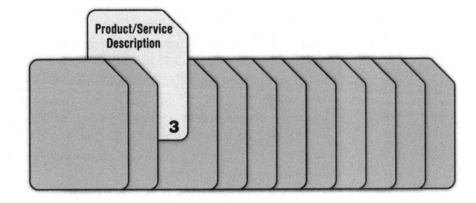

Product/Service Description
→ (length: approximately two pages)

The other sections of your plan that we have covered so far have called for brevity in summarizing what exactly your product or service is. Now is the time to build on those summaries and provide a clear and detailed picture of your core offering in two pages or less. Also included in this section is a portion of what will become the heart of your business: your value proposition. Even if your reader is an expert in your industry, take your time to ensure that he or she fully understands what it is you do.

It is important to be detailed and specific in this section, but that doesn't mean it is a good idea to get bogged down with extremely detailed technical specifications or descriptions. Your audience will want to assess that kind of information during the due diligence process, not in the first pass of reading your business plan. You can put more detailed technical specifications in an appendix or save them for the due diligence process. I discuss due diligence in further detail in chapter 17.

What to Include
Your product/service description should be broken into two sections. Section 1 is a detailed introduction to your product, proprietary rights, and pricing strategy. Section 2 includes a summary of your competitive advantage and your value proposition.

The introduction should answer the following key questions:

» **What exactly is your product or service?**
Of course, no introduction in this section would be complete without definitive information explaining exactly what your venture is offering. Build on the summaries you have presented thus far and ensure that there is no way your audience could put down your business plan without a complete understanding of what your product or service is.

Stay away from vagueness such as "our product is the future of XYZ" or "our service is the next evolution of ABC." These kinds of statements do nothing to answer your reader's questions or shed light on what it is that your product has to offer. Focus on concrete statements that don't waste words or use excessive jargon.

» **Where is your product or service within its life cycle?**
Is your product market-ready or is it still in development? Does it have a long life cycle or a relatively short one? Do you have plans to mitigate declining sales as the product life cycle runs its course?

If your product or service is still in development, how far along have development efforts come? What remains to be completed, and are there any obstacles in the way?

» **Pricing strategy**
Pricing is a strategic decision that has far-reaching implications for the success of your venture. Pricing is further complicated for new ventures because in many cases the products offered are new to the market. Entire books could be (and have been) written on the topic of pricing strategy, and an exhaustive examination of the topic is beyond the scope of this book; however, a brief primer on pricing strategies is included in chapter 5.

Be sure to detail your pricing strategy and be sure to explain why it will be effective with regard to your target market and your competition. Keep in mind that it is very rare for new ventures to sustain a cost advantage over their competition.

» **Proprietary rights**
What, if any, proprietary rights do you have to your product? Proprietary rights include patents, copyrights, trademarks, and trade secrets. If you are licensing proprietary property from another entity, the specifics of

that relationship should be detailed here. Don't forget to include any proprietary knowledge or skills in this section as well. Copies of the legal documents that certify these proprietary rights (patent filings, agreements, etc.) should be included in the appendixes. Most new ventures do not have significant proprietary rights. If this is the case for your venture, this subsection can be omitted.

Q: What's the difference between various proprietary rights?

Answer:

» *Patents* are the exclusive rights to exclude others from manufacturing something useful and novel that you have invented. Patents are issued and controlled by the US Patent and Trademark Office, which stipulates that in order for a concept to be patentable it must be new, useful, non-obvious, and "reduced to practice." This last criterion means that the person or entity filing for the patent must be able to construct the item or demonstrate the construction of it. Ideas are not patentable because they *cannot* be reduced to practice.

» *Copyrights* provide the right to restrict persons from copying material that has been published, such as books, articles, photographs, web pages, and other media, including "works of art on a fixed medium." Copyrights protect the expression of an idea, not the idea itself. They are automatically granted when the work is published.

» *Trademarks* can be applied to any symbol, name, or other configuration used to distinguish one company's product from another. A trademark must continue to be used and protected to remain valid.

» *Trade secrets* consist of any information, process, apparatus, or formula that gives an advantage to a company over its competitors. Trade secrets can be enforced through the use of nondisclosure agreements, but not everything qualifies as a trade secret. Trade secrets must not be generally known, must be of demonstrable value, and management must have already made some effort to protect them in the past.

The previous points are brief descriptions of the major classes of legally protected intellectual property. More detailed discussion of these topics is beyond the scope of this book.

A comprehensive description is not complete without the laying out of your venture's competitive advantage and value proposition in the second section of your Product/Service Description. This section is particularly important because these two elements of your venture are the core of your business plan. There are many factors of starting a new venture that are contributory to success, but the health and longevity of your venture are built on the robust quality of your competitive advantage and value proposition.

Because the specifics of this section are informed by later sections of your plan, if you are writing your plan sequentially it is best to leave this section blank through your first draft. The steps to developing your value proposition are outlined in the next section.

This section is a more detailed description of your venture's products or services. Even if the reader is an expert in your industry, he or she will not be familiar with your product, so describe it carefully. This is particularly important because (hopefully) your idea will be something that is new to your market or industry. Although you want to provide solid, factual information in this section, never lose sight of the fact that your business plan is essentially a sales document—never miss an opportunity to get the reader excited about what you are trying to do! There will be time for extremely detailed technical specifications and descriptions during the investor's due diligence process, so don't get bogged down here.

You may draft this section in the beginning of the business planning process, but many of these items will be further developed as you dive deeper into your analysis in subsequent sections. Expect to revise this section many times during the business planning process. Don't be afraid to take a stab at these areas in the beginning, knowing that you will be revisiting them as you progress.

Chapter Recap

» The length and specifics of your business plan depend on the nature of your product or service and the industry you are in, but it will follow a standard format. A comprehensive business plan can be divided into three main sections: Introduction of your venture, your value proposition, and your business model, along with specifics included in attached appendixes.

» The Executive Summary portion of your business plan should be one page or less and act as a hook for your audience. The executive summary is arguably the most important part of your business plan because it may be the only part that is read—your audience may make a decision on your opportunity after reading only the executive summary. Additionally, despite coming first sequentially, it is a summary of everything to follow, so when crafting your business plan, it should be written last to summarize your findings.

» Your elevator pitch, while not a formal part of your written business plan, is an important networking tool. Think of your plan's elevator pitch as a summary of your summary—keep it concise and stick to the key points.

» Your pitch deck is the short PowerPoint-style presentation that you make to investors if the need arises. Like your executive summary and elevator pitch, it should be concise and to the point. Be prepared to augment your presentation with answers to questions from your audience.

» The Company Overview portion of your business plan comes directly after the executive summary and shouldn't exceed two pages in length. It details the legal form of your company, its history, and other pertinent details. This can be summarized in paragraph form.

» The following section details your product or service. In the product/service portion of your business plan it is a good idea to be detailed, but make your words count. Keep this section under two pages in length, and don't waste your audience's time. Be sure to detail exactly what your product or service does, where it is within its life cycle, and the pricing strategy you are using.

| 16 |
Writing Your Value Proposition

Chapter Overview

»   The market analysis portion of your business plan
»   Your industry analysis
»   Presenting your value proposition

As we discussed in chapter 8, your value proposition is the heart of your venture. It is composed of the answers to two questions:

»   Who is your target customer?
»   How are you different from your competition?

In this section of the business plan, you will give your readers specifics about your markets, customers, industries, and competitors. You will then develop a concise one-paragraph value proposition.

fig. 38

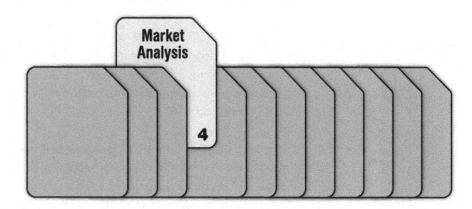

Market Analysis
→ (length: approximately two pages)

The Market Analysis and the Industry Analysis (following section) go hand in hand, but they are distinct, and it is important for new entrepreneurs to address them separately. Your industry analysis focuses on your *competitors* and your market analysis focuses on your *customers*. The market analysis is an examination of the people who will buy your product and the solution that you provide for them.

Remember that successful firms always solve a problem for their customers—even if the customer is not aware of the problem! Don't be a solution searching for a problem. If you can't think of a problem that your product solves, why would anyone buy it?

For both the market and the industry analyses, it is very important that all statements or claims made are *supported by primary or secondary research*. Of course, the entire business plan document should be as accurate as possible, but in certain areas it is necessary to make educated guesses or even WAGs (wild-ass guesses). The industry and market analyses are not the places for such estimations.

When compiling these sections, keep the following tips in mind:

- Focus on quantifiable facts. The market and industry analyses should focus exclusively on quantifiable facts. This is not the place for guesses, opinions, or conjecture.

- Show your work. Don't make your readers search for evidence that you have done your research, but don't overwhelm them either. Because the information from this section is often drawn from online sources, it can be mentioned right in the text (no long citations needed).

- Be prepared to talk through objections. Many of the objections that your readers may have can be settled through careful analysis and insight. Focus on the facts and try not to embellish when discussing the way your business will face the challenges that competitors pose.

Your market analysis should answer the following questions:

» Who wants your product?
» How much will they buy?
» What will they pay?
» Can you find a niche in this market that is big enough to make money?

This information will be communicated by first presenting a summary of how you define your target market, then a detailed look at how you define your target customers. This section will also provide critical insight into the development of your value proposition, or the core of your business.

Start a document now titled "Assumptions." Note all assumptions for your financial calculations as you make them from this point forward. Include this document as an appendix to your final plan. This is critical for your personal use as well as for other readers trying to understand your plan. You need to remember the basis for your numbers, and the best way to do it is to keep a running tally. This is critical preparation for your pitch and the due diligence process.

Defining Your Market

Your initial market will likely be a small segment of the market as a whole. For example, if you are opening a restaurant, your market will be limited in various ways, such as to the people within the city where you operate or even just within one neighborhood; the type of food and the price point; the style and customer perception of the restaurant; and many others. Unlike your industry analysis, which can largely be done with online research, gathering information related to your market is more involved. The bulk of your data here will come from interviews with potential customers, suppliers, and even competitors. With the right questions and the right approach, you will find many people who are happy to share what they know or discuss their area of expertise.

Market segmentation should *never* be a top-down process. Saying that you need a very small percentage of a very large market to be successful (although quite common) indicates to the reader that either you have not done your analysis correctly or you do not understand the nature of market segmentation. You must initially focus on a relatively small segment in which you can maintain a sustained competitive advantage. Expansion into other markets, and other industries, will be covered in the Growth Plan section.

Your market analysis should answer the critical questions that your readers will have. Include the following in your opening paragraph:

» **How do you define your market?**
Your product or service isn't a perfect fit for everyone. How do you define your market? The answer to that question should reflect characteristics of your product or service. Is your market based on geographic boundaries? What about demographic information such as age or gender?

» **What is the size of your market?**
Is your market large or small? How fast is it growing? If your market is shrinking, that is a warning sign. If there are fewer and fewer people willing to buy your product, how can you expect to grow your business?

» **How do you segment the market?**
All industries and markets can be segmented in a variety of ways. Pick the segmentation method that makes the most sense for your venture and your product.

» **What are the most important trends within your market?**
What does the future of your market look like? Remember, you will be competing and doing business in the future. Historical data from the market's past can be a helpful tool, but ultimately all markets are dynamic, and your business will be operating in the future. In what ways are you prepared to capitalize on current and emerging trends within your market?

Market segmentation techniques are covered in greater detail in chapter 6 of this book.

Defining Your Customer

The next subsection of your market analysis defines and segments the current customers in your market or market segment(s). Use interviews and secondary research to develop this section. These secondary sources include market research reports, industry publications, and data from trade groups. This information will tell you how others in the industry define, identify, and segment their customers.

» **Who are your customers?**
What segmentation method makes the most sense for your venture? What motivates buying decisions for your target segment(s)? These motivators

are responses to specific "pain points" or critical problems that your customers need solved (whether they know it or not). Are your customers sensitive to price? Are they interested in convenience, or quality?

» **Why does your value proposition resonate with this customer group?**
In what ways are customers dissatisfied with current offerings in the market, and how does your value proposition fill in these gaps? What customer needs are currently unmet by your competitors? This section will help you develop your value proposition, so in the first pass of writing this section, the information won't be available.

» **What emerging customer groups are being ignored?**
How is your product or service a good fit for the needs of these emerging segments?

These questions must be answered with facts, not supposition. It is very common for nascent entrepreneurs to create a narrative of customer problems and their desire for a specific solution based on what they think, not what actually is. You've created your idealized customer avatar—now support it with facts. Your market analysis isn't just busywork or context for your reader. This section is a key element in the development of your value proposition—the core of your business. Understanding your market, your customers, and their problems are critical to the success of your business.

Where to Find Customer Information

The best data is a mix of qualitative and quantitative—that is, data that represents opinions or emotions along with numbers-based data. Unfortunately, quality information about customer preferences can't be found simply with an internet search. The following sources of customer data are arranged from least expensive to most expensive.

» **Historical Data**
Historical data, such as known data about certain customer segments or information in trade publications and journals, can be a useful starting point. Just keep in mind that while this information may be easy to access and may include qualitative and quantitative data, it may lack current industry trends and will never be as timely or accurate as information derived directly from your customers themselves. It can be used to establish a baseline or to flesh out a background, but it should never constitute the only source of information for your market analysis.

» **Surveys and Questionnaires**

Surveys and questionnaires are cost-effective alternatives to more expensive and time-consuming interviews. With the benefit of tech-enabled solutions, they can be administered to a large group of people and targeted to certain specifications, and the resulting data is easier to explore than ever before. Surveys are great because they are very current, and the questions you use can help you capture exactly the information you are looking for.

» **Interviews**

When it comes to uncovering information about your customers, there is absolutely no substitute for talking to people. Interviewing is also the most time-consuming method of uncovering customer information. Interviews don't have to be formal—simply talking to people who are using similar products or services and asking them what they like, dislike, would like to see more of, etc., counts as an interview. Pay special attention to criticisms of existing market offerings, as these may present opportunities for you to outmaneuver the competition.

Suppliers are often more than willing to talk about the market they operate in, and even competitors can be sources of information. Look at their offerings, and purchase those that are most similar to your own. How does their buying process work from start to finish? What support do they offer, and how is their product or service process tailored to the people they serve? While competitors may be unwilling to discuss their business in an interview format, consuming their goods or services can be a way to reverse-engineer their customer avatar. Calling successful ventures in your space who aren't direct competitors, such as those in a different location, etc., can also be very useful. Everyone wants to talk about how they succeeded!

Sources of Customer Information

fig. 39

HISTORICAL DATA	SURVEYS & QUESTIONNAIRES	INTERVIEWS
Good starting point	Ability to target specific people	Best source of information
May not represent trends	Lots of quantitative data	Time-consuming
Not as helpful as surveys or interviews	Not good at capturing new insight or nuanced opinion/emotion	Real time and very current source of information

Q: What if I have little to no marketing experience?

Answer: Ideally, if marketing isn't your strong suit, you can find a team member, partner, or other advisor who can steer you in the right direction and act as a guide for your venture. There are numerous online resources, classes, and technical courses, both free and paid, to help expand your knowledge base, but nothing beats having an experienced marketer on your founding team.

GRAPHIC

fig. 40

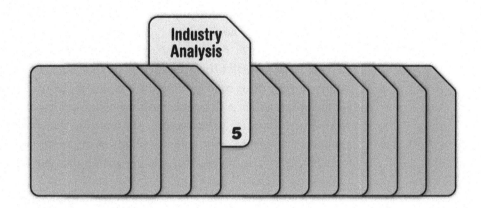

Industry Analysis

5

Industry Analysis
→ (length: approximately two pages)

So far, your business plan has been focused on your business and your customers. The Industry Analysis portion focuses on the competitive environment in which your business will operate. This means trends within the industry, but more importantly it focuses on your competitors and the ways in which you will differentiate yourself from their existing offerings. No business is an island, and competition is an inevitability of undertaking a new venture.

CAUTION

An industry analysis is not a market analysis. It is easy for new entrepreneurs to conflate the two. An industry analysis focuses on *competitors*, and a market analysis focuses on *customers*. The two sections are often used together in a finished business plan to describe a firm's potential for future success, but when researching and compiling your business plan it is best to tackle them separately so as not to mix them up.

Most of the research you do for this portion of your business plan can be conducted using internet sources. Government statistics, agency findings, and trade organizations' reports are all great primary sources of information, particularly *quantitative* information. Other helpful sources of information are suppliers who sell to the industry, financial analysts, and even competitors. Libraries often have access to statistical and financial databases, especially if you live in a larger city. A free library card can save you a lot of time and money here. These latter sources offer a mix of both quantitative and qualitative data—that is, a mix of numbers-based data and insight-based data. Together, these reliable primary and secondary sources inform your analysis to produce a big-picture overview of the size and scope of your industry, along with the role and position of competitors.

If the focus on documentation and citation seems excessive in these two chapters, consider this: the success of your business is dependent on the ability of your venture to survive the stresses of the marketplace. Operating on faulty information or unsubstantiated assumptions can pose jeopardizing risks down the line. What's more, the insights that your industry analysis produces are used to inform and develop your value proposition—the core of your business. That is certainly not something that can be based on a WAG (wild-ass guess)!

Your industry analysis is important in another way: insight gleaned from it forms the second half of your value proposition. The market analysis answers the question "Who will buy your product or service?" The industry analysis answers the question "How are you different (and better) than your competitors?"

Your first paragraph should address the following:

» **How do you define your industry?**
To ensure that your readers are on the same page and to provide important context, briefly outline how you define your industry. If relevant, what are your SIC and NAICS codes?

» **How is the industry segmented?**
And how are these segments defined? All industries and markets can be segmented in a variety of ways. You must select a segmentation that is relevant for you.

» **What are current trends and important developments?**
What role is technology playing in this industry? How are customer preferences changing?

» **What national and international events are influencing your industry?**
Are they boosting the industry, or will they create problems in the future?

» **What are the growth forecasts for the industry?**
Is it growing or shrinking? Why is this an advantage right now?

Competitor Analysis

In this section, identify potential direct and indirect competitors in your industry. Focus on why they are your competitors and where you differ. Try to include all direct competitors. If there are numerous existing competitors, pick several that produce products most closely related to yours. Of course, it goes without saying that having numerous competitors who are very similar to you is a worrisome sign.

Either in this section or in the appendixes, provide a chart showing the attributes and characteristics of these competitors and their products. Include basic information such as their size, location, target market(s), and other important characteristics. For each competitor's products or services, identify price, quality, features, distribution, and other important attributes. What you are trying to show with this chart is that your product has one or more unique features not offered by your competition, so be sure to highlight the attributes that make your product unique.

Make sure that you acknowledge the strengths of your competitors and their products, as well as the weaknesses or gaps that will create an opportunity for you. It is not desirable to appear overconfident or dismissive of your competition.

When conducting an analysis of your competitors, keep three key pieces of information at the forefront of your mind:

» **You *do* have competitors.**
It is common for entrepreneurs, especially those starting new ventures that offer unique products or services, to state with confidence that they do not have any competition. This isn't true, and it demonstrates to your reader that either (a) you have not correctly researched your competitors or (b) you do not understand the nature of competition. Every business has competitors, even if their product is unique.

Consider this: if your product is so unusual that nothing like it has ever been seen before, what were your customers using before your offering was released? Nothing. And nothing is a powerful substitute. However, "using nothing" is rarely the case. Apple transformed the music industry with the introduction of the iPod and the iTunes store—a unique product and service offering. People had plenty of music listening options prior to the iPod. Those were Apple's competitors.

» **Try to consider all of your direct competitors.**
Try to include each of your direct competitors in the Competitor Analysis portion of your industry analysis. If direct competitors are numerous, select those that compete with you most directly. That is to say, the competitors that produce products most similar to yours or offer very similar services. It should go without saying that if you are faced with the prospect of sifting through piles of competitors to pick the "best" ones, that's a worrisome sign for your future success.

» **Remember why your readers care.**
Your readers want to know *why* the competitors you chose are your competitors, and you want to *sell* them on the fact that you offer something better and different. Don't just focus on why they are your competitors; also focus on the areas where you differ.

For each of your direct competitors, include a small blurb that covers basic information such as name, size, location, and target market. Then summarize the key metrics of their offering and compare it to your own. The easiest way to do this is via a side-by-side comparison chart. If the chart can be presented in a compact manner, it can go right into this section. If not, then it should be placed in the appendixes.

There are no hard-and-fast rules that dictate what information should go in your competitor comparison chart. The objective is to demonstrate to your readers that your offering has one or more unique features not offered by the competition. So, pick whichever attributes are relevant. Common candidates for comparison are price, quality, features, and distribution. Whichever set of attributes best helps you highlight the ways your offering is unique is the right set to choose for your comparison chart.

What Not to Include

The Industry Analysis section is best kept to two pages or less, so if you find yourself with five pages of competitor analysis you have a problem.

Did you focus on your *direct* competitors? Would your competitor comparison charts be better served by being placed in your business plan's appendixes? If your competitor analysis is long because you simply have a high number of direct competitors, that's another problem all its own. High-competition industries that are jam-packed with entrenched competitors are tough environments for new ventures to tackle.

Be sure to acknowledge the strengths of your competitors and their products, as well as the weaknesses or gaps that will create an opportunity for you. Appearing overconfident or dismissive of your competitors is not a good look. Remember, *you're* the new, unproven venture. The simple fact that they are one of your competitors is proof that they have a sustainable business, at minimum.

Other Competitive Forces

In this subsection of your Industry Analysis, you should acknowledge two other competitive forces from the Five Forces model that was discussed in detail in chapter 7: the threat posed by new entrants and the potential of substitute products. All five forces will make it into your plan; the competition between industry actors, the threat of new entrants, and the potential of substitute products are covered here. The relative power of customers and suppliers is addressed in the Operations Overview portion of your plan.

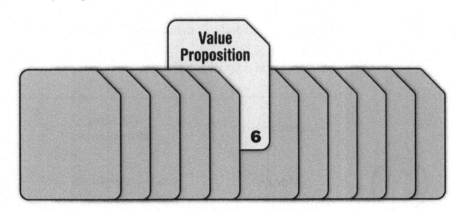

fig. 41

Constructing Your Value Proposition

We discussed the concept of a value proposition briefly at the beginning of this chapter and at length in chapter 8, and you've gathered the data necessary for it in the previous three chapters. Now you're ready to write a concise, impactful value proposition statement for both yourself and other stakeholders.

Determining your value proposition is an inflection point in the business planning process. This is the point where you ask yourself some tough questions: Is this something real? Can this be a healthy and sustainable business, or should I go back to the drawing board? Being honest with yourself and relying on the honest input of friends, family, peers, and mentors can save you lots of money, lots of time, and lots of frustration.

Your value proposition is the answer to two fundamental questions:

» Who is your target customer?
» How are you different from your competition?

Those are the two questions that make or break new ventures. Without a firm, confident answer to both, your marketing plan, your operations plan, and all of the other parts of your business plan that have yet to be written don't matter.

To construct your value proposition, you will take information from your Product/Service Description, Market Analysis, and Industry Analysis sections. This information will be turned into a concise statement that answers both of the above questions. This statement should leave nothing to the imagination. It should make sense to you first and foremost, but it should also make sense to investors down the road. It should make sense to your customers, and it should make sense to your team. In short, you value proposition should be instantly understood by anyone who reads it.

Your value proposition exists in three parts:

fig. 42

Introduction	Who are you? What do you do?	This comes from your: **Company Description**
Market Definition	Who is your target customer? What problems are you solving for them?	This comes from your: **Market Analysis**
Competitor Differentiation	Who are your competitors? How are you different from them?	This comes from your: **Industry Analysis**

Even though your value proposition is totally dependent on the work you have done so far drafting your business plan, it should make sense standing completely alone. A good way to test this is to print it out on a single sheet of paper. Does it make sense? It should. Does it reference any part of your business plan? It shouldn't.

Introduction

The introduction tells your reader who you are and what you do. This information is presented in your Company Description section, but remember, your value proposition must make sense as a coherent statement independent of your business plan. The introduction is a single sentence that gets right to the point. That doesn't mean that it has to be boring or that you can't cast your venture in a positive light. It does mean, however, that your introduction should be more than just the name of your venture. Under no circumstances should it be a slogan or a tagline or be jam-packed with jargon. A slogan is not a value proposition. Furthermore, leaving the jargon at the door means that anyone—investors, team members, suppliers, and customers—can get right to the bottom of who you are and what it is you do without being an industry expert.

To illustrate the value proposition construction process we will be using a fictional pet specialty e-commerce retailer named Rex. Rex focuses on hard-to-find items for unusual (not dogs, cats, birds, etc.) pets.

"Rex is an online pet product retailer focused on nontraditional and exotic pets."

Market Definition

The information from your market analysis informs this section of your value proposition. First, identify your target customer. Your target customer may or may not be the end user of your product. They may be a consumer (B2C) or a business (B2B). For the purpose of your value proposition, your target customer(s) can be identified in a single sentence.

"Our product assortment is perfect for friends of pets that are neither a dog nor a cat who need specialized products to live happy, comfortable lives."

Next, define the problem that your target customers have, and how that problem is a pain point—how does it make them feel? Again, this information is drawn from your market analysis. If you asked one of your target customers today, they should immediately identify with the pain point(s) your value proposition addresses.

"Owners of nontraditional pets struggle to find an adequate, affordable assortment of supplies and accessories in one place. They end up wasting time and money traveling to expensive specialty stores or searching online for the products they need."

"Their current choices are limited to expensive specialty stores, big box retailers with limited stock of the products they are looking for, and e-commerce sites such as Amazon. Frustrated pet owners often have to spend an inordinate amount of time and money tracking down the supplies they need."

Competitor Differentiation

Based on the competitor analysis within your industry analysis, who are your competitors? Use direct competitors for your value proposition. Keep it concise. Your competitor may be called out by name if it is large enough or well-recognized. On the other hand, if you are competing with a number of smaller firms within an area, just say so.

"Rex competes with local specialty pet stores, big box pet retailers such as Petco, and online outlets such as Chewy and Amazon, but it has distinct advantages over each of these categories."

Based again on your industry analysis, define the ways in which you are different from your competitors. This list is for you and will be summarized in your finished value proposition. Focus on features and benefits that relate to your target customers' pain points that were outlined in the market definition. The features are only an organizing tool for you. Customers do not buy features. They only buy benefits. If a feature does not provide a benefit that is relevant to your target customers' pain points, then it is not a point of differentiation—it is not a reason that a customer would choose you over a competitor. Once you have listed your key features and benefits, summarize them in a concise sentence format.

"Specialty pet stores are expensive and don't exist in most places. Big box pet retailers have limited shelf space, highly rotational products, and a preference for popular pets. Online retailers like Amazon may have the products, but the search is difficult and customers may end up having to buy from multiple outlets. The specialty selection that Rex offers presents unique supplies and accessories that fill the needs of nontraditional pet owners and are affordable and easy to find."

The Complete Value Proposition

To produce your completed value proposition, put together each of the statements you have already written into a single, succinct statement.

"Rex is an online pet product retailer focused on nontraditional and exotic pets. Our product assortment is perfect for friends of pets that are neither a dog nor a cat who need specialized products to live happy, comfortable lives. Owners of nontraditional pets struggle to find an adequate, affordable assortment of supplies and accessories in one place. They end up wasting time and money traveling to expensive specialty stores or searching online for the products they need. Their current choices are limited to expensive specialty stores, big box retailers with limited stocks of the products they are looking for, or e-commerce sites such as Amazon. Frustrated pet owners often have to spend an inordinate amount of time and money tracking down the supplies they need."

"Rex competes with local specialty pet stores, big box retailers such as Petco, and online outlets such as Chewy and Amazon, but it has distinct advantages over each of these categories. Specialty pet stores are expensive and don't exist in most places. Big box pet retailers have limited shelf space, highly rotational products, and a preference for popular pets. Online retailers like Amazon may have the products, but the search is difficult and customers may end up having to buy from multiple outlets. The specialty selection that Rex offers presents unique supplies and accessories that fill the needs of nontraditional pet owners and are affordable and easy to find."

Chapter Recap

» The Market Analysis portion of your business plan is the section where details concerning your customers are laid out. This section should focus on quantifiable facts. This section should answer the following questions: who wants your product, how much will they buy and at what price, and is there a big enough niche within this market to make money?

» It is important to demonstrate how and why you chose to define your market in the way that you have. This means outlining how you define the market, how you segment it, and why this method of segmentation is relevant for your product. Be sure to clearly define the size of your market, along with important trends.

» Shifting from the focus on your market, use your market analysis to define your customers—who are they, why does your value proposition resonate with them, and is there an emerging customer group that is being ignored by competitors? As with the information you present with regard to your market at large, it is important that details about your target customers are grounded in facts, not sweeping generalizations or unfounded assumptions.

» The Industry Analysis portion of your business plan follows the market analysis and focuses on your competitors as well as the industry at large. As with your market, be sure to identify the ways in which you define and segment your industry, as well as important developments, forecasts, and emerging trends.

» The Industry Analysis portion of your business plan should also include a competitor analysis that directly compares your offerings with that of both your direct and indirect competitors.

» For the Value Proposition section, recall that your value proposition is the central "why" of your business and that it should answer two fundamental questions: who your target customer is and how you are different from your competitors. For your business plan, your value proposition is pulled from your market analysis (defining your target customer) and your industry analysis (how you are different from your competitors) and is summarized in a direct and succinct statement.

| 17 |

Your Business Model

Having read to this point in your plan, the reader is clearly interested in your idea and intrigued by the potential market for your product or service. Now they want to be convinced that you and your team can achieve your financial goals; the next section of your plan does just that. The upcoming Operations and Marketing Overviews along with the Growth Plan help convince them in three ways:

»   These sections demonstrate that you understand the practical aspects of running this business throughout every phase of the value chain.

»   These sections demonstrate that you understand the critical assumptions you are making and the leverage points required to be successful.

»   These sections demonstrate that you understand where your competitive advantage truly lies, and that you and your team are willing and able to execute accordingly.

After you have completed these three sections, you will be able to clearly present your *business model*—a concise statement of how you will achieve your financial goals. Thinking back to chapter 15, this is your refined business model that belongs in your Company Overview.

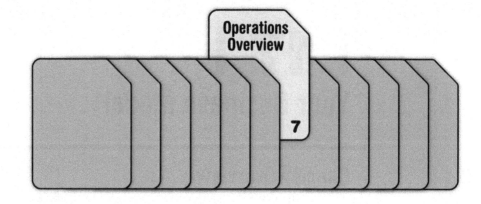

fig. 43

Operations Overview
→ (length: approximately two pages)

Operations are defined as the processes used to deliver your products and services to the marketplace and can include purchasing, manufacturing, marketing and sales, customer service, etc. Be sure that you carefully link the design of your operations to your value proposition. Since you are building your business around a point of differentiation from your competition that is critically important to your target customers, make sure you design your operations to maximize this point of differentiation, not necessarily to minimize costs.

Don't go crazy with nitty-gritty details. The most critical aspect of the Operations Overview is to show an understanding of where your competitive advantage is coming from and how you have designed your business to take advantage of it. Other nonessential activities can be purchased, outsourced, or simply eliminated. This section should demonstrate that you understand this and have a solid grasp of how to run your business.

Internal Operations Strategy
In this subsection, describe how you will use your firm's internal operations to create value for your target customers. It will be helpful to show your firm's value chain and describe how you intend to run each area of the business.

External Operations Strategy
In this subsection, describe how your firm will interact with suppliers and partners in your industry group, including the following:

» **What you will produce internally and what you will purchase?**
Essentially, this is a question of what you will make versus what you will buy. More importantly, why do these decisions make sense for your particular business?

» **How do you fit into the industry's supply chain?**
What is your relationship with vendors, suppliers, partners, and other service providers? Again, more importantly, why does your operations strategy make sense for this position?

» **What critical partnerships will you have to develop in order to be successful?**
What outstanding critical partnerships are yet to be developed? What progress has already been made and what remains to be completed?

fig. 44

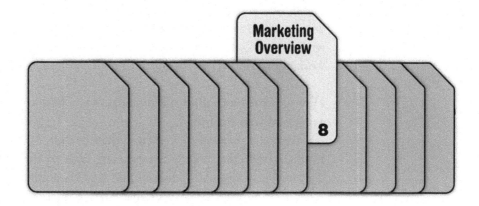

Marketing Overview
→ (length: approximately two pages)

In marketing class, students are often taught that the marketing mix consists of the "4 Ps": product, price, promotion, and place. Your plan has already covered the product and price portions of the marketing mix in the Product/Service Description. This section covers the remaining two: place (your distribution strategy) and promotion (sales, advertising, and public relations).

The marketing mix and the 4 Ps of marketing are covered in greater detail in chapter 10 of this book.

Distribution Strategy

The Distribution Strategy section of your marketing overview should answer the following questions:

» **How is your product/service going to get to the customer?**
Remember, your customer may not be the end user. Will you distribute your product through digital channels? Are you going to sell to a wholesaler or distributor who then delivers to retailers, or does it make more sense to only sell direct? Explain why you selected the distribution method(s) you did, why it is a good fit for your business and your customers, what distribution channels are involved, and how you will access them.

» **How does your chosen distribution strategy fit into the larger set of your business goals?**
For example, if your pricing strategy and overall objective is to gain market share fast through the use of a penetration pricing strategy, how does your distribution strategy support that objective? Perhaps it goes without saying, but the greater the number of business elements you have working in concert, the higher your goal completion will be.

» **How will the method(s) of distribution you have chosen impact other aspects of your business?**
Are there distribution-related costs that invalidate your pricing strategy? If this is the case, it may mean going back to the drawing board on distribution. How will a distribution lead time affect production? Does a distribution lead time affect the way you prepare for or execute your service? Are there packaging or labeling concerns that may arise based on the chosen distribution method(s)? Are there minimum inventory levels that must be adhered to for a particular distribution method to be viable?

Sales Strategy

Channels of distribution may get your product to your customers, but an effective sales and promotion strategy generates demand. Unless it is crystal clear in the minds of your customers how your product or service solves their problem(s), they will be reluctant to buy. There is no such thing as a product that sells itself, and a comprehensive sales strategy is needed to get startups off the ground.

» **The Sales Cycle**
In addition to answering the above critical questions regarding your sales strategy, another aspect of the sales process that you must understand is the sales cycle. The sales cycle is the process that a company undergoes from the initiation of a sale to the close of that sale. To put it another way, your sales cycle is the blueprint that your sales force follows to generate sales.

If some entrepreneurs are guilty of overlooking their distribution strategy and chalking it up as a noncritical part of the business planning process, then far too many have done the same thing to their sales strategy. Selling is a critical function that is often overlooked by new ventures. It is not uncommon for new entrepreneurs to either badly underestimate the time and expense that an effective sales effort requires, or worse, ignore the task of developing a sales strategy altogether.

The Sales Strategy portion of your marketing overview should answer the following questions:

» **How will you reach your target customers?**
Start by looking at industry norms. Are others in the same space using cold calls? Do they have a large presence at trade shows or do they tap into large networks to generate sales? Whatever approach you choose, it must reflect your target customers as well as the product or service you offer.

» **Who will do the selling?**
Who will actually be responsible for carrying out sales activities? Is this going to be a responsibility of members of the founding team, or will your venture rely on an internal sales team? Are sales and selling something you are comfortable outsourcing to external product representatives? No matter the decision you make, back it up with a sound rationale.

» **How will you administer your sales force?**
What is your plan to recruit, train, and compensate your sales force? Electing to outsource sales to external product representatives may mean that you are not responsible for recruiting the individual members of your sales team; however, you will still need to train and educate them.

» **How will you support your sales force?**
In what ways will you support the efforts of your sales team? Support could include customer service, maintenance plans, warranties, etc. How will the costs of sales support be recouped?

Promotion, Advertising, and Public Relations Strategy

New ventures rarely have the financial means to launch a full-scale multimedia advertising campaign; instead, entrepreneurs must learn and develop effective guerilla marketing techniques. Just like guerilla warfare tactics, the objective of guerilla marketing strategies is to compete with other market players who have more resources by using unconventional, outside-the-box, and inexpensive approaches.

The world of marketing and advertising is full of buzzwords and solutions-driven mindsets. It can be easy to focus on finding an advertising solution for every exposure issue that ails you (especially if you have a member of the ad industry in the room). Don't forget the power of a good public relations campaign. PR is often low cost—even free—and may carry more credibility with your customers than advertising materials prepared by the company.

Your Promotion, Advertising, and Public Relations Strategy section should outline the following in summary-level detail:

» **Your Advertising Strategy**
Your advertising strategy consists of the methods and channels you will use to promote your product. This is a strategic decision, but keep in mind that as your venture grows and your product matures, your strategy may shift. Changes in the industry, along with shifting customer attitudes and interests, can also spur changes in a promotion and advertising strategy. Make sure that your reader understands the scope of your advertising strategy and why each decision was made, especially with regard to the ways in which specific aspects of your advertising plan fit into the overall business objectives of your venture. This may mean touching on a summary of the digital consumption habits of your target market—the way they spend their time online and where in digital space they hang out.

It is a rare venture that can survive in today's business landscape without a strong digital presence. Don't leave out the ways in which you will leverage digital marketing/advertising solutions such as a content marketing strategy, an SEO plan, a programmatic ad plan, or a social media promotion plan.

» **Your Plan to Administer Your Advertising Strategy**
Will a member of the founding team administer the advertising strategy, or will dedicated staff be hired? What percentage of sales revenue will

be allotted for advertising efforts? Is this more, less, or in line with the industry average? If it is exceptional, why?

fig. 45

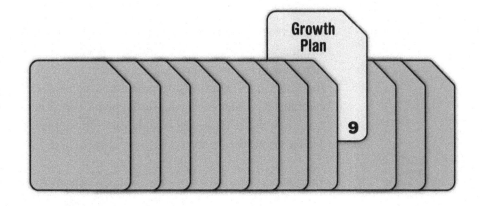

Growth Plan
→ (length: approximately two pages)

There are two related but distinct parts of this section. In the first—the Development Strategy—you will outline the steps you need to take to get your business up and running. In the second—the Growth Vision—you can discuss the ways in which you may be able to grow and expand the business in the future. This is your opportunity to be a little creative or visionary (which should come as a relief after carefully documenting your sales and market assumptions!)

Development Strategy
This subsection outlines the steps you have to take in order to launch your firm and get your initial product to market, as well as the factors that need to come together to make the concept work. This should contain a development timeline showing your timetable for launching your company. List major milestones that will have to be met in order to get your business up and running. Some type of graphic such as a *Gantt chart* is often useful here, but don't waste space!

Growth Vision
Once you have met your goals of launching your firm and getting some traction with your initial product in your initial market, where do you go from there? What are your growth plans and what steps will you have to take to achieve them? How big do you think the venture can become? What other areas can you expand into after succeeding with your initial

market segment? Besides your initial product, are there others that can be developed using the same technology platform or brand? Finally, if applicable to your venture, discuss your potential exit strategies.

Recall that I have encouraged you to focus on one product or service and one market segment throughout this document. Now is your chance to suggest other markets that you can penetrate and new products or services that you can offer in the future. As noted above, these do not have to be as carefully documented as your initial plans. Feel free to be a little visionary here. Let the reader understand your future plans and why you are so excited about this venture.

NOTE

This section provides more detail for areas that you first addressed in the Company Overview. Now may be a good time to revisit that section and make sure you are being consistent throughout the plan.

GRAPHIC

fig. 46

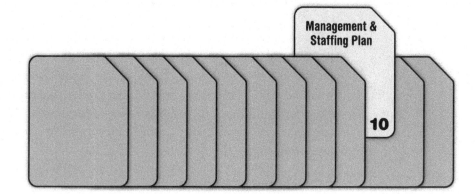

Management & Staffing Plan

10

Management and Staffing Plan
→ (length: approximately two pages)

The Management and Staffing Plan portion of your business plan is where you discuss the people that will bring your business opportunity to life. The purpose of this section is to convince your audience that you have a great management team to complement your outstanding venture concept. If your business plan is still in the just-for-you stages, then this portion will be used to organize your staffing plan, identify weak areas or gaps in expertise, and plan your salary-related expenses.

In two pages or less, your Management and Staffing Plan addresses the two key staffing-related areas of your venture: organization and staffing, and your management team.

Organization and Staffing

This section describes how your company will be organized. It should answer the following questions:

» **What is the ownership structure of your company?**
Basically, who owns what? How is equity—non-cash compensation in the form of ownership shares of the company—distributed among the founding team? Is equity in the startup being used to compensate members of the management team as well?

» **Who are your advisors?**
A board of directors is mandatory for corporations (both S corps and C corps). If your venture does have a board of directors, who will be on it? Regardless of whether you have a formal board of directors, you should have an informal board of advisors. Who are these people, and how do they provide value to your organization? How active a role will they play in the management of the organization?

Lack of expertise in the founding team can be mitigated to a great extent by recruiting a seasoned board of advisors. Now is a good time to begin putting your board together. It goes without saying that you should not list someone as a board member unless they have already agreed to work with you.

» **What does the organization chart look like?**
An organization chart (org chart) is a visual representation of the people within your organization. It is often organized as a hierarchy and demonstrates a clear chain of command. Is your org chart consistent with those of other firms in your industry? Is it taller or flatter than others in your industry, and why? A flat org chart would be one with more staff members on the same "level," and a taller one would include more supervisors or managers in a vertical chain of command.

» **Who will be responsible for each functional area?**
Tying in with the org chart, which critical members will be responsible for each functional area of the business? What gaps, if any, exist? What is your plan to fill these gaps?

The overall purpose of this section is to convince the reader that you have a great management team to complement your outstanding venture concept. This is not the place for modesty. Highlight your accomplishments and capabilities while mitigating any obvious shortcomings or weaknesses. When readers are finished with this section, you want them to be confident that your venture is in good hands and will be competently managed. To reinforce this point, include bios or condensed résumés of key team members in your plan's appendixes.

NOTE

Your audience will be experienced professionals. Don't gloss over gaps or try to explain them away. Be honest and clearly present your plan to address staffing gaps. Identifying gaps in expertise and presenting a definitive plan to fill said gaps is a clear indication to your audience that you are not overconfident and that you understand what it will take to succeed.

Transparency regarding gaps in your management team isn't just a trust measure for the readers of your business plan. It is also a vital undertaking for the success of your venture. The best way to think about the management team is in terms of competencies or capabilities. Which capabilities do you absolutely need in order to be successful? From this "capabilities wish list," which ones do you already have in the founding team? Which will you have to acquire right away, and which will you need in the future, at specific milestones?

EXAMPLE

Most high-growth technology startups will need to recruit a seasoned industry professional as CEO at some point for the venture to fully reach its potential. Investors will expect you to understand this and will expect you to be willing to take a back seat for the good of the venture if necessary.

Unless you have significant startup and industry experience, representing yourself as the only one who can move the venture forward will come across to seasoned investors as egotistical and immature rather than confident or capable.

NOTE

Successful high-growth ventures will generally not reach their potential without recruiting outsiders to key positions at the appropriate phase in the firm's life cycle. Identifying which positions will need to be filled and when is an important part of this section.

Management Team

Moving on from the Organization and Staffing subsection of your Management and Staffing Plan, the next topic to cover is the composition of your venture's management team. Here you will describe the founders and principal managers who will run your firm. This subsection should answer the following questions:

» **Who are the key managers, what will they do, and what skills do they bring to the table?**
The key managers could be members of the founding team or they may include outside hires. What will their main duties and responsibilities consist of? What unique skills do they bring to the venture? How will they be compensated? Compensation could include stock as well as a standard salary. As with other key people, include brief résumés in the appendixes.

» **What additions to the management team are planned?**
Not only what additions do you plan, but when do you plan to implement them? What milestones will trigger this decision?

In most cases, you will not be planning to hire during the startup phase of your venture. However, if it is to grow significantly, you will eventually have to hire to fuel that growth. Think carefully about what skills and activities will likely be needed and when. This will have a good deal to do with the skills and interests of the founding team.

For example, if the founders largely specialize in technical skill sets, the next logical step might be to hire a sales team as the growth of the business warrants it. On the other hand, if members of the founding team predominantly enjoy being on the road talking to customers, they may want to hire operational talent to round out the team.

Describe the founders and principal managers who will run your firm.

» Who are the key managers? (Include brief résumés in the appendixes)
» What will be their duties and responsibilities?
» What unique skills do they bring to the venture?
» How will they be compensated?
» What additions to the management team do you plan? When?

Compensation is often a tricky issue for entrepreneurs. While there is general agreement that the management team must receive enough salary to live on, investors are extremely reluctant to put money into a venture that will be immediately taken out in the form of salary expenses.

Moreover, inserting high salary estimates into your plan indicates to the investor that you may not be careful stewards of their resources;

it may even remind them of the "bad old days" of the internet boom/bust. Take as little as you can possibly manage—your rewards will come later when the venture takes off.

GRAPHIC

fig. 47

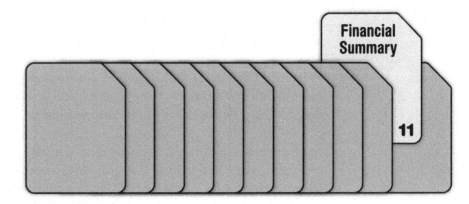

Financial Summary

11

Financial Summary
→ (length: approximately two pages)

You've outlined a great business concept, demonstrated a real need in the marketplace, shown how you will execute your ideas, and proven that you have the right team to manage the venture. However, no one will invest in your venture unless they see a real possibility of earning an adequate return, and you shouldn't invest your own funds without this possibility either!

Entrepreneurs often misunderstand the true rationale behind the financial projections in the business plan. The figures you provide here are estimates, and highly biased ones at that. Every entrepreneur is enthusiastic and optimistic about his/her venture. Investors don't necessarily "believe" that these projections will actually occur. Neither are they checking to see if you have the "right" figures, because there are no right figures. Your financials serve two critical purposes:

1. To show how big your venture could be if everything goes as planned. If you can't show that your great concept has the potential to make a lot of money, your readers will quickly lose interest. Investors are taking a huge risk when they back a startup. They simply will not do it if there is not the possibility of a big reward. It's the same with any stakeholder—bankers, government-grant-writing agencies, key potential hires, suppliers, etc., all want to be confident that your venture is on good financial footing.

2. To show that you understand what the business model is and how the business will operate, and that you have thought through critical details.

The financial plan is at the end of the business plan because it cannot be completed until the other sections are in place. However, the financials are very complicated, and a great deal of the information should be compiled before the plan is written. It is very difficult to complete this section in a short period of time. You will need a full set of pro forma financial statements projecting three to five years into the future, with all assumptions rigorously supported. A full discussion of developing your financial model is outside the scope of this book.

Finances

Most of the "meat" of your financials is in the appendixes in your pro forma financial statements, but you should summarize them and highlight important areas in the body of the plan. Prepare a summary of your financial projections to be included in this section.

Follow your summary with a paragraph or two highlighting the main things you want the reader to grasp when they read your summary. Will you break even quickly? Generate good cash flow? Have healthy earnings? Now is the time to point this out.

Finally, write a description of the vital financial drivers of the venture. What key assumptions have you made that will determine its financial success? You will document all of your assumptions carefully in the appendixes, but list critical ones here. For example, what minimum number of customers per day is assumed, and what average selling price? What level of cost per unit must be achieved? What are the customer acquisition costs? What is the development cost of your product? What is the sales cycle for your target customer group, and how long will it take you to make a sale?

Business Risks

The Business Risks section is really part of your assumptions but is often included as a separate section. The key is to show that you understand the risks to the successful implementation of your plan and have a contingency plan in case things don't work out as expected (which they won't!). They may be technological risks (your product doesn't work), cost risks (it costs way more than you thought), competitive risks, regulatory risks, etc.

Entrepreneurs often seriously oversell this subsection. Focus on risks that are unique and important to your venture, not the ordinary operating risks faced by any venture (for example, everyone understands that there is a risk that no one will buy your product!). This should be a short, hyper-focused section of the financial plan.

Some sort of sensitivity analysis may be appropriate here. In other words, what will happen if things do not go as planned? What are some obvious factors that could go wrong, and what effect would these have on the plan? What contingency plans have you made?

Much of the detailed part of the financial plan belongs in the appendixes. Only the financial summary and business risks belong in the body of the plan.

Sources and Uses of Funds

Potential sources of funding and how they may best be deployed are discussed in chapter 13 of this book.

In the Sources of Funds section of your plan, describe the specific funding you will need to get your venture to full independent sustainability. Include funding you have already received as well as anticipated sources of funding. There is no need to be overly specific about future plans—something to the effect of "We intend to raise $XX from angel investors by X date" is sufficient.

In the Uses of Funds section, provide a brief and general summary of how the funds will be used. Include an analysis that summarizes the major capital expenditures, and categorize other expenses such as product design, R&D, marketing, capital expenditures, inventory or working capital, losses due to burn rate, etc.

The Appendixes
→ (length: no more than ten pages)

The appendixes are the place to put all of the documentation that supports the body of your business plan. As with the plan as a whole, it should be complete, but succinct. Include those documents that are required (e.g., pro forma financial statements), those that are helpful (e.g., results of customer surveys), and those that assist in selling your idea (e.g., pictures or diagrams of your product).

fig. 48

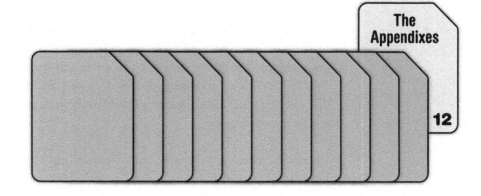

Don't include lots of tangential information, such as articles or tables of data, unless they serve to bolster your plan. One way to deal with information that is voluminous and/or lengthy (such as a large market research study) is to summarize it and note in the plan that the complete document is available upon request. Don't worry—if you're looking for funding, it will all come out in the due diligence process.

Required items (organized here roughly in the order of presentation):

» Key assumptions sorted by relevant section
» Pro forma financial statements
» Yearly income statement, balance sheet, and statement of cash flows for five years
» Monthly income statement and statement of cash flows for one year
» Break-even analysis
» Ratio and vertical analyses
» Brief résumés of key employees
» Competitor analysis (if not contained in the body of the plan)
» Copy of intellectual property protection documents (if applicable)

Optional items to include in your business plan appendixes:

» Surveys and survey results
» Development timeline
» Product photos, diagrams, or schematics
» Sample menus, web pages, advertisements, etc.
» Anything else that will help to illuminate and/or sell your plan, anything that won't easily fit in the body of the document

Key Assumptions

Although investors will not expect you to have firm answers on most of these items at this point in the planning process, they will want to understand where the numbers come from and how you arrived at your conclusions. Keep a running list as you prepare your plan. Thorough documentation of all assumptions made in the course of writing your plan is absolutely critical!

What assumptions have you made in putting together your financial forecasts? Describe how you arrived at such things as the following:

- » Industry and market projections
- » Revenue forecasts (prices, volume, discounts, margins)
- » Cost of goods sold (materials, labor, major indirect expenses)
- » Salaries and operating expenses
- » Sales and marketing expenses
- » Startup costs
- » Extraordinary income and expenses (including grants)
- » Tax rate
- » Capital expenditures (major expenditures, depreciation)
- » Working capital (accounts receivable, inventory, payables)
- » Any other assumption that you have made

Guessing at or inventing numbers will show a lack of due diligence on your part and readers will simply not take you seriously. Everyone knows these numbers are estimates, but they must come from a credible source or a logical conclusion, not inspiration.

Pro Forma Financial Statements

Pro forma financial statements should be prepared for three to five years into the firm's life. As a rule of thumb, your financial projections should extend into the future to the point where your business is expected to achieve stable operations, or at least until you reach your projected break-even point. Five years is standard.

After you have prepared the annual projections, forecast the first year of your financial projections month-by-month, since cash flows are critical in the early stages of any startup. Be sure that your financial projections are consistent with the other sections of your plan!

The following pro forma financial statements are required and should be placed in the appendixes:

- » Income Statement
- » Balance Sheet
- » Statement of Cash Flows

A common problem with first-time entrepreneurs' business plans is showing very large cash accumulations following the break-even point. Although high-growth ventures must have revenues that grow much faster than operating costs, they also generally incur significant initial losses and require large ongoing capital expenses in order to do so. If you find your pro forma statements showing large cash accumulations by year four or five, you should carefully examine your assumptions and adjust your plan accordingly.

- » **Ratio Analysis**
  To help to validate your financials, compare critical financial ratios from your plan to those of your industry. Be able to explain and justify significant differences. Adjust financial statements if necessary. Compare cost of goods sold, margins, earnings, and other key financial ratios for your industry with your figures. This is also a good place to include your vertical analysis to show that your expenses are in line with industry norms. Differences from industry averages are generally fine, but they should be explained and justified. As noted earlier, this can be a powerful tool to help you complete your financial statements.

- » **Break-Even Analysis**
  Most business plans contain some kind of break-even analysis, but it doesn't have to be as complicated as it might seem. Investors just want a rough idea of when your revenues will cover your operating expenses. You may also want to include the point at which you plan to achieve positive cash flow.

A common error made by entrepreneurs in high-growth ventures is to show break-even too quickly. Investors want the venture to make money, but they don't expect profits right away. Breaking even too quickly may even be a sign that you are too focused on short-term profits at the expense of investing in the business for the long haul. Breaking even in two to three years is common for technology ventures. Biotech or medical ventures that have a long testing and regulatory approval process will take longer. Restaurants, fitness centers, and other ventures with high up-front capital costs often break even far in the future, if at all.

Templates and descriptions of essential pro forma financial statements can be accessed in the digital asset materials designed to accompany this book. Access your digital assets at go.quickstartguides.com/startingbusiness.

Brevity is the soul of wit.

- HAMLET, ACT II, SCENE II

A Note on the Due Diligence Process

Until now, I have continually urged you to condense, shorten, paraphrase, and otherwise make all of your points as succinctly as possible. There is a good reason for this—people have short attention spans and get bored easily. You're trying to hook them into getting interested in your venture and wanting to learn more. Nevertheless, at some point people who are considering making a serious financial or other commitment to your venture are going to want more details, and you need to be prepared to answer very specific questions. This is called *due diligence*, and it's a standard part of the venture investment process.

During the due diligence process, there can be no secrets or vague, misleading answers, or your potential investors will run for the hills. An informal term for this is "opening the kimono," since you need to be prepared to bare all, even things you're not necessarily proud of.

Since you've taken my advice and carefully documented all of the assumptions leading to your business and financial models, you should have answers to any questions you will get. Resist the urge to sugarcoat unflattering news or potential difficulties. You want these people to be your partners, and a partnership can't be built on mistrust. This is also your chance to reinforce how well-thought-out your projections are.

A Thought Experiment:

Consider two hypothetical due diligence processes with the same investor for two similar startups.

Investor: "You are projecting sales of $10 million by year three. Where does that figure come from?"

Entrepreneur A: *"The worldwide market for my product is $1 billion per year. All I need is 1 percent of that to get sales of $10 million."*

Investor: "Why do you think you'll get 1 percent of the worldwide market?"

Entrepreneur A: *"With a disruptive technology such as ours, we feel that 1 percent of the market is a highly conservative projection. We actually think it'll be closer to 5 percent."*

Investor: "Do you have any other data to back up that projection?"

Entrepreneur A: *"We've spoken to numerous contacts we have in the industry, and all of them have assured us that our product is unique and paradigm-shifting."*

Investor: "Thanks. Let's move on."

Investor: "You are projecting sales of $10 million by year three. Where does that figure come from?"

Entrepreneur B: *"As you know, the worldwide market for our product is $1 billion. We segment the market into three basic groups: millennials, baby boomers, and gen Z. Most of our competitors are focused on the first two groups, which currently comprise 85 percent of the market. However, studies show that gen Z is the fastest-growing segment of the market and will grow to 25 percent, or $250 million, in the next three years. Our product is primarily focused on gen Z and is poised to dominate that segment.*

We've done surveys that show that 75 percent of gen Z purchasers of our product category are familiar with our brand, and 90 percent of them have a favorable *impression of it. That gives us an addressable market of around $170 million in year three. Our current penetration is 1.5 percent of this market, and it's doubling every year, so in three years we expect to achieve 6 percent of the market, or a little over $10 million.*

We intend to use 25 percent of the funding we're asking for on a marketing campaign, so we expect our penetration to accelerate. However, we're basing our projections on our current growth rate."

Investor: "Thanks. Let's move on."

Q: **Which entrepreneur do you think gets funded?**

Chapter Recap

» Operations are the processes used to deliver your product or service to the marketplace. The Operations Overview is designed to convey to your audience where exactly your competitive advantage is coming from, and the ways in which you have designed your business to take full advantage of it.

» The Marketing Overview portion of your business plan addresses how your product or service will reach your customers and how you will entice them to buy.

» The Sales Strategy portion of your plan should discuss your sales cycle—is it long or short—how your sales and promotion efforts will reach your target customers, and who will actually be doing the selling.

» The Growth Plan portion of your business plan gives your audience an idea of where your organization is headed and what steps you still need to take to get there.

» The Management and Staffing portion of your business plan describes the people who will bring your venture to life, as well as any gaps in the management team that may still exist. Don't forget to include any additions you have yet to make to the management team or any gaps that have yet to be filled.

» In the Financial Summary portion, summarize your financial projections. The details of these projections belong in the pro forma financial statements that should be included in the appendixes of your plan. Be sure to include business risks.

» Dedicate a brief section to the sources and use of funds that have been raised and have yet to be raised, and the ways they will be deployed.

» All supporting documentation belongs in the appendixes. This section should consist of no more than about ten pages. Don't go overboard.

Conclusion

Real questions from my Quora queue:

» "If most startups fail, why risk starting one?"
» "What are the best IT startup ideas?"
» "If I explain a business idea to a possible provider and they steal my idea, can I sue them?"
» "What's your go-to industry for startups as an entrepreneur?"
» "How do you make a million-dollar startup?"
» "What would be a good name for a sea captain?"

As someone who knows a little about entrepreneurship, I often get requests on Quora to answer questions about starting a business. I try to answer when I can. In most cases, though, the actual premise of the question shows a misunderstanding about the process of launching a venture that is so profound that any answer I give would automatically be wrong. This is the reason I wrote this book.

I can teach anyone the steps to writing a business plan, but without understanding why you're doing it or how to achieve your goals, you're doomed to failure, or at the very least to a long and frustrating learning experience. My hope is that readers of this book can identify the logical fallacies inherent in these questions (except the sea captain one. That one has nothing to do with entrepreneurship, but it does make you think!).

"Risk," "idea," and "opportunity" are all common words in the English language, but they mean different things to different people. I have tried to show how successful entrepreneurs frame these issues, and why it is critical to have the right mindset before jumping into the startup world. Starting a business can be lonely and grueling, or it can be liberating and exhilarating. How you view it, and your motivation for doing it, have far more to do with your success than any cool technology you've invented. Mindful entrepreneurs who know what they are doing and why they are doing it already have a huge competitive advantage over the average person and are already well on their way to achieving their goals and leading an authentic, fully actualized life.

Having determined *why* you're starting a business, the next step is *how*. There are a series of practical considerations you must address in order to get your business off the ground. There are also the standard strategic forces that apply to all businesses. These issues can be coalesced into two basic tools: your value proposition and your business model. Thinking these tools through honestly and carefully is critical to your success.

Once you have a solid concept of your value proposition and business model, the next issue you will face is how to communicate them effectively to potential stakeholders. Having a communications tool kit including an elevator pitch, executive summary, pitch deck, business plan, and fully documented assumptions for the due diligence process will help you do just that.

I view entrepreneurship as the ultimate creative act, very much analogous to any sort of artistic endeavor. Like art, entrepreneurial success requires passion and vision, but it also requires some technical skills. In this book, I've tried to balance cognitive factors with the basic economic realities faced by all new ventures. My hope is that it helps you achieve your dreams.

REMEMBER TO DOWNLOAD YOUR FREE DIGITAL ASSETS!

 Complete Sample Business Plans

 Business Plan Creation Checklist

 Pro Forma Financial Statement Template

 Useful Cheat Sheets

TWO WAYS TO ACCESS YOUR FREE DIGITAL ASSETS

Use the camera app on your mobile phone to scan the QR code or visit the link below and instantly access your digital assets.

or go.quickstartguides.com/startingbusiness

 SCAN ME

VISIT URL

About
The Author

KEN COLWELL, PhD, MBA

Ken Colwell, PhD, MBA is a seasoned strategic and operational leader with extensive experience working within entrepreneurial ecosystems and interacting with relevant private and public sector stakeholders at all levels in order to accomplish objectives.

He has consulted for hundreds of start-up ventures and is the principal of Innovative Growth Advisors.

Dr. Colwell is currently dean of the University of Houston-Victoria School of Business Administration. He has held past decanal posts at School of Business at Central Connecticut State University and the School of Business, Public Administration and Information Sciences at Long Island University–Brooklyn. Prior to taking his current decanal post, he was director of entrepreneurship programs at the University of Miami School of Business Administration and a professor of strategy and entrepreneurship at Drexel University.

Dr. Colwell holds a PhD in strategic management from the University of Oregon and an MBA from San Francisco State University. He has taught strategic management, entrepreneurship, new venture planning, and entrepreneurial consulting at the undergraduate, graduate, and executive levels.

About QuickStart Guides

QuickStart Guides are books for beginners, written by experts.

QuickStart Guides® are comprehensive learning companions tailored for the beginner experience. Our books are written by experts, subject matter authorities, and thought leaders within their respective areas of study.

For nearly a decade more than 850,000 readers have trusted QuickStart Guides® to help them get a handle on their finances, start their own business, invest in the stock market, find a new hobby, get a new job—the list is virtually endless.

The QuickStart Guides® series of books is published by ClydeBank Media, an independent publisher based in Albany, NY.

Connect with QuickStart Guides online at www.quickstartguides.com

Glossary

4 Cs Model
A service-focused alternative to the 4 Ps of Marketing model. The four Cs represent the marketing mix for service businesses. Product translates to Customer Solution, Price to Customer Cost, Promotion to Customer Communication, and Place to Customer Convenience.

4 Ps of Marketing
The standard marketing mix. Together, Product, Price, Promotion, and Place form a high-level overview of the considerations that marketers must make when crafting a marketing plan. Different products have a different mix of spending and focus on each of the four Ps.

Barriers to Entry
Obstacles that prevent new ventures from entering and participating in an industry. These obstacles could include prohibitively expensive initial costs, pressure from entrenched firms within the industry, or restrictive government regulation.

Brand Collateral
The various digital and physical elements that make up your brand. These include a company's logo, brand color palette, website, business cards, and other branded elements.

Break-Even Point
The point at which costs equal revenue. At this point, a business can begin to turn a profit.

Burn Rate
The negative cash flow that a startup experiences while covering startup expenses before the venture becomes profitable, or at least produces enough revenue to sustain itself.

Business Model
A strategic design that outlines the method by which a business profitably solves a problem for specific customers. A successful business model acts as a template that includes considerations for operational, technical, and financial aspects of the business.

Competitive Advantage
The sum of conditions that put one business in a superior or favorable position over another. Competitive advantage stems from resources, competencies, or capabilities that are valuable to the customer, rare, not easily imitated, and not easily substituted.

Customer Avatar
A fictional profile that represents the qualities that your perfect customer would exhibit. This customer persona is designed to guide efforts to identify the target market for a product or service, as well as to refine marketing efforts.

Dilution
The devaluation of every member of a founding team's equity when a new member joins the team. Because total ownership of equity in a venture cannot exceed 100 percent, when a new equity-sharing member claims a portion, every other portion becomes smaller.

Direct Competitors

Competitors who compete in a one-to-one capacity. These firms offer the same solution to a customer's problem, for example, two pizza shops in the same neighborhood. The customer problem is hunger—a problem for which there are many solutions—and two pizza shops offer the same solution.

Distinctive Competencies

The source of competitive advantage. Distinctive competencies are a combination of best practices and technical skills that come together in a valuable and creative way that is difficult to beat by competitors.

Due Diligence

The comprehensive, specific, and often technical questions that investors ask entrepreneurs regarding the nature of their startup. It is important that these questions be answered truthfully and as accurately as possible, as the answers are material to investor decisions about whether to invest in a venture or not.

Effectuation

The opposite of causation. Instead of starting with a goal and gathering resources to accomplish that goal, effectuation is the process of developing a goal based on the resources at hand.

Foreign Qualification

The practice of registering a business in a state where it is not physically based.

Entity Classification

The legal form of a business. Different legal forms offer different advantages in the form of personal liability protection, tax liability advantages, and methods of acquiring capital.

Entrepreneurial Thumbprint

The unique blend of background, talent, insight, and perspective that positions an entrepreneur to turn an idea into an opportunity.

Flow

A state of elevated focus and elation that stems from a match of competency and challenge for a particular task. Learning and productivity are maximized when a flow state is achieved, along with a feeling of accomplishment.

Gantt Chart

A visual representation of a project or series of milestones. This type of chart is especially useful to demonstrate a sequence of dependent tasks.

Graphic Identity

The sum of a business's visual elements such as logos, business cards, visual messaging elements, color palette, and visual themes.

Indirect Competitors

Competitors who offer a different solution to the same customer problem. For example, a pizza shop and a sandwich shop both solve the problem of hunger, but they offer different solutions. Both establishments indirectly compete with grocery stores and other restaurants as well—other businesses that help customers solve the same problem but offer different solutions.

Kaizen

A philosophy of continuous improvement. Kaizen favors constant incremental change that can be implemented immediately and with minimum disruption over large sweeping changes that can often cause disruption. In addition to being an engine for improvement, the philosophy of kaizen teaches practitioners to embrace change—a critical mentality for entrepreneurs.

Liquidity Event

An exit strategy that transforms equity into cash. Common liquidity events include acquisitions, mergers, and initial public offerings (IPOs).

Marketing Collateral

All the sales sheets, brochures, articles, and case studies that are used to promote a brand, product, or service.

Marketing Mix
Elements of the exchange that exists between a brand and its customers. Traditionally, the marketing mix is made up of four key elements collectively referred to as the "4 Ps": product, price, promotion, and place.

Outsourcing
The process of relying on third-party firms to carry out processes that do not directly contribute to a venture's value chain. Outsourcing plays a critical role in the development of many startups and is cheaper and easier than ever before.

Porter's Five Forces
A conceptual framework designed to help business decision makers better understand the ways in which the pressures of competition influence an industry or industrial sector. The five forces are the intensity of competition within an industry, the bargaining power of suppliers, the bargaining power of buyers, the threat of substitute products, and the threat of new industry entrants.

Price Ceiling
The highest price a firm can charge for its product or, effectively, the highest price the market will bear.

Price Floor
The lowest price a firm can charge for its product while maintaining a profitable margin.

Price Sensitivity
The degree to which price factors into the buying decisions of a market segment. A high sensitivity to price means that low or affordable prices are very important. Low price sensitivity means that other product features are more important than price.

Primary Activities
The operational activities in a value chain that contribute directly to the creation of value for customers. In a value chain analysis, these activities include inputs, operations, distribution, marketing, and service.

Promotional Mix
The combination of various forms of promotion that are particular to a product or service. The promotional mix consists of advertising, public relations, personal selling, and sales promotion.

Runway
The amount of time a venture can stay in business before its burn rate surpasses the amount of cash it has raised.

Sales Cycle
The process that a firm undergoes from the initiation of a sale to the close of that sale.

Sensitivity Analysis
An exploration of the impact particular variables have on a forecasted outcome. These analyses are used to gauge how reliable a plan is and what vulnerabilities it may have.

Shiny Object Syndrome
The practice of adjusting focus and shifting a plan to accommodate the newest, flashiest tools. It is important to be ready to pivot when the situation calls for it, but constantly adopting new systems results in wasted energy and spinning wheels.

SMART
An acronym that stands for specific, measurable, achievable, relevant, and time-bound. These qualities represent a best practice for effective goal setting. Vague, unrealistic, or open-ended goals are not only unlikely to be accomplished but represent a lack of focus and strategy.

Support Activities
Activities within a value chain that indirectly add value. These include areas of a firm such as financial and legal, human resources, development, and procurement.

Top-Level Domain

The suffix of a web address. Common top-level domains include .com, .org, .info, .edu, and .gov.

Value Chain

The journey that a firm's inputs take through operational processes. This journey transforms them from raw materials into outputs that have value for the firm's customers. All firms have a value chain, but the specifics will vary from firm to firm (even within the same industry).

Value Proposition

The *why* of a venture. It is the answer to two key questions: who is your target customer and how are you different from your competition? A venture's value proposition is at the heart of its success.

WAG

An acronym for the phrase "wild-ass guess." Your business plan should have as few of these as possible, although your audience will understand that certain elements of your plan will be an educated guess out of necessity.

References

CHAPTER 1:

1   Lewis, T. (2015, September 21). "Qualcomm Lays Down Start-Up Gauntlet with Founding Story." Retrieved from Global Corporate Venturing: https://globalcorporateventuring.com/qualcomm-lays-down-startup-gauntlet-with-founding-story/

2   Lowry, T. (2006, October 30). "ESPN's Cell-Phone Fumble." Retrieved May 5, 2018, from Bloomberg: https://www.bloomberg.com/news/articles/2006-10-29/espns-cell-phone-fumble

3   Alexander, L. (2016, January 11). "Why It's Time to Retire 'Disruption', Silicon Valley's Emptiest Buzzword." Retrieved April 15, 2018, from The Guardian: https://www.theguardian.com/technology/2016/jan/11/disruption-silicon-valleys-buzzword

CHAPTER 2:

4   Klein, M. (2003). *The Change Makers: From Carnegie to Gates, How the Great Entrepreneurs Transformed Ideas into Industries* (1st ed.). New York, New York: Henry Holt and Company.

CHAPTER 3:

5   Csikszentmihalyi, M. (2000). *Beyond Boredom and Anxiety: Experiencing Flow in Work and Play* (25th Anniversary Ed.). San Francisco: Jossey-Bass.

6   Gillett, R. (2014, April 16). "Arianna Huffington On The Struggle To Find Work-Life Balance." Retrieved June 5, 2018, from Fast Company: https://www.fastcompany.com/3029144/arianna-huffington-on-finding-work-life-balance

CHAPTER 4:

7   Bullock, J. W. (2015). Delaware Division of Corporations 2015 Annual Report. Retrieved June 1, 2018, from State of Delaware: https://corp.delaware.gov/Corporations_2015%20Annual%20Report.pdf

8   Pinterest Business. (2018, October 23). Pinterest Audience Demographics. Retrieved from Pinterest Business: https://business.pinterest.com/en/audience-demographics-user-stats

CHAPTER 6:

9   Halbert, G. (2014, July 17). The Boron Letters - Chapter 6. Retrieved May 15, 2018, from The Gary Halbert Letter: http://www.thegaryhalbertletter.com/Boron/TChapter6.htm

10   At time of writing, Google Trends can be accessed at *www.trends.google.com*

11   At time of writing, Consumer Barometer can be accessed at *www.consumerbarometer.com*

12   At time of writing, Google Public Data can be accessed at *www.google.com/publicdata*

13   At time of writing, The New York Times census visualizer can be accessed at *http://www.nytimes.com/projects/census/2010/map.html*

14   At time of writing, the Pew Research Center can be accessed at *www.pewresearch.org*

15   At time of writing, Statista can be accessed at *www.statista.com*

16   At time of writing, the Nielsen My Best Segment program can be accessed at *www. segmentationsolutions. nielsen.com/mybestsegments*

CHAPTER 7:

17   At time of writing, the NAICS classification directory can be accessed at *www.census.gov/eos/www/naics/index.html*

CHAPTER 8:

18   Miller, D. (1992, January/February). "The Generic Strategy Trap." *The Journal of Business Strategy*, Volume 13 Issue 1, p. 37.

CHAPTER 13:

19   Graham, P. (2007, August). "How Not to Die." Retrieved from Paul Graham : http://www.paulgraham.com/die.html

20   The American Angel Campaign. (2017, November 30). The American Angel Campaign. Retrieved June 27, 2018, from The American Angel: http://docs.wixstatic.com/ugd/ecd9be_5855a9b21a8c4fc1abc89a3293abff96.pdf

21   At time of writing, AngelList can be accessed at *https://angel.co*

22   At time of writing, Gust can be accessed at *www.gust.com*

23   Deeb, G. (2013). *101 Startup Lessons*. Chicago: BlogIntoBook.com.

24   Fundable. (2017). Startup Funding. Retrieved from Fundable: https://www.fundable.com/infographics/startup-funding

25   Kickstarter. (2018). Stats. Retrieved from *www.kickstarter.com*

Index

WHAT DID YOU THINK?

We rely on reviews and reader feedback to help our authors reach more people, improve our books, and grow our business. We would really appreciate it if you took the time to help us out by providing feedback on your recent purchase.

It's really easy, it only takes a second, and it's a tremendous help!

—— NOT SURE WHAT TO SHARE? ——

Here are some ideas to get your review started...

- *What did you learn?*
- *Have you been able to put anything you learned into action?*
- *Would you recommend the book to other readers?*
- *Is the author clear and easy to understand?*

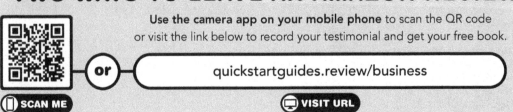

TWO WAYS TO LEAVE AN AMAZON REVIEW

Use the camera app on your mobile phone to scan the QR code or visit the link below to record your testimonial and get your free book.

or

quickstartguides.review/business

SCAN ME

VISIT URL

GET YOUR NEXT
QuickStart Guide®
FOR FREE

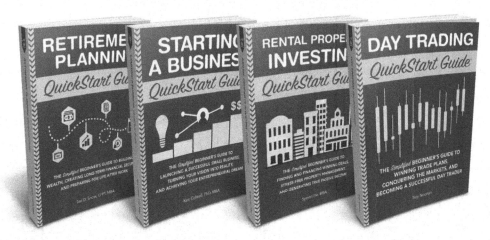

Leave us a quick video testimonial on our website and we will give you a **FREE QuickStart Guide** of your choice!

RECORD TESTIMONIAL

SUBMIT TO OUR WEBSITE

GET A FREE BOOK

TWO WAYS TO LEAVE A VIDEO TESTIMONIAL

Use the camera app on your mobile phone to scan the QR code or visit the link below to record your testimonial and get your free book.

SCAN ME

or

go.quickstartguides.com/free-qsg

VISIT URL

SAVE 10% ON YOUR NEXT

QuickStart Guide®

USE CODE: QSG10

https://quickstartguides.shop/real-estate

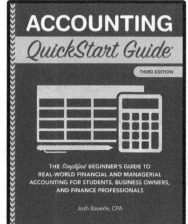

https://quickstartguides.shop/accounting

https://quickstartguides.shop/investing

https://quickstartguides.shop/html-css

Use the camera app on your mobile phone to scan the QR code or visit the link below the cover to shop.
Get 10% off your entire order when you use code 'QSG10' at checkout at www.clydebankmedia.com

LISTEN TO *QuickStart Guides* ON THE GO

NEW AUDIBLE MEMBERS
GET THEIR FIRST AUDIOBOOK

FREE!

TWO WAYS TO SELECT A FREE AUDIOBOOK

Use the camera app on your mobile phone to scan the QR code
or visit the link below to select your free audiobook from Audible.

or

www.quickstartguides.com/free-audiobook

 SCAN ME

VISIT URL

CLYDEBANK MEDIA

QuickStart Guides®

PROUDLY SUPPORT ONE TREE PLANTED

One Tree Planted is a 501(c)(3) nonprofit organization focused on global reforestation, with millions of trees planted every year. ClydeBank Media is proud to support One Tree Planted as a reforestation partner.

Every dollar donated plants one tree and every tree makes a difference!

Learn more at www.clydebankmedia.com/charitable-giving or make a contribution at onetreeplanted.org.